Researching Education for Social Justice in Multilingual Settings

Researching Education for Social Justice in Multilingual Settings

Ethnographic Principles in Qualitative Research

EDITED BY JEAN CONTEH

Bloomsbury Academic
An imprint of Bloomsbury Publishing Plc

B L O O M S B U R Y
LONDON · OXFORD · NEW YORK · NEW DELHI · SYDNEY

Bloomsbury Academic

An imprint of Bloomsbury Publishing Plc

50 Bedford Square	1385 Broadway
London	New York
WC1B 3DP	NY10018
UK	USA

www.bloomsbury.com

BLOOMSBURY and the Diana logo are trademarks of Bloomsbury Publishing Plc

First published 2018

© Jean Conteh and Contributors, 2018

British Library Cataloguing-in-Publication Data
A catalogue record for this book is available from the British Library.

ISBN:	HB:	978-1-3500-0263-0
	PB:	978-1-3500-0264-7
	ePDF:	978-1-3500-0267-8
	ePub:	978-1-3500-0265-4

Library of Congress Cataloging-in-Publication Data
Names: Conteh, Jean, editor.
Title: Researching education for social justice in multilingual settings : ethnographic principles in qualitative research / edited by Jean Conteh.
Description: London, UK ; New York, NY : Bloomsbury Academic, 2017. | Includes bibliographical references and index.
Identifiers: LCCN 2017015068| ISBN 9781350002630 (hb) | ISBN 9781350002647 (pb) | ISBN 9781350002678 (ePDF) | ISBN 9781350002654 (ePub)
Subjects: LCSH: Multilingual education–Research. | Qualitative research–Methodology. | Social justice.
Classification: LCC LC3715 .R47 2017 | DDC 370.11/5–dc23 LC record available at https://lccn.loc.gov/2017015068

Cover image © Bob Small Photography / GettyImages

Typeset by Integra Software Services Pvt. Ltd.

To find out more about our authors and books visit www.bloomsbury.com. Here you will find extracts, author interviews, details of forthcoming events and the option to sign up for our newsletters.

This book is dedicated to all teacher-researchers, whose passion for social justice it acknowledges and encourages, and may even spur to action. In particular, I wish to dedicate it to those teacher-researchers who completed the MA in English as an Additional Language and Education during its short but productive life at the University of Leeds, UK, from 2012 to 2016.

CONTENTS

FIGURES

LIST OF CONTRIBUTORS

Samyia Ambreen is a doctoral researcher in the School of Education at the University of Leeds, UK. Prior to this, she served as a teaching fellow in the Department of Education in Fatima Jinnah Women's University in Rawalpindi, Pakistan. As a specialist in teacher education, she has experience of doing small-scale qualitative research projects in various educational settings in Pakistan.

Jessica Bradley is a doctoral researcher in the School of Education at the University of Leeds, UK. Her academic background is in modern languages and translation studies, and she worked in higher education in outreach and educational engagement for a decade. In 2016 she received the Faculty of Education, Social Studies and Law's nomination for postgraduate researcher of the year.

Jean Conteh is a Senior Lecturer in the School of Education at the University of Leeds, UK. She has extensive experience in teacher education and development and has published widely in the areas of multilingualism and social justice in education.

Chisato Danjo is a Lecturer in the School of Languages and Linguistics at York St John University, UK. Her research interests are in the area of sociolinguistics, applied linguistics and educational linguistics, especially on the topics of multilingualism, language policy and practice, family language planning and maintenance, and language issues relating to culture and identity.

Katherine Fincham-Louis is an ESL practitioner turned academic, with over twenty-five years of practice. She completed her Doctorate in Education at the University of Edinburgh, UK, in 2012, exploring the role of language and identity for bilingual children in state elementary schools in Cyprus. She is currently a Lecturer at the University of Nicosia, Cyprus, and her research interests include multilingualism, translanguaging, language and identity and social justice in education.

Nasir Mahmood is an ESRC-funded PhD student at the School of Education, University of Leeds, UK. He completed his Masters in educational policy at the University of Sheffield, UK, and has worked in the UK secondary schools as an EAL/Inclusion support tutor for more than eight years. His PhD deals with the misrecognition phenomenon of identities, agency and belonging in the lives of British-Pakistani Muslim teachers.

Indu Vibha Meddegama is a Lecturer in Applied Linguistics and TESOL in the School of Languages and Linguistics at York St John University, UK. She teaches in the areas of World Englishes and Language Teaching Methodology. Indu's research interests lie in multilingualism, TESOL and English as a lingua franca.

Valerie Nave completed her PhD in language education at the University of Leeds, UK in 2016. She taught English as a second language abroad, and then moved to the UK, where she developed the urge to be a researcher and gain an insight into the reasons why multilingual families often struggle to maintain their mother tongue in 'monolingualising' societies.

Janica Nordstrom was awarded her PhD from the University of Sydney, Australia, in 2016, where she is currently teaching courses at the Faculty of Education and Social Work in the field of information technologies in schools, language, literacy and diversity. She continues to research in the field of languages and multilingualism in higher education, primary and secondary education and in community language schools.

Ambreen Shahriar is a Associate Professor at the University of Sindh, Pakistan, and Research Fellow at Goldsmiths, University of London, UK. She is interested in researching multilingualism, multiculturalism, issues of identity, individual learner differences and motivation.

Robert Sharples is a Lecturer in Linguistics at York St John University, UK. His research focuses on migration, language and education, with a particular interest in English as an Additional Language.

Yi XiLaMuCuo is Vice Professor in the School of Tibetan Language and Culture in the Northwest University for Languages, China. She completed her PhD at the University of Leeds, UK in 2015 and continues to research the experiences of Tibetan-Chinese bilinguals in education in China. She is currently preparing a book based on her PhD thesis.

LINKS TO CONTRIBUTORS' THESES

Note: *The completed theses for Ambreen, Bradley, Mahmood and Sharples will appear on etheses.whiterose.ac.uk*

Ambreen, S. (2017) Analysing the Nature of Pupils' Interaction in Different Fixed and Mixed Ability Groups in Primary Classroom, Jessica Bradley's academia page: (https://leeds.academia.edu/JessicaBradley).

Danjo, C. (2015) A Critical Ethnographic Inquiry into the Negotiation of Language Practices among Japanese Multilingual Families in the UK: Discourse, Language Use and Perceptions in the Hoshuko and the Family Home, http://nrl.northumbria.ac.uk/27269/

Fincham-Louis, K. (2012) Bilingual Greek/English Children in State Elementary Schools in Cyprus: A Question of Language and Identity, https://www.era.lib.ed.ac.uk/bitstream/handle/1842/7567/Fincham -Louis2012.pdf?sequence=2

Mahmood, N. (2017) A Critical Ethnographic Study Exploring the Misrecognition Performance of Identities, Agency and Belonging in the Lives of Four British Pakistani Muslim Teachers in Their Educational and Social Contexts.

Meddegama, I.V. (2013) The Enactment of Status and Power in the Linguistic Practices of Three Multilingual, Malayali Families in the UK, http://etheses.whiterose.ac.uk/id/eprint/5550

Nave, V. (2017) How Do Multilingual Families and Different Schooling Contexts Shape Young Children's Beliefs and Attitudes towards Multilingualism?, http://etheses.whiterose.ac.uk/17375/

Nordstrom, J. (2015) Re-thinking Community Language Schools Moving from In-between to beyond the Nation-states, https://ses.library.usyd .edu.au/handle/2123/14316; http://hdl.handle.net/2123/14316

Shahriar, A. (2013) Making a Better Life: the Stories of People from Poor Rural Backgrounds in Sindh, Pakistan, http://ethos.bl.uk/OrderDetails .do?did=1&uin=uk.bl.ethos.586871

Sharples, R. (2017) Rethinking 'English as an Additional Language': An Ethnographic Study of Young Migrants, Language and Schools,

XiLaMuCuo, Y. (2015) Becoming Bilingual in School and Home in Tibetan Areas of China: Stories of Struggle, http://etheses.whiterose.ac.uk/id /eprint/9744

FOREWORD

Passion is not usually at the forefront of books on methodology. Indeed, it is often avoided or regarded with suspicion in the aim to achieve validity, objectivity or distance, even in qualitative work. Yet, it is passion, particularly passion for social justice that makes a story worthy of being told and thus makes a study important. What makes the chapters in this book unique is that they put passion and social justice in the middle, yet simultaneously show how rigour and attention to detail cannot be compromised. The stories told in different chapters often come from communities or countries which we know little about, whose ordinary people have little official voice and who often remain invisible. These stories come to life through the tellers, who themselves often share part of the background of their participants and who care passionately for their plight. Unlike traditional ethnographic work, these authors' roots are often deeply and intricately intertwined with those of their participants. They speak from personal experience and their passion is expressed from the heart, rather than the reasoning of an 'outsider'. Indeed, issues relating to the role of the 'insider/outsider' are central to their discussions as are notions of reflexivity and trustworthiness of data as it is both collected and analyzed.

Unusually, in a book on methodology, we are not told *how* to conduct an ethnographic study but are invited into *the process* of seeing how others have gone about conducting one; we experience the 'messiness' of conducting fieldwork with real people, the dilemmas of things going wrong and how we can learn from our mistakes. We see how the authors learn to remain ethically sound while still being trustworthy to others. We learn how we are not alone in wondering whether our theories and methodologies are rigorous enough and in decisions to include other non-ethnographic approaches within our framework. Finally, we see how the authors gradually realize that any type of data investigation, including statistics, can be viewed through an ethnographic lens. Throughout all this we learn how to become true to ourselves and, in so doing, become true to our participants. Through our apprenticeship in ethnographic work, we slowly become members of a long-standing community of educational ethnographers originally inspired by the work of Dell Hymes (1964), Shirley Brice Heath (1983) and Brian Street (1984). Like them, the authors in this book are not afraid to admit dangers, difficulties and sometimes despair. It is this that makes the collection such a valuable one in the field.

Eve Gregory, Professor Emerita of Language
and Culture in Education, Goldsmiths,
University of London, UK

References

Heath, S.B. (1983), *Ways with Words: Language, Life, and Work in Communities and Classrooms*, Cambridge: Cambridge University Press.

Hymes, D., ed. (1964), *Language in Culture and Society: A Reader in Linguistics and Anthropology*, New York: Harper and Row.

Street, B.V. (1984), *Literacy in Theory and Practice*, Cambridge: Cambridge University Press.

ACKNOWLEDGEMENTS

Samyia Ambreen wishes to thank her research supervisors (Dr Martin Wedell and Dr Jean Conteh, School of Education, University of Leeds) for encouraging her to write her chapter. She is very grateful to Dr Wedell for reviewing the chapter and giving her useful insights to improve her work. She would like to say a huge thank you to the participants of her study, who gave her permission to use their ideas and reflections on group work.

Jessica Bradley's research was conducted as part of the Translation and Translanguaging (TLANG) Project, funded by the Arts and Humanities Research Council (AHRC) (AH/L007096/1). Jessica wishes to thank the Leeds-based AHRC TLANG team, in particular James Simpson. She would also like to thank her critical colleagues Lou Harvey, Emilee Moore and Piotr Wegorowski for their careful comments on her writing. Finally, she is grateful to Faceless Arts and to the Ana Monro Theatre for their hospitality and welcome.

Chisato Danjo is deeply grateful to her research participants, especially to the family which this chapter focuses on. Chisato also acknowledges the productive discussions she held with Chris Moreh regarding researcher positionality, whose anthropological perspectives have been very helpful in shaping this chapter.

Nasir Mahmood is immensely thankful to his research participants Saima, Naila, Majid and Raza for their life histories. He also wishes to thank his supervisor Dr Jean Conteh and the anonymous reviewer for their very helpful and constructive comments.

Indu Vibha Meddegama acknowledges her parents:

> To ammi and appachchi, my parents: 'Brahmā ti Mātāpitaro, Pubbācariyā ti vuccare' ('Mother and Father are our creators and very first teachers')
> Pali Verse from the *Anguttara Nikāya*

Valerie Nave acknowledges that a large number of people helped her with her chapter. The first is Dr Jean Conteh, who has been a great source of inspiration and support. Her participants, their families and teachers in the complementary and mainstream schools have also been key elements in the work, in particular her daughter, who showed much patience and goodwill. She also wishes to thank her husband, who constantly reminded her of the importance of education.

Janica Nordstrom wishes to thank Mike Baynham for his valuable feedback on an earlier version of this chapter.

Ambreen Shahriar wishes to express her warmest gratitude to both her supervisors, Professor Eve Gregory and Dr John Jessel, who were unfailingly positive and supportive throughout, both academically and personally. Special thanks are due to Dr Jean Conteh, in whom she has gained a lifelong friend and mentor.

Robert Sharples acknowledges Jean Conteh and James Simpson, for their patient guidance through the PhD process, and the staff and students of the International Group, for everything they taught him.

Yi XiLaMuCuo wishes to thank her grandmother for her love, which inspired her to finish her PhD.

Finally, **Jean Conteh** wishes to thank all the contributors to the book. For many, this is their first academic publication. They all responded to the invitation enthusiastically, and generously gave their time when they were often very busy with other demands of life and work. She also acknowledges the contribution of the anonymous reviewers whose efforts were often beyond the call of duty and whose critical and sympathetic comments made a major contribution to the final shaping of the book. They were: Oksana Afitska, Mohammed Ahmadian, Piet van Avermaet, Mike Baynham, Mike Beaumont, Clare Cunningham, Constant Leung, Vally Lytra, Gee Macrory, Gabriela Meier, James Simpson and Martin Weddell.

INTRODUCTION

Overview of the book

This book aims to provide models for ethnographic research in multilingual settings through showing the reader how others have done it, rather than attempting to lay down specific guidelines to follow. The eleven case studies, which form the main content of the book, have been selected to illustrate methodological principles and provide practical examples of research projects that address questions about social justice in multilingual contexts, with relevance to education. The purpose of Chapter 1 is to set the scene by presenting fundamental methodological principles for the kinds of ethnographically informed, **interpretivist** research that afford the best opportunities to understand multilingualism and education in diverse settings in our globalized world, and to contribute to change for the better.

Following this, the main content of the book comprises eleven chapters, each written by an invited contributor who has recently completed a small-scale research project in a multilingual setting in home, school, family or community. These are all successful EdD or PhD projects, all with strong connections to education, though not all were carried out in educational settings. Though most of the authors have extensive professional experience, they are all at the early stages of their journeys as researchers, and, for most, their chapter in this book is their first academic publication. I appreciate their courage and trust in agreeing to write chapters as I believe there is great value for other doctoral students and novice researchers in seeing how their peers have worked through issues they themselves may be facing.

The eleven chapters are arranged in three parts, each with a brief, framing introduction that explains the purposes of the part in relation to what it shows about the overall trajectory of completing a doctorate. These sections also outline the links between the chapters the part contains, and discuss their significant methodological and substantive themes. The three parts are not really about the linear progression of doing a doctorate from beginning to middle to end, but are each intended to focus on a different aspect of the process. They are about the concerns and preoccupations that particular researchers have faced in framing, developing and sustaining their projects at key points along the way. They inevitably overlap and are not mutually exclusive. Here is a summary of each part.

Part 1: Looking forward – conceptualizing the research

The chapters in Part 1 focus on the processes that contribute to identifying the issues to be studied and the methodological framing of the thesis. The case studies in this part focus, in different ways, on the decisions made by the researchers when reflecting on their central research problem, identifying relevant literature, constructing theoretical arguments and making sure that these link to the methodology subsequently developed. In Chapter 2, Yi XLaMuCuo describes how she combined ethnographic principles with narrative method to collect and analyze the stories of five Tibetan individuals' journeys of becoming bilingual in the Tibetan areas of China at four different points in time from 1950 to the present. Following this, in Chapter 3, Nasir Mahmood outlines his process of developing a theoretical framework suited to his research questions, which were about the ways in which adult Pakistani-heritage British Muslims are stereotyped in political, social and educational discourses in England. Like Yixi, his research questions came directly from personal experience. A key theoretical starting point came with his growing understanding of how misrecognition theories illuminated his own life story. Once this understanding was achieved, Nasir was able to develop a theoretically informed and nuanced set of data collection strategies, which generated rich data in interviews with his participants to answer his questions. In Chapter 4, the final chapter in this part, Ambreen Shahriar reflects on her study, conducted with young men and women from economically deprived backgrounds who aspire to better lives in a multilingual Pakistani context. Her research gives voice to the perspectives and concerns of participants who are both economically weak and have a 'lower status' language in a multilingual context. In her chapter, she considers the methodological features that allowed her to see her participants as individuals and to capture their distinctive personal experiences.

Part 2: Developing the research processes

The chapters in Part 2 focus on the processes of conducting the research, what can be considered as the fieldwork. The authors illustrate the decision making with which they engaged, and how this played out in the processes of conducting the research. In Chapter 5, Chisato Danjo focuses on the negotiation trajectories of her research project, in which she worked with Japanese/British intermarriage families in the north of England. Focusing on the moment-to-moment processes of negotiating researcher **positionality**, the chapter highlights the impact that issues arising can have on data collection procedures. In Chapter 6, Indu Meddegama reveals the interview process she developed in her ethnographic research on home language use and its relation to status and power relations in three multilingual immigrant families in the north of England. She offers an insight into the pitfalls and triumphs she experienced when researching the inherently private home domain of the families, who originally come from the south-western region of Kerala, India.

The remaining two chapters in Part 2 come, in many ways, under the linguistic ethnography banner (see Copland and Creese 2015). Chapter 7 is a classroom-based study in which Robert Sharples discusses his work with migrant learners in a south London secondary school. Over two years of fieldwork, he developed a significantly rich and complex body of data that incorporated field notes, photographs, interviews and documents. The students' voices emerged more and more strongly in the course of his data collection, and the challenge changed from 'working inwards' into the daily experiences of a marginalized group to 'writing outwards', so that those voices might be heard, more clearly than at present, in discussions of policy and curriculum. In Chapter 8, the final one in Part 2, the context moves from the classroom to the street. Jessica Bradley explores the processes of conducting linguistic ethnographic research in street performance and visual arts settings with a grassroots community arts organization. Taking Ingold's principles of 'educational correspondence' and 'generous attentiveness' (2014) as a framework, she shows how her research methodology developed through close collaboration with those with whom she was working and reflects on the effect of 'liquid settings' (Bauman 2000) on methodology.

Part 3: Looking back – reflections on processes and outcomes

The chapters in Part Three all look back on the completed studies and identify the key methodological (as well as the substantive) issues that emerged. The writers reflect critically on what they learned about conducting research for social justice following ethnographic principles in multilingual settings. In Chapter 9, Samyia Ambreen considers the findings of her study, which was designed to explore the nature of pupils' interactions in group-based activities in a state-run, multilingual primary school in northern England. Her discussion sheds light on the importance of understanding the relationships between pupils' distinctive social and cultural backgrounds and their classrooms. Personal identity is a strong theme in Chapter 10, where Valerie Nave shares her journey as a mother researcher who – in many ways – is in a position of power in relation to her participants. Valerie explores the experiences of three multilingual primary pupils in the north of England, whose daily languages are English and French. Her longitudinal study highlights the tensions children, parents and teachers face in living and learning multilingually in a monolingual society. Following this, in Chapter 11, Janica Nordstrom describes her research in a Swedish community language school in Australia. She explores how participant observations can be carried out to gain insight into multilingual educational settings, involving the researcher not only observing, but taking part in the common (and uncommon) activities in the field over time. In the final case study chapter in the book, Katherine Fincham-Louis reports in Chapter 12 on a participatory case study which explores language use and identity among a select group of Greek/English bilingual/bicultural children in state elementary schools in Cyprus. She opens out methodological issues and concerns in researching with children, and also adds to the literature on research which focuses on the voices of children in school, rather than teachers, policy makers or administrators.

The concluding chapter to the whole volume, Chapter 13, returns to the ethnographic principles introduced in Chapter 1, highlighted in the framing sections to each part, and then played out in the case study chapters. It draws out some general themes in qualitative, interpretivist research following ethnographic principles and discusses the role of writing in ethnographic research. It considers what it really means to research with teachers and to be a teacher-researcher, and concludes by considering ways of moving forward in order to disseminate findings and generate impact and change in order to promote social justice. In this way, I offer concrete ways of contesting some of the positivist challenges to the kinds of research that this book is about.

For long enough, interpretivist, ethnographic research in education has been held to account by the wrong evaluative criteria – those generated by positivist frameworks of research – and thus inevitably found wanting. Thus, its importance and relevance are undervalued. I hope that this book can contribute to changing this unhelpfully narrow model for assessing the quality of research in increasingly complex, multilingual contexts. The kinds of research illustrated in this book need to be judged by their trustworthiness, relevance and value for those set to gain directly from their outcomes; that is, those involved in constructing meanings and facing challenges in living multilingually every day. Rampton et al. (2015: 45) offer a set of conditions for 'good research', which are valuable for considering the work presented in this volume:

Good research should be careful, logical, accountable, explicit, sceptical, well-informed, comparative and original, leading to the production of interesting claims that people (in some determinate discourse community) can trust.

A note about reading the book

You don't need to read this book from start to finish. It can be read in different ways. If you are interested in gaining a general understanding of what it means to do ethnographic research, you could begin by reading Chapter 1, but you may get a better sense of how it feels to do such research by reading one of the case study chapters first, perhaps one in which the topic, themes or questions link with your own work. The overview above will help you decide which chapter to begin with. You may be interested in reading in more detail about particular aspects and issues in researching in multilingual settings; if so, you could read through all the chapters in the part which offers the most relevant thematic focus for you. These are the thematic focuses of each part:

Part 1: Making the familiar strange-developing praxis

Part 2: Researching multilingually-positionality

Part 3: 'Validity', 'reliability' and ethics

If you wish to pursue the ideas in any of the chapters further, there is a list of the titles of all the completed PhD theses and links to where they can be downloaded on page xii.

To support your reading of the book as a whole, there are **reflection and discussion points** for each part at the end of the introductory framing sections, and **guiding questions** at the start of each chapter. You may also find the questions raised here useful for peer group discussions or seminars. Finally, words and phrases highlighted in bold are explained briefly in the **glossary**.

Where data are presented in the case study chapters, I have retained the approaches of the authors, and have not attempted a uniform 'house style' across the chapters.

References

Bauman, Z. (2000), *Liquid Modernity*, Cambridge: Polity.

Copland, F. and Creese, A. (2015), *Linguistic Ethnography: Collecting, Analyzing and Presenting Data*, London: Sage Publications.

Ingold, T. (2014), 'That's Enough about Ethnography!', *HAU: Journal of Ethnographic Theory*, 4 (1): 383–395.

Rampton, B., Maybin, J., and Roberts, C. (2015), 'Theory and Method in Linguistic Ethnography', in J. Snell, S. Shaw and F. Copland (eds), *Linguistic Ethnography: Interdisciplinary Explorations*, 14–50, London: Palgrave Macmillan.

CHAPTER ONE

Principles and Processes of Ethnographic Research in Multilingual Settings

Jean Conteh

Starting points

This is a book about how to do research in multilingual settings following ethnographic principles, but it is not a methodology textbook in the conventional sense. It does not tell you how to do research, nor does it offer specific guidelines for carrying out a research project from start to finish. Instead, it shows you first-hand how others have carried out their own projects to investigate a wide range of issues around multilingualism, mostly in education settings, and how they addressed the inevitable problems that arose along the way. A key aim of the book, very important to me personally, is to show how research can contribute to the furtherance of social justice and possibly to social change. In this introductory chapter, I spend quite a bit of time considering the researcher's role, and the importance of developing the right relationships with those you are researching with and for. I believe that these are two key elements in constructing a successful ethnographic research project. In doing this, I quote extensively from texts that I have found very helpful in learning how to do research and being a researcher, mainly because of the quality of the authors' voices and the ways they opened out the processes for me. You may find these texts speak to you in the same way as they did to me, but they may not, and you will find your own such texts.

The idea for this book has grown slowly over the past few years as I have supervised a lively, responsive and collaborative group of doctoral students, first in the Department of Education at the University of York and then in the School of Education at the University of Leeds, all of them working in multilingual settings. But the book's origins are in the past, in the days when I was a PhD student myself. At the time I began studying for a doctorate in 1996, I was a full-time lecturer in a busy FE college, in the middle of a rather chequered career in education that had taken me to West Africa as a young volunteer teacher, then to various other places and finally, in 1988, to settle in West Yorkshire. Over the years, I have worked with students of all ages and in a great range of multilingual settings. I began with no formal background or qualifications in language education, and became increasingly fascinated with the complex ways that language seemed such an important and yet such a hidden factor in success in education. More generally – as Angela Creese puts it – I wanted to understand about 'the role language plays alongside other social constructs in reproducing or unsettling social inequalities' (Copland and Creese 2015: 3).

Becoming a PhD student happened for me by chance. It began when I read a book chapter about assessing bilingual learners in the National Curriculum, written by the academic who became my supervisor, Eve Gregory. What she wrote impressed me greatly, and then I met her at an event in the early days of the National Association for Language Development in the Curriculum (NALDIC), and she encouraged me to think about doing a doctorate. Eventually I registered at Goldsmith's with Eve as my supervisor. The odds seemed to be stacked against me completing successfully: I was registered part-time while working full-time at a very busy job, a mature student in my mid-forties, and my supervisor was 250 miles away – a much more significant disadvantage then, when sending an email was a major undertaking. Moreover, I had two teenage children, who between them at times filled up more space than the full-time job! But, by the time I completed my PhD in 2001, I had become so inspired and empowered by the processes of ethnographic research that I wanted to tell other teachers and students about them and encourage others to embark on the doctoral journey which, as I had come to realize, certainly did not end with the awards ceremony. A short while after completing, I collaborated with Eve and two of her other former PhD students, Chris Kearney and Aura Mor-Sommerfeld, in writing a book about the processes of doing a PhD project (Conteh et al. 2005). Over the years, it has been satisfying to receive positive feedback on that book, and to be told of its value for people thinking about and getting started on doctorates and also their tutors. In many ways, this book is the successor to that one; it takes many of the ideas further, attempting to offer more comprehensive guidance and providing a wider range of examples of interpretivist research that follows ethnographic principles.

A few years after completing the doctorate, I became a university academic. I began to learn what it meant to play the game of seeking funding through writing research proposals, publishing in 'high-status' journals and with the 'right' publishers in order to meet the demands of REF, RAE and whatever other ranking systems have been, and will continue to be, imposed on universities. I felt uncomfortable with the hierarchical approaches to knowledge assumed in the bidding processes of many of the big national funding bodies, which meant research projects had to fit with the predetermined roles of 'Principal Investigator', 'Co-investigator', 'Research Assistant' and so on. Even the division between 'researcher' and 'researched' felt awkward to me when in my own research I depended heavily on the expertise and knowledge of my co-researchers and other participants in the project. Indeed, I have never stopped feeling somewhat ambivalent about being identified as an academic and a researcher, preferring to identify myself as a teacher, though of course the two are certainly not mutually exclusive. For me, the core of academic life is in the relationships that are formed between students and teachers, or 'researchers' and 'researched'.

Such relationships promote a culture of learning where the **'funds of knowledge'** (Gonzalez et al. 2005) brought to the shared enterprise by all participants are equally valued, and new knowledge is constructed and shared in collaborative and mutually empowering ways. I began to understand that assertions such as these are not just personal, political and epistemological (though they are certainly that, in deep ways); they are also philosophical, ethical and theoretical. They have profound implications, not just for what is counted as knowledge, but for the questions we seek to investigate and the ways that research is conducted. This became more and more apparent to me the more I worked with doctoral students on shaping and carrying out their projects. I have written a lot about multilingualism over the years, and somewhat less about research in multilingual contexts. Over time, I decided I wanted to set down as clearly as I could what I had come to think about as key messages for research methodology that might bring about change and enhance social justice in multilingual settings – and so the book began to come together.

Aims and purposes of the book

This is a research methodology textbook. But it is different from the standard kinds of such texts, which usually aim to set out systematically information about different research methodologies and methods, and to offer specific guidelines for students to follow in carrying out their projects. Instead, the intention in this book is to show how research methodologies work in practice, rather than to tell readers how to do them. It provides **case studies** that demonstrate how particular research projects have been carried out, all of which engage with the daily lives of people in multilingual settings. In the spirit of Mishler's notions of **'validation'** and **'trustworthiness'** (1990: 417), the hope is that the reader, as part of a community of scholars, will recognize in the case studies similarities with and ways forward for their own work. The intended audience is researchers wishing to develop their understandings of what it means to carry out interpretivist research following ethnographic principles, whether Masters', EdD or PhD students and their tutors, or more experienced researchers perhaps working on funded projects. Through the case studies, the book provides examples of research projects that both demonstrate particular methodological principles and shed light on some important and substantive issues related to multilingualism in society as a whole and in education more specifically. It demonstrates how small-scale projects such as those described in the case study chapters, which pay attention to the fine detail of individual experience situated in particular contexts, have the potential to contribute to change in education in all its forms in globalized, multilingual societies.

The eleven case study chapters in the book have several themes in common:

- All are concerned with understanding how people make sense
  of their lives and everyday experiences in multilingual homes,
  communities and classrooms.

- All the studies, in different ways, see being multilingual as a normal
  and convivial way of living in local and global contexts, and all
  build on theoretical models of language as social practice, and of
  different languages as resources for their users in sociocultural
  contexts.

- All the researchers began with personal or professional experience of
  a problem that they had identified; usually something that appealed
  to their sense of social justice.

- The identities of the researchers are key to the success of the projects
  and so constitute a vital theoretical and practical strand that flows
  through the studies.

- All the studies set out to understand the ways in which language, as
  defined above, underpins opportunities for success in education, and
  how this can be enhanced or impaired for the participants through
  external forces.

These commonalities are woven through both the topics being researched and the processes of the research projects themselves that are the focus of the case studies. This reflects the two most important substantive aims of the book. The first is to contribute to the growing body of evidence about the positive benefits and the challenges of living and learning in multilingual societies. The second is to show how such evidence can be elicited through qualitative, interpretivist research processes, carried out following ethnographic principles.

Learning to be a researcher – Linking theory and practice

The discussion above is about the aims of this book in relation to its content. But the overarching aim of the book relates to its readers, and to the processes of learning to be a researcher. All of the authors, including myself, came to research through practical professional experience, mostly in teaching but also in other professional fields. This is an increasingly common trajectory as more and more students come to PhD and EdD work after several years of a professional career. The first lesson for such beginning researchers in our field is that in research – just as in teaching – theory and practice are not separate; the two always need to be considered as parts of a dynamic whole. It is vital that the different kinds of knowledge that practitioners and researchers bring to the table are equally valued. Unfortunately, this is not the case currently in most classroom-based research: Lefstein and Israeli (2015) illustrate some of the problems in constructing the right kinds of dialogues between teachers and researchers, and I take up this theme in Chapter 13 (p. 245). I have written previously about how my PhD research arose directly from my professional experience as a teacher in different settings, but mainly as a primary teacher in a multilingual city in England (Conteh 2003). I completed my doctorate part-time while working as a teacher educator in the same contexts as those I was researching. Throughout the whole process, my research findings were constantly tested through my practice and validated by the teachers and families I was working with. When I completed the PhD and was persuaded to write a book, which turned out to be *Succeeding in Diversity*, I was determined to write something that would speak to the students I was teaching, and the teachers and families who were participants in the research. The book earned a positive response from those audiences, which was very satisfying. It was also very satisfying that, a few years later, it was accepted in the first university Research Assessment Exercise in which I was involved.

Cohen and Manion (1994: 39) see theory in the interpretive **research paradigm** as 'sets of meanings which yield insight and understanding of people's behaviour, which are as varied as the situations and contexts supporting them'. Methodologies are the theories of research in action, in other words the praxis. They are the theoretical justifications for the practical processes through which researchers seek to uncover, understand and explain the phenomena they investigate. As such, they link the questions with the ways in which they can best be investigated. Glaser and Strauss (1965, 1967) argue that theory is formulated through the 'continually intermeshed' processes of data collection, coding and analysis. They were among the first to conceptualize theory as 'theorizing', a continually developing and iterative process and not a finished product. For them also, theory is **'grounded'** in and emerges from within the data. In the same way, in classroom practice, theory emerges from within the practice of teaching. Theorizing is a way of constructing explanations of the data and linking them with similar contexts, rather than having an external explanation imposed upon them. So, a crucial argument that runs through the book as a whole is that practice and theory in education research are two parts of one whole, linked in circular – not hierarchical – ways.

Kramsch (2002: 197) discusses the links between theory and practice in research processes themselves, in the ways the questions emerge and the project develops and grows. She argues that research questions often come from 'telling moments' in classrooms, which spark off questions that teachers cannot help themselves from exploring. Sometimes – perhaps most times, and for most teachers – this may remain an intuitive process. But, as Kramsch illustrates, it can also lead to more explicit processes of research which not only 'broaden[s] outlook on practice' (p. 232), but also '[have] a way of revealing other potentially intriguing moments', and so the cycle continues. Theory-informed practice leads to better practice in which the construction of richer theorization is a natural outcome. This then feeds back into practice in a continuous, virtuous circle. The main implication of this for me is that research in education which has real potential to bring about change and make a difference to both teachers' and pupils' opportunities for success needs to grow from practice in schools, homes and communities and to feed back into practice and – ideally – into policy making. Such research cannot be handed down from 'experts' outside the classroom (though experts often have a vital role to play). It needs to take account of the complexity and unpredictability of daily life in classrooms and other learning contexts (even the most orderly seeming ones). Finally, it needs to take account of the viewpoints of all the participants in the process, some of whom may not be present on the scene. In this way, we will begin to understand much more richly than we currently do how the lived experiences of people in families and communities influence their experiences in schools and their affordances for success in education.

This introductory chapter sets out my arguments for what I mean by ethnographic research and what this means for the kinds of data we need to understand the questions that arise in multilingual education settings. The rest of the chapter is organized in two main sections:

- Ethnography, ethnographic principles and ethnographic tools

- Understanding language in multilingual settings: data generation, collection and analysis in ethnographic research

Ethnography, ethnographic principles and ethnographic tools

Ethnography and democracy

In tying my colours to the mast of ethnography, I have often been asked, 'What makes a research project ethnographic, rather than simply qualitative?' I think my answer has sharpened over the years, perhaps because I have felt a greater sense of urgency in changing political times and with the increasing challenges to the importance of and need for ethnographic research. The first thing that appealed to me about ethnography, when I began reading it and about it, was how it allowed you to get close to the people being researched in a way that no other methodology seemed to do. We have all had the experience of reading texts that are mind changing at the time and that keep on feeding our thinking over the years. Shirley Brice Heath's *Ways with Words* (Heath 1983) is such a book for me. I remember my first reading of it and my amazement and pleasure at how it drew me into the communities of Roadville and Trackton as places where people actually lived. And, perhaps more importantly in learning how to be a researcher, it made me feel very close to the author. Heath's openness about herself and her differing roles in her research and writing was a second revelation to me. I was also impressed by the clear, open style of writing and wanted to be able to write like that. A second text that has stayed with me from those early encounters with ethnography is Trueba, Guthrie and Au's (1981) edited collection of ethnographic studies in schools and classrooms. For different reasons, two chapters in particular have been very influential; Hugh Mehan's (1981) chapter on ethnography of bilingual education and Dell Hymes's (1981a) reflection on the practical benefits of ethnographic research, summed up in the need for **'ethnographic monitoring'** (p. 58). Hymes's chapter was almost like a call to arms to me. In it he says that, among research methodologies, ethnography is

> the most open, the most compatible with a democratic way of life, the least likely to produce a world in which experts control knowledge at the expense of those who are studied. (p. 59)

For Hymes, ethnography is a collaborative practice which can make a contribution to social change through developing knowledge that is 'co-operative, cumulative and comparative' (Van der Aa and Blommaert 2011: 321). Hymes's concept of ethnographic monitoring (summarized in Van der Aa and Blommaert 2011: 322–323) is both a blueprint for methodology that values the voices of all the participants and a political statement about the importance of such research for change. A crucial requirement of both of these is that the findings become 'the possession of the school (*sic*) people who have contributed to their discovery' (Hymes 1981b: 6). This clearly has strong implications for the nature of the relationships between 'researcher' and 'researched' at all stages of the process and these are discussed in the section below on the researcher's role (p. 17–21). One practical outcome of Hymes's vision, in which Heath played a major founding role, is the annual student-organized Ethnography in Education Research Forum at the University of Pennsylvania, first convened in 1980, where teachers and students present their work alongside university academics. I was able to attend and present in 1999 and 2001, and was bowled over by the friendly, collegial ethos, very different from other large, international academic conferences I have attended since. Of course, such equal cooperation does not just happen automatically and straightforwardly. Van der Aa and Blommaert (2011: 326) hint at the 'obstacles of tradition', especially in academic contexts, the established positions and hierarchies that hinder the co-constructive processes of communication so vital to achieve the desired change. We could also add to this the normalized ideologies and stereotypes related to race, class, gender and so on that can still be intractable barriers to achieving equal and open interaction in academic contexts. Maud Blair's article on neutrality in educational research, cited below (p. 18), is a powerful reminder of this.

Anthropology to ethnography: Context and time

While ethnography can trace its origins to the discipline of anthropology, the two have developed in different ways. The most important change, perhaps, is that – unlike Malinowski studying the lives of the Trobriand Islanders during the First World War, or Margaret Mead setting off from the United States for Samoa in 1925 – most ethnographers now are studying contexts which are close to hand with which they may already be familiar and sometimes know very well. Heath (1983: 9) captures a second important difference, which is in the aims of both paradigms. She points out the contrasts between the aim of anthropology to 'study social life as and where it is lived' and that of ethnography to 'capture the influences and forces of history on the present' – the 'ethnographic present', as she terms it. So, while both anthropology and ethnography are interested in understanding social life in **context**, the ways they construct the concept of context differ. Cole's (1996: 132–136) arguments are helpful for understanding the distinctions. He suggests that the sense of context, which is perhaps the one most employed in anthropology, as 'that which surrounds' is somewhat reductive, something like the 'context as bucket' metaphor mentioned by Rampton et al. (2015: 30). It ignores the etymological root of the term *contexere,* which is 'to weave together'. This brings back to the word the dynamic, dialectical aspects of its meaning. Cole suggests that it is the interplay between context and event that is significant to understanding the role of context in ethnography. Rampton et al. (2015: 26) articulate how context is an active element in social interaction:

> [C]ontext here is an understanding of the social world activated in the midst of things, an understanding of the social world that is also interactionally ratified or undermined from one moment to the next as the participants in an encounter respond to one another.

They go on (p. 30) to argue that this way of thinking about context as 'context-in-process' needs also to 'be conceptualized' as layered and "multi-scalar" in research that seeks to address questions about language in society. This has important implications for the ways we need to think about data collection and, indeed, what will count as data, which I discuss in the section below about understanding language in multilingual settings (p. 23–26). The main implication I want to draw here is that an ethnographic project needs to take into account not just what is observable in the scene to the researcher's gaze, but also how all participants perceive what is going on. And to fulfil Heath's quest to understand 'the ethnographic present', we need to understand something of what everyone brings to the context in terms of their personal, social and cultural histories. This idea has many echoes with the 'funds of knowledge' (Gonzalez et al. 2005) approach to understanding teaching and learning in classrooms, and also Cole's notion of culture as 'history in the present' (Cole 1996: 110). Holland and Lave's (2001) concept of 'history in person' is also illuminating in thinking about context in this way, especially in situations of 'contentious local practice' (p. 5), where individuals are trying to make sense of experiences that involve tension and uncertainty.

Erikson (1973, 1984: 58–59) trenchantly argues that 'traditional ethnography' is inadequate for the study of schools, classrooms, and – we can add – family and community contexts that are already familiar to us as members of such communities. The main reason, he suggests, is that school ethnography, unlike traditional ethnography, begins with a ready-made 'unit of analysis' (i.e. the institution of schooling, or other specific social settings), rather than a society as a whole. He also argues that traditional ethnography does not insist, as school ethnography does (or should), on making the processes of decision making, selection and abstraction in the research sufficiently transparent. This is important, because we all feel, with justification that we already know about schools, classrooms and other such places. We tend to take for granted what Erikson describes as the 'arbitrary nature of [the] ordinary everyday behaviour' (p. 66) as it is displayed in the daily life of the social contexts we have ourselves inhabited. For ethnographers heading off to 'foreign lands', unsure what they will encounter, the arbitrariness is much more apparent. In a famous – and often wrongly attributed – statement, Mehan (1981: 47) elegantly describes the stances ethnographers must take, contrasting the 'anthropological' ethnographer working in exotic settings in distant lands with the ethnographer of more 'local' scenes:

> The ethnographer working in a foreign land is attempting to make the strange familiar, while the ethnographer in local scenes must reverse the process and make the familiar strange in order to understand it.

The fact that many researchers contemplating ethnographic research are already familiar with the contexts of their projects can undoubtedly be an advantage. But there are attendant cautions and constraints, which are discussed below in the section on the researcher's role (p. 17–23).

There are many reasons why it may not be feasible to carry out a full-blown ethnography as part of an EdD or PhD project, and the one that is most frequently raised is time. Like many writers on ethnography, Mehan (1981: 47) stresses the point that there is a need for 'an extended period of time', for 'long periods' of study in the contexts being explored in order to gather enough data for an ethnography. Indeed, some would say that ethnographic projects are never finished, they are only left, their findings always provisional and their conclusions tentative. Despite carrying out her fieldwork over a decade, Heath (1983: 13) cautions the reader to see *Ways with Words* as:

> an unfinished story, in which the characters are real people whose lives go on beyond the decade covered in the book, and for whom we cannot, within these pages, either resolve the plot or complete the story.

The pressures of completing an EdD or PhD in three years mean that Malinowski, Mead, and even Heath, no longer offer transferable models, not just because of the distances they travelled to carry out their research, but because of the amounts of time they could devote to it. Time pressures relate not only to doctoral projects, but also to funded projects which are required to produce their conclusions within tight time constraints. Despite this, there are ways in which research projects can still develop along ethnographic lines. Jeffrey and Troman (2004) offer practical suggestions for ways that researchers can make the most of the time they have available. They identify three modes of time that can accommodate the needs of ethnographic practice when time is limited; 'compressed time', 'selected intermittent time' and 'recurrent time'.

In terms of methodology more broadly, Green and Bloome (1997) identify three distinctive approaches to ethnography:

- **doing ethnography**, which refers to the traditional model of research, involving a broad, in-depth and long-term study of a social group;

- **adopting ethnographic perspectives,** which entails a more focused approach in which particular aspects of the everyday life of a social group are studied, guided by theories of culture and ethnographic practices of inquiry;

- **using ethnographic tools,** which refers to the use of data collection techniques derived from ethnographic fieldwork.

These distinctions are helpful for thinking practically about how to do research ethnographically when it is not appropriate to carry out a full ethnography and open up possibilities of different ways of planning an EdD or PhD project following ethnographic principles within the time available. The case study chapters in this book mostly fall into the second category: the authors all show in different ways how they developed ethnographic perspectives in their research within particular constraints of time and other resources.

In my view, research that can satisfy the claim to adopt ethnographic perspectives and follow ethnographic principles needs to meet two main criteria. First, it needs to develop understanding of what is happening in a particular setting from the perspectives of all the participants, respecting their knowledge and expertise as equal in importance to the researcher's own and maintaining transparency about the researcher's own role. Second, it needs to demonstrate a commitment to understanding the importance of what participants bring to the contexts of which they are members, and how personal experiences are mediated and influenced by their contexts – social, cultural, political and historical. In the rest of this section, I discuss these two criteria under two subheadings, which I have worded as practical principles:

- Make the familiar strange: recognize the significance of the self in the research;

- Strive to understand the local in the global and the global in the local.

Make the familiar strange: Recognize the significance of the self in the research

All ethnography is part philosophy and a good deal of the rest is confession.

This is one way in which Geertz (1973: 346) articulates the significance of the researcher as a unique individual in ethnographic research. Peshkin (1988: 17) describes **subjectivity** as 'a garment that cannot be removed' and stresses – indeed – the importance of self awareness for all researchers, not just those proposing to take an ethnographic perspective. He argues that:

researchers, notwithstanding their use of quantitative or qualitative methods, their research problem or their reputation for personal integrity, should systematically identify their subjectivity throughout the course of their research.

Because of the ways in which the academy reflects the ideological stereotypes of the wider society, these subjectivities are sometimes, inevitably, glaringly obvious. Writing from her experience as a minority ethnic, female academic, Maud Blair (1998: 20) concludes that neutrality is a myth in educational research. Though given fire by her personal and professional experiences, her arguments relate to us all. Researcher identity is a crucial factor for all researchers, even those who – as Blair (p. 14) points out – just seem somehow to understand the rules of the game and whose identities may never be called into question. My supervisor, Eve Gregory, saw the articulation of personal investment as vital, especially at the beginning of the project. This is how she described the discomfort she felt when, as a young teacher, she read an academic text which she felt drew misleading conclusions about the area of London where her family had lived for many years:

> The beginnings of an ethnographic study are often rooted in anger, even fury, and, as such, are partisan. (Conteh et al. 2005: x)

This was one of the starting points for her PhD. Her powerful sentiments echo the sense of indignation that drove me to begin my own PhD, but my anger had a different source. In my teaching career, particularly during a spell as a primary teacher in a multilingual school in England in the late 1980s, I had become more and more unhappy and angry about things I encountered on a daily basis. I perceived them as injustices to individual pupils and to particular groups of learners and their teachers. My problem was about what I perceived as the systemic inequalities of opportunity for the children I taught. This fed my anger, and I readily recognized that my own history, beliefs and attitudes were part of the reason why I felt the way I did and so were part of the data. Doing a PhD was not a career move for me. From the start, 'the satisfaction of personal needs' (Peshkin 1982: 55) was the strongest motivating force. It was only when I had finished that I realized I wanted to have further opportunities for writing and research and so moved on from the FE college I had been working in to an academic post.

But anger is not obligatory for starting an EdD or PhD. I appreciate that there are many very different, and equally legitimate, motivations. These days, instrumental reasons may often dominate, and perhaps quite rightly so. Whatever the initial motivation, the recognition of one's own subjectivity (or subjectivities), of the self in the research, is crucial from the start. Eve invited all her students, at the start of the PhD, to write an autobiographical piece, a sort of position paper of the self, a 'why am I here?' statement. I found this hugely empowering, and it is something I have asked all my own students to do. It gave me the confidence to:

> see how autobiographical exploration and writing is not self-indulgent, but an excellent way to begin to understand the problem and define the important research questions which will help to illuminate it. (Conteh et al. 2005: 9)

I learned from Eve how personal and professional experiences are valid starting points for research, and also how righteous indignation can feed positively into questions that can be researched. The ethnographic researcher's recognition of the ways in which their subjectivities influence their perspectives is a vital aspect in the process of 'making the familiar strange'. It is also fundamental to the ethnographic quest to develop **emic** (insider), as well as **etic** (outsider), stances necessary in the attempt to reflect the perspectives of the members of the culture being studied. But it is not as simple as it may sound. **Subjectivity** can become a barrier to seeing clearly. Duranti (1997: 85) highlights the 'apparently contradictory qualities' of the participant observer's need to maintain some level of detachment while at the same time constructing an emic view of events. Peshkin stresses the importance of 'tamed subjectivity' (1988: 20), which is necessary to 'avoid the trap of perceiving just that which my own untamed sentiments have sought out and served up as data'. This mirrors Erikson's concept of 'disciplined subjectivity' (p. 61), which, he suggests, is vital for identifying the features of the context that the researcher may find 'intolerable', but which at the same time are 'probably the key to the difference between that culture and one's own'. Mercer (2007: 4) shows how etic/emic perspectives are not diametrically opposed but 'constantly move back and forth along a number of axes, depending on time, location, participants and topic', and helpfully discusses several dilemmas in insider research. What is needed is a strong **'subjective monitoring'** on the part of the researcher, a clearly articulated awareness of the range of subjectivities which they bring to the context, and which are either mirrored or undermined in the responses of other members of the community as the data collection proceeds. What is certainly not needed is the attempt to develop some self-imposed kind of objectivity in order to make the claim that subjectivity has been eliminated. This would not only be pointless, but impossible to achieve.

This leads to the second main dimension of 'making the familiar strange', that of constructing appropriate relationships between the researcher and the researched. Barron (2013: 118), reminding us of the inevitable power differentials, quotes Lassiter and Campbell (2010: 10), who sum up the paradoxical nature of the researcher/researched relationship well:

Ethnographers seek to reflexively offset colonial modes of research by engaging research participants as dialogic partners in projects (still) largely initiated by the researcher.

I argued above that inequalities are often entrenched in the ways that research projects are traditionally funded and planned (p. 9). This can also be the case in the procedures through which doctoral projects get ethical approval, but EdD and PhD students can have considerable room for manoeuvre in the ways they set up and develop their projects. A small but significant change that can be made is in the words you use to describe those whom you engage with in your research. There is a wide range available – subjects, sample, participants, informants, respondents, sources, to suggest a few. Each has its own connotations and associations. As you read published research, notice what different words the writers use, and consider their effects on the views you are forming about the relationships between the researcher and the researched implied in the text.

In a seminal book, Cameron et al. (1992) argue that there are three kinds of relationships that researchers can construct with their study participants; **ethics, advocacy** and **empowerment**. The nature of the relationships is summed up in the prepositions, respectively 'on'; 'on and for'; and 'on, for and with'. They conclude that the only position consonant with research that strives towards social justice is that which promotes empowerment through focusing on the 'with' relationship. Research 'on' denies the agency of the people being researched, and research 'for' can risk silencing their voices. Cameron et al. (pp. 147–150) propose three precepts for researchers committed to social justice, which help them consider how they can change the terms of their research in ways that will empower their 'subjects', rather than treat them merely as sources of data. The first of these is the use of interactive methods in order to nurture a dialogue between 'researcher' and 'researched' about the nature of the data, as well as how it is being collected. The second is the need to valorize participants' own agendas, but always with the recognition that there may be situations where participants do not wish to share them (p. 148). The final precept relates to the need to share the data as it emerges and to provide opportunities for feedback in the thick of things, as well as at the end of fieldwork.

Feedback is often informally woven into the processes of the research, but it also needs to be done in more overt, formal ways. Torrance (2012: 114) formalizes the feedback process, naming it as **'respondent validation'** (it is sometimes also called **'member checking'**), and stressing that this approach has ethical, as well as theoretical, salience. He suggests there are two purposes for respondent validation. First, research participants can check the accuracy of the data, adding anything they may feel has been missed or asking to delete anything they would prefer not to be included. Second, they can respond to the interpretive claims being made, which may lead to changes in the analysis. Torrance also reminds us of the need to take account of the relationships between participants, as well as between participant and researcher (p. 128). Ways of doing respondent validation are suggested below in the following section (pp. 38).

There is no doubt that the practicalities of positioning yourself as outsider or insider can be fraught. Researchers have found different strategic ways of resisting the power differentials in their research design. Carrasco (1981: 169) stresses the value of 'teacher collaboration' in classroom research, with the teacher being able to offer insights on events that may not be available to the 'outside' researcher. Corsaro (1981: 130) provides an engaging account of his efforts to make himself 'one of the family' in the nursery in which he conducted his research, and goes on to describe how he was careful to ensure that the children's perceptions of his role were different from those they had of the teachers and other adults in the setting, in the hope that he could capture behaviour from the children that they might otherwise suppress 'for fear of negative reactions'. Similarly, in my study, I remember working to establish a slightly less 'teacherly' relationship with the children in the classrooms in the hope that this might lead to more open responses on their part. This caused problems when the class teachers sometimes popped out for a few minutes, or asked me to lead activities with groups of children. I then had to keep some semblance of order, and the situation verged on chaos at times. I remember one slightly exasperated child, looking up at me one day and asking, 'Mrs Conteh, when are you going to be a proper teacher?'.

Strive to understand the local in the global and the global in the local

So far, the focus of the discussion has been on the importance of understanding the fine detail of the contexts being studied from the points of view of all the participants. But, to satisfy the criteria I outlined above, and to understand the significance of the emerging data in terms of social justice, the perspective must also be broader. Blackledge and Creese (2010: 67) argue that the detailed study of local issues needs to lead to 'tying [our] observations to broader relations of power and **ideology**'. With Erikson's 'disciplined subjectivity' in place, this entails the need to take a contextually informed, critical stance on the data. In my own reading, my first encounter with critical ethnography was Ogbu's (1981) **'multi level' study** of the underachievement of children from ethnic minority communities in schools in the United States. The key aim of Ogbu's research was to take into account the ways in which historical, sociopolitical and economic forces influence what goes on in classrooms. He was struck by the mixed messages the children in his study were receiving. On one hand, there was constant verbal encouragement from their parents to do well in school. On the other, ethnographic description of their family contexts and of their actual 'texture of life' (p. 21) revealed that doing well in school did not lead anywhere.

The same kind of confused signals came to the children from school, where grades they were given always seemed to be at the same mediocre level, despite the efforts they made and the quality of their work. I found his conclusion to his study (p. 23) powerful:

> [C]lassroom events are built up by forces originating in other settings … how they influence classroom teaching and learning must be studied if we are ever to understand why a disproportionate number of minority children do poorly in school.

This put into words something that, at the time I first read it, I had dimly perceived but not been able to articulate. Ogbu's starting principle in analysis was that, to consider classroom interaction as if it were self-contained, separated from and uninfluenced by events outside its four walls leads to an analysis which is uninformative in revealing the causes of children's success or failure. Such a position helps us understand why *only* changing classroom practice is of limited value in improving many children's educational opportunities.

But, as I became more immersed in my data and reading, I began to realize that the trajectory from local to global may not be as simple as the quote above suggests:

> The value of traditional ethnography lies in exploring a particular perspective on the world; however, a global analysis includes multiple perspectives of different types distributed across widely different social locations.

Thus Agar (2005: 19) raises the issue that, in a research project, each participant's awareness of the links between the local and global in relation to their situation can be very different from others. He argues that it is crucial to try to understand what these dissonances indicate. His article shows how 'local discourse and global theory are linked in numerous ways' (p. 3), and that 'going from the global to the local' is sometimes the more appropriate way to travel. He cautions (p. 17) that some participants may have 'more pressing problems to deal with' than considering global explanations for their situations. Through **discourse analysis** on interviews with participants he knew well from previous research, about the reasons for the persistence of substance abuse in a particular context with which he had been familiar for many years, he demonstrates the ways in which his global knowledge often differed from that of his interviewees. He suggests that, at times, the detailed data generated by the research in the local contexts can only be understood with 'a prior global analysis' (p. 8), and that to see the research process as always a progression from the local conversations to the global interpretations may mean that vital understandings are missed. His analysis shows how it is sometimes in the interplay between local and global, as well as between interviewer and interviewee, that the full story emerges. He also shows the importance of being alert to the significance of global factors that may emerge in the words of participants that at first may seem tangential to the focus of the research.

One valuable lesson I take from Agar's article is the need to engage with participants as mediators of the global, as well as the local, and to try to figure out what this means in their responses to the questions which are the focus of the research. This became very clear to me with a student I was supervising at the time when the London bombings of 7/7 (2005) had just happened. A non-Muslim, she was in the early stages of interviewing Muslim parents (mainly mothers) about their perceptions and experiences of home – school relationships. This involved her travelling to a town about 30 miles away from where we were based to meet her participants. One day, during our supervision, we had a conversation about the fact that one of the London bombers had been identified as coming from this particular town. The student was concerned about how to respond if the subject of the bombings and thus Muslim fundamentalism came up during her conversations with the mothers. I was surprised when my co-supervisor, an eminent historian, suggested that this was not very likely as they would not be very interested in such remote events. Surely, he suggested, the mothers would have enough on their plates with looking after their children, cooking and shopping. When the student came back from her fieldwork, she told me that 7/7 was just about the only thing the parents wanted to talk about. More significantly, through their conversations, she had come to realize how differently they saw it from her and, indeed, how momentous it was in their daily lives. This realization, backed up by data from her interviews and observations, became one of the main 'rich points' (Agar 2006: 4) in her data. It led to a much more nuanced analysis and more powerful conclusions about the gaps between home and school for many Muslim pupils in schools in England than would have been the case without it. The notion of 'rich points' is an important one in thinking about data collection and analysis, and is discussed in the following section (pp. 35).

Understanding language in multilingual settings: Data generation, collection and analysis in ethnographic research

Language as resource: Identity, culture and ideology

In this section, I provide a brief overview of ways of thinking about language as social practice and consider what they mean for understanding language as data in ethnographic research in multilingual settings. Following this, I discuss the processes of doing data collection and analysis ethnographically that best fit these ways of thinking about language. All of the case studies in this book, in different ways, see being multilingual as a normal and convivial way of living in the local and global contexts they investigate. The questions they ask, in line with ethnographic research in general, are not about language itself, but about how people make sense of their worlds and lives, the factors that enhance or impair their opportunities to achieve their goals, and how language is an integral part of all this. Language is conceptualized not just as sounds, words and syntax, but as socially situated practices which people construct together to accomplish their purposes in specific sociopolitical and cultural contexts (e.g. Heller 2007; García 2009; Blackledge and Creese 2010; Blommaert and Backus 2011). The research presented in Chapters 2–12 is all grounded in theoretical models of language as social practice, and of different languages and language varieties as resources for their users in sociocultural contexts. The ways they make sense of their data to understand how their participants use language to accomplish their goals go well beyond the features of language as a self-contained system. My own realization of the need for such an approach came when I was stuck in trying to make sense of an interview I had done with a teacher where the words she spoke seemed to make no coherent sense, and even to be contradictory. As I listened over and over again to the recording, I began to realize that the meaning was not in the words she was saying, but in *how* she was saying it and in what she had not said. The paralinguistic features of the text began to reveal the sense to me: the ways the teacher used pitch, intonation, stress and pausing were laden with significance and helped me to realize the struggle she was having in making sense of a situation that actually made no sense to her (Conteh 2003: 105–107). This led me to see how I could use Fairclough's model of **critical discourse analysis** (Fairclough 1995) to explain what was going on in my data.

Rampton et al. (2015: 25) sum up the way we need to open out the range of features involved in a model of language for ethnographic research:

> [W]ord denotation, the formal structures of grammar and the propositional meaning of sentences still count, but they lose their traditional supremacy in linguistic study, and, and instead become just one among a large array of semiotic resources available for the local production and interpretation of meaning.

Shifting the focus from linguistic features to 'semiotic resources' opens out the possibilities of what is available for data generation and analysis, and calls into question the traditional model of languages as separate, sealed systems. It links with current ways of theorizing language such as **translanguaging** (see García 2009), which shift the focus to the people and the goals they are seeking to accomplish through language. It also breaks down distinctions between people as 'monolingual', 'bilingual' and so on by proposing that the resources and processes of translanguaging are available to everyone. This resonates with Blommaert and Backus's (2011) reconceptualization of the sociolinguistic concept of repertoire, in which they construct languages as part of individuals' 'indexical biographies' as they move across and between different social contexts in their lives. For many, the significant elements of their biographies are not different languages, but different varieties expressed through accent, dialect and other resources. Rampton et al. (2015: 28) remind us of the powerful indexicality of these particular linguistic features, particularly in the United Kingdom. Indeed, they argue that 'the relationship between varieties and social structure' is powerfully indicative of the ways that linguistic features are 'aligned with the interaction of form, ideology and situated action' and so move us away from the 'separate-but-connected' model of the relationships between language and social structure to a much more nuanced one, which reflects the model of context I discussed above (pp. 14–15).

The main implication of the arguments developed above is that there are powerful associations between language, identity and culture for all of us. Language is an inextricable part of all our personal and social lives; of the cultures we live in and of who we are. It is part of the way in which we develop a sense of where we belong in the social contexts that we inhabit. The ways we use languages and in what social contexts we use them shape our identities as we constantly (re)organize a sense of who we are and how we relate to these social and cultural contexts. This also has implications for the ways we understand data in ethnographic research. Copland and Creese (2015: 14) argue that language and culture are 'a single unit of analysis' and conceptualize the links between them in this way:

> Culture is not a fixed set of practices essential to ethnic or otherwise defined groups. Language is not an unchanging social structure unresponsive to the communicative needs of people. Rather, languages and cultures are practices and processes in flux, up for negotiation but contingent on specific histories and social environments.

Copland and Creese go on (p. 17) to make the fundamental point that, while language and languages are experienced and observed through 'microsociological encounters or interactions', they are also the conduits through which 'macrosocial processes always operate'. Moreover, as Piller (2016: 3) convincingly argues, investigating the intersectionalities between language and their contexts is a key factor in exposing the **ideologies** that underpin social justice (or the lack of it), because 'language intersects with race, socio-economic status, legal status and gender in complex ways'. Through exploring the complexities of how these sociopolitical concepts are both constructed through language and also contribute to the ways we use language in our daily lives, we are able to reveal and come to understand the systemic inequalities in a particular setting. Rampton et al. (2015: 18) make essentially the same points, while reminding us that the contexts need to be counted as data, as well as the interactions that are situated within them:

> the contexts for communication should be investigated rather than assumed. Meaning takes shape within social relations, interactional histories and institutional regimes, produced and construed by agents with expectations and repertoires that have to be grasped ethnographically.

By recasting language as 'communication' and foregrounding the co-construction of 'meaning' as the prime goal of communication in the contexts they research, Rampton et al. clearly allude to some of the ways in which 'language' needs to be perceived and conceptualized in ethnographic research – many of which are illustrated in the case studies in this book – as conversation, narrative, performance, classroom discourse and interaction, online interaction, translanguaging, multimodal texts, interview transcripts, field notes, policy documents and so on.

From language to data

Freire's (1985: 43) construction of praxis in teaching and learning resonates with the way we need to think about the iterative processes of theorizing, fieldwork and analysis in ethnographic research. For Freire, praxis is based on understandings that are shaped partly by practice, and partly by critical reflection. The quality of this process depends on the extent to which teachers are able to take ownership of the contexts in which they are working, to engage in reflection which 'sends us back ... to the given situation in which we act'. In the same way, ethnographic research processes are always context-based and contingent, proceeding through repeated cycles of data collection, reading, analyzing, theorizing and writing and requiring that the researcher 'makes a wise and prudent practical judgment about how to act in *this* situation' (Carr and Kemmis 1986: 190). This is the essence of the kind of research that is illustrated in this book.

The notion of 'writing up' at the end of the data collection and analysis process is not a very helpful one in ethnographic research. Writing is an important element throughout the research process. Much of the data collection involves writing in different forms and genres, as I show in the section below on data, and the construction of the written outcomes to the research needs to grow from the process, as well as the findings. This is part of the kind of reflection that Freire talks about in his model of praxis. Alasuutari provides a useful section which illuminates how the process of writing is an integral part of the research (1995: 177–192). He begins by making the important point that 'talking and writing are tools of thinking not just ways for expressing one's thoughts', and ends by reminding us that 'researchers always become blind to their texts and thoughts'. Asking others (and not just supervisors) to read drafts from an early stage is vital.

I want to make one more general point about writing before getting down to the detail of data generation, collection and analysis. It is that ethnography is not really a methodology, nor a method, in the same way as others that we talk about, such as interviewing, observing or conducting surveys. It is the only research approach that is spoken about as both process and product. The word 'ethnography' can refer both to a way of doing research and to a written artefact in a way that a study following other kinds of research processes cannot. For example, we entitled our book about educational ethnographic research, *On Writing Educational Ethnographies* (Conteh et al. 2005). Similarly, Barron (2013: 17) talks about producing a representation of his data in a 'full ethnography'. In this chapter, I have been talking about taking an ethnographic perspective and following ethnographic principles, not 'doing an ethnography' in the full sense. I hope it is becoming clear what I mean by this. Essentially, an ethnographic perspective is a particular way of looking at the world. In our book (Conteh et al. 2005), we traced the development of our different methodological frameworks from the common starting point of ethnography to the different approaches we took to understanding our data. As Eve suggests (Conteh et al. 2005: xxii), 'an ethnographic lens is needed through which data should be viewed', but 'each of us needed to search for a second methodology or approach to explain what was happening in the data'. Rampton et al. (2015: 22) explain the changing ways that ethnography has been perceived and how it is currently conceptualized:

> Before, ethnography could simply be seen as an additional method of data collection, supplementing the otherwise standard procedures of elicitation and analysis in linguistic science. But as we become more conscious of the social and historical particularity of knowledge, ethnography gains foundational weight as a way of seeing, building on dialogue and on a reflexive recognition of the researcher's own positioning.

Thinking about ethnography in this way means that it becomes meaningless to talk about qualitative or quantitative methods of data collection as if they related to two different kinds of methodology. Using a method ethnographically can apply to conducting a survey, a questionnaire, an interview, an observation, or writing field notes or analyzing documents. Numeric data collected by 'quantitative' processes can be examined through an ethnographic lens, just as can data collected by 'qualitative' processes. For example, one of my main areas of interest is multilingual learners in mainstream classrooms. The Government publishes annual statistics taken from the Schools Census returns (e.g. NALDIC 2013), which are widely quoted and used to support many different arguments – sometimes opposing ones – about language education. The kinds of questions I have in mind as I look at these figures are:

- What's the history of collecting data about children's languages in schools?
- Who makes the decisions about collecting the data?
- How are the data collected?
- What changes have been made to the ways the data are collected over the years?
- Who are involved in collecting the data (children, teachers, parents, local authority officials, school managers)?

Such questions constitute an ethnographic perspective on the statistical data contained in the census. They reveal how these statistical data have histories and are situated in specific political, social and cultural contexts. Addressing them in my research means that the figures will appear in my ethnographic accounts not as simply neutral data, but linked to the findings that emerge from other **data collection strategies** in the study and to the developing arguments about the ways in which the contexts are part of the ways in which success is mediated for multilingual pupils in mainstream classrooms.

Data generation and collection: Field notes, participant observation and interviews

The best way to learn about the basics of data generation, collection and analysis is to collect some data for yourself. The next best way is to read studies by other researchers who show how they have done it. In this section, I briefly discuss the three main **strategies for data collection** that form the basis of ethnographic research, and provide references that can be followed up for fuller accounts of the issues and processes. My intention is to indicate some general principles and offer some practical examples about each strategy and also to suggest some useful further reading. The case study chapters then illustrate in detail how the strategies work out in practice. Finally, in the last chapter of the book, I synthesize the ways in which they have been illuminated in the case studies and draw some general conclusions.

Field notes

The first kind of data, field notes, are the fabric of the whole research project, from which all the other data arise and through which they are interwoven. But, despite their omnipresence, as Barron (2013: 120) points out, 'there is very little agreement amongst ethnographers regarding how to go about recording what happens in the field'. Rather than worrying about this, think about it as liberating. It means that there is no right or wrong **method** of writing field notes and you can devise your own ways, dependent on the nature of the situations and interactions that emerge in your research contexts. Your field notes, in essence, are a record of your own ways of making sense of the context you are studying. Field notes are very personal, they will change and develop as your research proceeds. As you read the case study chapters, notice how the authors use field notes to support their more 'formal' data collection and interpretation. What researchers choose to write down is inevitably partial and indicative of how they position themselves in relation to the research context as a whole. Creese illustrates this in her example of researchers working in teams (Copland and Creese 2015: 41–43) where she shows the different, but complementary, field notes of three researchers observing together in one setting.

There are clearly advantages to working collaboratively, but most EdD and PhD students work alone on their projects. The important thing is to develop a critical stance on your own field notes as you write them and adapt the process of writing accordingly. This is part of the 'making the familiar strange' process. It can be demanding: Copland describes it as 'like performing on stage: you had to be aware of your own performance and simultaneously free of it' (Copland and Creese 2015: 98). Barron provides a full account of his own field note taking which reveals some of the challenges he faced, particularly that of recognizing his own assumptions which, as he noticed, differed according to the settings he was visiting (2013: 120–123). The actual forms that field notes take vary greatly. I remember, in my PhD fieldwork, devising a strategy to capture an aspect of my research context that involved talking to myself into a tape recorder as I drove home. Then, as soon as I got home, I listened and made notes, adding anything else I could remember. This arose because I had fallen into the habit of staying behind in the classroom after my regular Wednesday afternoon visits, chatting with the two teachers I had just been observing. These chats sometimes went on for a long time and I began to get the sense that the teachers, intuitively, were signalling important issues to me in what they were saying. I did not feel able to take out my notebook and pencil and start taking notes during our conversations, so I tried to hold as much as I could in mind until I got in the car.

Observation

As Copland shows, field note taking and observation tend to merge into one another (Copland and Creese 2015: 99). But there comes a point when, as a researcher, you realize that you need to negotiate with your participants to engage in a more formal process than sitting in the corner and writing notes – this is when the observation often begins. In my PhD fieldwork, this point came seven months in (I was doing it part-time so my data collection period was stretched out over a period of almost two years). In my quest to understand why some 'EAL' pupils seemed to get on well in school and others didn't, I had struck lucky in finding a vertically grouped class as my main research site. The children stayed there for two years and – even better – were taught by two teachers who job-shared, so I had the opportunity to watch two different teachers with the same pupils in the same classroom. For the first seven months I visited every Wednesday afternoon and sat in the classroom, took a lot of notes, chatted with people, helped out with classroom activities and collected documents. Despite all this, I still felt quite unsure at times what I was actually looking for. But I began to realize that the ways the teachers talked to each other constituted some kind of 'rich point' (see below p. 35). I was not sure what or why, but I felt I had gained the teachers' trust, so I asked if I could record them, and this is when the observations began.

Observation forms an essential part of most research projects and deserves more status as a research strategy than it often gets. Watching what is going on underpins research in many fields, not just in ethnographic research. There are many reasons why: it is easy to manage, it doesn't need complex equipment or preparation and it can provide the basis for further kinds of data collection. Observation can be done in a wide range of ways, from 'unstructured' to highly 'structured' with a predefined schedule. Such schedules do not fit into ethnographic research: the observation needs to be open in order to capture the complexity of what is happening and to contribute to the quest of understanding all the different perspectives at play. A predefined schedule would close down the interpretative process of 'unriddling' that Alasuutari (1995: 133–139) characterizes as allowing the researcher to 'see beyond the horizon of the self-evident', and as generating the 'all-important why-questions' about the observational data. Alasuutari goes on to suggest some useful ways of generating the why-questions that – he suggests – will lead to a rich analysis of the data.

The central issue to consider in observation is what role you take as the researcher. Labov's (1972: 209) famous 'observer's paradox' defines the central dilemma:

> The aim of linguistic research in the community must be to find out how people talk when they are not being systematically observed; yet we can only obtain this data by systematic observation.

This raises the key question of how you can most effectively position yourself as the observer in relation to the setting you are observing.

The traditional model of the ethnographic researcher is as a participant observer, and you need to work out what kind of participant you are. This will change in relation to the events, and the participants, you are observing. Subjective monitoring (see pp. 19) is vital throughout. Teacher-researchers, for example, have great advantages in classroom-based observation as they begin from a strong position of familiarity with the context. But, as Lefstein and Israeli show, the temptation to hang on to the teacher's role of judging the quality of the teaching and learning, rather than developing a more open observation of the scene can be strong (2015: 197–198).

Objectivity is no more than the agreement of everybody in the room.

I saw this remark on the notice board of one of my colleagues at Leeds, and immediately copied it and put it on my own board. It is attributed to Edward Boyle, minister of education from 1962 to 1964 and vice-chancellor of Leeds University from 1970 to 1981. I like it because it neatly sums up the key dilemma of ethnographic participant observation. Observers inevitably bring their own values and interests to the task and this is a positive feature, at the same time empowering and full of responsibility. But you need to remain keenly aware of the limitations of this. Sevigny (1981: 69) suggests that there are four possible 'research stances' for the participant observer:

- Complete participant;
- Participant as observer;
- Observer as participant;
- Complete observer.

and that the kinds of data gathered will depend in part on the extent of participation along this continuum. I would question the fourth stance – I am not sure that it is possible to be a 'complete observer' in the full sense, especially as you get to know your context and participants more deeply. You need to maintain throughout the awareness that your presence in the situation is changing it, and so your role is always an interactive one. This resonates with what Hymes regarded as an essential aspect of ethnographic monitoring (Van der Aa and Blommaert 2011: 332–323):

Ethnographic monitoring starts from the requirement that the analyst participates, and does not just observe, because the analyst is very much part of the social environment in which the research takes place and to which it must be fed back – not as a matter of choice but as a matter of political, theoretical and methodological requirement.

In my PhD fieldwork, I needed to maintain the awareness that I was known in schools in the community as a tutor from the local college who went round observing and assessing student teachers. This meant not only that I needed to find schools which, ideally, did not have partnership relationships with the college, but also that, while observing, I had to remove my tutor hat and put on my researcher one, while still processing what was happening through the lens of my familiarity with the local scene.

Interviews

Observing raises awareness of the perspectives of the participants in the context, and interviews are often the way that these perspectives are understood and **triangulated** with the findings emerging from other emerging data. In my PhD fieldwork, the progression from field notes to observing to interviewing seemed natural, with most of the more formal interviews taking place towards the end of each phase of the fieldwork in each school setting, and in the children's homes. By this time (from about six months in), I felt I knew the teacher-participants and the parents well enough simply to ask them from time to time to share their views on particular issues, rather than have to set up a formal interview and then arrive with a set of questions, though I did do this once or twice. Handbooks on research methodology often characterize types of interviews as ranging from 'structured' to 'unstructured' with a progression from a list of closed questions in a schedule that needs to be rigorously followed to something like a free conversation. I think the idea of an 'unstructured interview' is rather strange as even the freest and most open conversation has a structure, albeit a very complex one. In ethnographic research, interviews can take different forms; they can be brief and conducted 'on the hoof' while fieldwork is going on; they can be iterative where the interviewer conducts a series of interviews with the same participants, building on the data generated in each successive interview. Interviews need to be open in order to allow space for the views of the interviewee to be clearly represented, and equal, so that the interviewee is empowered to express their views confidently. Spradley's famous description of the ethnographic interview is that 'it shares many features with the friendly conversation' (1979: 58). Saeko Toyoshima and I invented the term 'structured conversations' (2005: 23) to describe the kinds of interviews we conducted in order to understand the perspectives and motivations of teachers in two very different contexts.

The quality of ethnographic interviews is strongly determined by the relationships between interviewer and interviewee. As I said above, as far as possible, there needs to be an equal sense of power between the participants. This means that the data that emerge are dependent to some extent on who is interviewing whom. Shah (2004: 553), discussing cross-cultural interviewing, reminds us of an aspect of this that is sometimes forgotten; the whole interview itself is a cultural construct involving 'particular codes of conversation and patterns of behaviour'. But more than this, the whole framework of the interview may be alien to members of some cultural groups:

> [T]he western concept of the researcher's power in the interview context associated with control over research direction, data and dissemination may not have similar connotations in the cultures where sources of power differ widely from those in the western capitalist societies.

In her article, Shah gives us an honest account of her own struggles in cross-cultural interviewing, and some useful advice for others trying to do the best interviews they can in complex, uncertain and unsettling circumstances:

> Learning to be a good researcher, to avoid assumptions based on familiarity, and to bring a critical eye to the research context is a developmental process, but cultural knowledge is a matter of habitus, which cannot be acquired except by living.

Like Shah, you may feel the need to redo interviews, to return to your participants and engage their perspectives more fully, and there is no harm in this. In the end, the important thing is to be open and transparent about what you have done, about who is interviewing whom, and as clear as you can be about the implications of this for the ensuing data while developing the 'critical eye' that Shah advocates.

Foster (2004: 255) discusses her own 'insider' research with African-American teachers, which – she claims – was more effective in allowing them to speak 'in their own voices' than previous work done by White academics. Reflecting on her experiences as a researcher (pp. 256–260), she points out how insider/outsider roles are always 'intricate and intertwined' and how the researcher must maintain vigilant awareness of this. She also warns, however, of the dangers of assuming that the data obtained in an interview constitute an 'authentic candid version' (p. 262) of the interviewee's experiences, simply because interviewer and interviewee share the same cultural backgrounds. In a project I carried out with bilingual teachers, I arranged for the interviews to be done by teachers themselves rather than myself, as I am not a bilingual teacher in the way this was defined in the project. In preparation, we agreed on a set of broad questions for the teachers to follow, and discussed ways of encouraging participants to share their own views on issues that we may not have thought of. I transcribed all the interviews, and it was very clear to me that the teacher-researchers were able to elicit much richer and more illuminative data with their interviewees than would have been possible for me, who was not an insider in the same ways.

Towards analysis

When it comes to analyzing interviews, the key point to remember is that, within an ethnographic framework, they need to be understood, not just from the point of view of their content, but also as socially constructed discourses between interviewer and interviewee. Copland and Creese (2015: 36) sum up the implications of this:

> The central point from this perspective is that data created in an interview must be taken as a joint construction so that both the content of the interview and also the process of the interview, that is how the interview is interactionally accomplished, are analyzed.

Paying attention to the linguistic features of the interview, in the way that Rampton et al. (2015: 18, see p. 26 above) suggest, opens out the interpretation, providing analytic insights that are not available from considering just the content itself. For example, in the transcript I provide in Figure 1.1 (p. 37), which is taken from an interview that lasted almost two hours, I knew by listening to her voice as she spoke and later listening on the tape that 'Sandra' was finding it very difficult to say what she felt. Paying attention to the prosodic features of her language revealed the way she was struggling with intractable contradictions in her professional experience.

Another issue that every ethnographic researcher has to grapple with is the sheer amount of data that accumulate as the research progresses. Keeping things organized is essential so that you can keep track of things and avoid undue stress to yourself as the data mount up. All the time, label, list and catalogue your data in ways that make sense to you. Before you begin formal analysis, you need make yourself very familiar with your data by listening to your recordings and reading through your field notes several times. Though time-consuming, this will save you a lot of time in the long run, as you will be able to identify and track themes across the data more easily and ensure that your interpretations are intuitively strong, as well as theoretically grounded. While doing this, you can also begin to identify which parts of the data you need to go back to for deeper consideration and perhaps more detailed analysis. This leads to the issue of transcription – which I discuss in detail below – as part of getting to grips with your data. Though it is laborious and time-consuming, the benefits of doing your own transcribing cannot be overestimated. You do not need to transcribe every word of the data that you collect in your sound files, but you need to be able to justify the choices you make, both theoretically and methodologically.

Rich points in the data

As you listen to your sound files, be alert to what Agar (2006–4) calls the 'rich points' in the data:

> What happens is, people do something in a situation that we don't understand. For years I've called such moments *rich points*. Those moments of incomprehension and unmet expectations are the fuel that drives ethnographic research.
>
> There are a lot of ways that an outsider might explain a rich point. The people might have made a mistake, an error. It might be something that is stupid or crazy. It might be that the people don't know any better. It might be that they're trying to pull a fast one. It might be some kind of -ism, a prejudice that *that* kind of person never makes any sense, so what would you expect?

As many authors remind us, the processes of interpretation and analysis begin as soon as we begin collecting and organizing data, and the rich points can become key drivers in the collection of further data and in the analysis. Sometimes a rich point jumps out at you; at other times it only emerges through carefully and repeatedly sifting through your data. I mentioned above (p. 23) how the 7/7 bombings were a particular rich point for one of my PhD students. One of my own rich points, as I suggest above (p. 24), was the realization that I needed to pay attention to the paralinguistic features of the discourse, as well as the words that were spoken.

Into analysis: Transcribing

Transcribing of recorded data, particularly of conversations, is part of methodology. Interpretation and analysis are involved in the decisions made about how the oral text on the recorder is to be turned into a written text on the page. Ochs (1979: 44) reminds us that 'transcription is a selective process reflecting theoretical goals and definitions'. It is a way of developing your arguments about your theoretical perspectives about language, as well as about the substantive issues within the data, and thus a step to developing the process of analysis that best suits your questions. There are many ways of coding, formatting and laying out transcripts. Richards (2003) provides a good, comprehensive set of coding conventions as a starting point. Graddol et al. (1994) see transcription essentially as an intuitive, impressionistic exercise (p. 181), and warn against the over-rigid use of coding conventions. They stress the value of adapting your coding as you progress. Trying out different coding conventions is a useful exercise, as is adapting those you read about, or constructing your own. Sometimes, the way a transcript looks on the page can be a useful indicator of its arguments and themes. In my

---

Conventions used for coding the transcripts

The following prosodic features of spoken language emerged from the data as significant for indicating implied meanings. Their extent varied from speaker to speaker:

- The relative speed and pacing of delivery – speeding up and slowing down within and across utterances;
- The stress given to particular words and phrases;
- Pausing.

In addition, the occurrence of overlapping utterances between speakers occurred more often in some conversations than in others. It seemed to be significant for indicating sections of the discourse where the participants were closely identifying with each other's meanings, or where there was the sense of negotiating towards an agreed meaning.

I have indicated these features in the transcripts in the following ways:

1. *Speed* – *italics* for words or phrases delivered with differences in speed from the surrounding text – *s-t-r-e-t-c-h-e-d* for slower speed and *condensed* for faster speed.
2. *Stress* – **bold** for words given stress when this would not occur in a normal, unmarked delivery.
3. *Pausing* – 1 dot(.) for short 'syntactic' pause (i.e. when a comma, full stop or other punctuation would be appropriate in written text); 2 or more dots (....) for longer pauses – the number of dots is an estimate of the length of the pause.

FIGURE 1.1 *Example of coding conventions*

own coding of some of my interviews with teachers from my PhD data, I identified features of stress, pitch, pausing and intonation as significant to the meaning, and devised a system that represented these visually on the page. Here are the coding conventions (Fig. 1.2) I used for many of my interviews, and an example of a coded transcript.

Graddol et al. (1994) provide examples of a range of ways of coding and laying out transcripts, showing how choices can be made to foreground different aspects of the linguistic and paralinguistic features considered salient in the discourse. In the case study chapters in this book, the coding conventions of the authors have been left in place, so you will see a variety of ways of doing it. A particularly important feature of many of the chapters is that the researchers themselves were multilingual and had to make decisions about which languages to use in conducting their interviews, transcribing their recordings and analyzing their transcripts. Of course, the final outcome had to be produced and presented in English, but decisions along the way

01	Sandra:	Increasing numbers of children who don't seem to be able to
		listen ... as well .. listening skills seem to be quite ... quite *poor*
		.... and there's probably a lack of levels of maturity as well ..
		which is *something to be said for those with the behavioural*
		problems as well ... increased children with special needs
05		...um ...
	JC:	And is that something you've noticed over the years?
	Sandra:	Mm .. **definitely** definitely it's ... getting worse .. definitely
		... and *I suppose to some extent* .... um ... the level of the
		children who we've been getting into the class .. they're
		generally not functioning at the level that you would
10		expect of children of that age and that's a **worry** .... especially
		when ... you're supposed to be preparing them for middle school
		.. you think well middle school are going to have these children
		and they will expect them to do this *this and this* and they *c-a-n-t*
		... do that because they've come in at this level and you can't
		possibly get them up to *that* level when they've come in at **this**
15		*level* .... you can only do your **best** and move them on from
		where they *a-r-e* ... but ... um ... I suppose that's a pressure to
		some extent .. that the children **a-r-e n-o-t** working at the level
		that .. would be expected .....
	JC:	Do you think that's because of ... um ..... external factors?
	Sandra:	Um .... it's difficult .. I think we have had a c-h-a-n-g-e in the ....
		not the
20		catchment area but the ... the *h-o-u-s-i-n-g* within the catchment
		area I think that might *h-a-v-e* ... some *e-f-f-e-c-t* ... on it .... um ....
		children coming from perhaps different backgrounds ..... um ....
		we *s-e-e-m* to be getting more children <*cough*> who have been
		..... um..... you know .. who have some .. sort of difficulties .... or
		um .. with <*indecipherable*> or whatever ... um .... *I*
25		*don't* .... um... *it's difficult for me to say really* .... at this point
		... um ... I mean we.. we've got ... I suppose we've got an
		increasing *number of Asian children* .. as well ... um ... with
		the **l-a-n-g-u-a-g-e** difficulties but ... it's not that it's .... it's not
		necessarily **that** I don't think ... um.

FIGURE 1.2 *Example of coded transcript*

could enrich their data and analysis. I discuss the issues around researching multilingually in the introduction to Part 2 (p. 97).

Arguing that 'variability in transcription practice has analytic, social, and political meanings that we would do well as researchers to examine more closely', Bucholtz (2007: 801) shows how the same raw data can be transcribed in different ways for different purposes. For her, this 'variation' is a positive factor, but one that needs careful consideration. My example of a coded transcript above is a very short extract from an interview I did with a teacher. After listening to the whole interview many times and taking notes, I selected this one particular piece of data to present in my thesis because I wanted to use it to show a 'rich point', an idea that had emerged from the long interview and was also emerging from other parts of my data, and which seemed to me very important at the time for understanding the bigger problem I was interested in. It became a significant aspect of the findings of my thesis as a whole. This idea linked to my research questions and was situated in the theoretical framework I had developed. I devised the coding to reveal the aspects of the piece of data that I decided were salient in expressing all of this. The coding was intended to reveal more about *how* things were being said than *what* actually was being said, because this was what seemed significant to me. Someone else might have taken other extracts from the interview and argued different things, and this would have been as valid as my own interpretation of the interview, if their arguments were found to be rigorous. This is what I think Bucholtz means by saying that transcription is 'a sociocultural discourse practice' (p. 788), and it keys into Cook's contention (2011: 440) that 'any analysis of language in use is discourse analysis of some kind'.

Strengthening analysis: Respondent validation

As you amass the data, you need to think about how you are going to ensure that your participants have the opportunity to share their own views on them, and how they can be empowered to make a meaningful contribution to shaping the data, the analysis and findings. I discussed the purposes of respondent validation on pp. 21. Here, I will briefly illustrate how you can make it part of your research processes. You can share your data in an ongoing way by inviting your participants, whenever possible, to read the transcripts or listen to the sound files that relate to them, but you also need to have more formal occasions where you invite your participants to look at your data so that they can tell you about anything they do not wish to be included in the final dataset. Of course, confidentiality means that you must not share data from one participant with another without overt permission. These occasions can also be an opportunity to invite your participants to contribute to analysis. If this involves data from focus group discussion or classroom discourse with several participants, this could lead to valuable dialogue about the actual data. I did this with the bilingual teacher interviews that I mentioned above (p. 33). For one particularly interesting interview, I invited the two participants to take part in a post-interview discussion, which was recorded with their permission (Conteh and Toyoshima 2005: 30–31). This led to some valuable iterative data that could be triangulated in other project interviews, and which fed into the analysis and conclusions of the project as a whole.

As with every other aspect of the research process, there are times when the respondent validation process leads you to the need to make uncomfortable ethical decisions. This happened to me with one focus group interview that took place towards the end of my PhD fieldwork and which I had completed only with some difficulty. It contained data that I felt could be explosive, if used in the wrong way. The interview was with a group of four teachers, and some of their comments could easily have been interpreted as racist. I struggled to decide what to do: was my analysis unjustifiably negative, and – moreover – had I uncovered issues that I, as a teacher trainer, needed to 'do something about'? My subjectivity as a teacher educator was aroused and ready to go. Clearly, however, one thing I urgently had to do was resist the urge to run an in-service workshop on institutional racism. I was encouraged by my fellow PhD students at one of Eve's intercollegiate seminars to maintain the researcher role and follow ethical research processes as carefully as I could. So, I gave the transcripts of the interview back to the teachers, along with my initial thoughts about analysis, and invited them to respond. I assured them I would leave out anything they felt unhappy about, and that I would be very interested in hearing their views on the issues that came up in the interview. To my surprise, all four teachers reassured me that my transcript was a fair record of the interview, that there was nothing they regretted saying and would like taking out, and indeed that the views emerging were a reasonable account of their perspectives and perceptions of the issues. One of them even went on to comment on how helpful she had found the interview, and what an interesting view on the issues had emerged. So, my responsibility as a researcher was to report the findings, which I did in the PhD thesis. In due course, I published them for a different audience (see Conteh 2003: 110–114). But I still feel anxious that in some way I might have betrayed the trust of my participants in revealing views that are easy to condemn as racist and stereotypical.

I have only made brief mention in this chapter about actual analytic frameworks and strategies. In the introductions to each part, I discuss further the ways the analyzes were developed in the studies discussed in the chapters, and you will see many examples of analysis in the case study chapters themselves.

References

Agar, M. (2005), 'Local Discourse and Global Research: The Role of Local Knowledge', *Language in Society*, 34(1): 1–22.

Agar, M. (2006), 'Culture: Can you Take it Anywhere?', *International Journal of Qualitative Methods*, 5(2), Article xx. Available at: http://www.ualberta. ca/~iiqm/backissues/5 2/pdf/agar.pdf (accessed May 11, 2017).

Alasuutari, P. (1995), *Researching Culture: Qualitative Method and Cultural Studies*, London: Sage Publications.

Barron, I. (2013), 'The Potential and Challenges of Critical Realist Ethnography', *International Journal of Research and Method in Education*, 36(2): 117–130.

Blackledge, A. and Creese, A. (2010), *Multilingualism: Critical Perspectives*, London: Continuum.

Blair, M. (1998), 'The Myth of Neutrality in Educational Research', in P. Connolly and B. Troyna (eds), *Researching Racism in Education: Policy, Theory and Practice*, 12–20, Buckingham: Open University Press.

Blommaert, J. and Backus, A. (2011), 'Repertoires Revisited: "Knowing Language" in Superdiversity', *Working Papers in Urban Language and Literacies*, 67, King's, London. Available at: http://www.kcl.ac.uk/innovation/groups/ldc /publications/workingpapers/download.aspx (accessed 29 December 2016).

Bucholtz, M. (2007), 'Variation in Transcription', *Discourse Studies*, 9: 784–807. doi:10.1177/1461445607082580.

Cameron, D., Frazer, E., Harvey, P., Rampton, M.B.H. and Richardson, K. (1992), *Researching Language: Issues of Power and Method*, London: Routledge.

Carr, W. and Kemmis, S. (1986), *Becoming Critical: Education, Knowledge and Action Research*, Basingstoke: Falmer Press.

Carrasco, R.L. (1981), 'Expanded Awareness of Student Performance: A Case Study in Applied Ethnographic Monitoring in a Bilingual Classroom', in H.T. Trueba, G.P. Guthrie, and K.H. Au (eds), *Culture and the Bilingual Classroom: Studies in Classroom Ethnography*, 153–177, Rowley, MA: Newbury House.

Cohen, L. and Manion, L. (1994), *Research Methods in Education*, 4th edn, London and New York: Routledge.

Cole, M. (1996), *Cultural Psychology: A Once and Future Discipline*, Cambridge, MA: Harvard University Press.

Conteh, J. (2001), 'Success in Diversity: Culture, Language and Learning in Ethnically Diverse Primary Schools', PhD Thesis, Goldsmiths, University of London.

Conteh, J. (2003), *Succeeding in Diversity: Culture, Language and Learning in Primary Classrooms*, Stoke-on-Trent: Trentham Books.

Conteh, J. and Toyoshima, S. (2005), 'Researching Teaching and Learning: Roles, Identities and Interview Processes', *English Teaching Practice and Critique*, 4 (2): 23–34. Available at: https://edlinked.soe.waikato.ac.nz/research/journal /view.php?article=true&id=91&p=1 (accessed 29 December 2016).

Conteh, J., Gregory, E., Kearney, C. and Mor-Sommerfeld, A. (2005), *On Writing Educational Ethnographies: The Art of Collusion*, Stoke-on-Trent: Trentham Books.

Cook, G. (2011), 'Discourse Analysis', in J. Simpson (ed) *The Routledge Handbook of Applied Linguistics*, 431–444, London: Routledge.

Copland, F. and Creese, A. (2015), *Linguistic Ethnography: Collecting, Analyzing and Presenting Data*, London: Sage Publications.

Corsaro, W.A. (1981), 'Entering the Child's World – Research Strategies for Field Entry and Data Collection in a Pre-school Setting', in J.L. Green and C. Wallat (eds), *Ethnography and Language in Educational Settings*, 117–146, Norwood, NJ: Ablex.

Duranti, A. (1997), *Linguistic Anthropology*, Cambridge: Cambridge University Press.

Erikson, F. (1973, 1984), 'What Makes School Ethnography
"Ethnographic"?'*Anthropology and Education Quarterly*, 15: 51–65.
Fairclough, N. (1995), *Critical Discourse Analysis: The Critical Study of Analysis*,
London: Longman.
Foster, M. (2004), 'The Power to Know One Thing Is Never the Power to Know
All Things', in G. Ladson-Billings and D. Gillborn (eds), *The RoutledgeFarmer
Reader in Multicultural Education*, 252–265, London: RoutledgeFarmer.
Freire, P. (1985), *The Politics of Education: Culture, Power and Liberation*,
Westport, CT: Bergin and Garvey.
García, O. (2009), *Bilingual Education in the 21st Century: A Global Perspective*,
London: Wiley-Blackwell.
Geertz.C., ed. (1973), *The Interpretation of Cultures: Selected Essays by Clifford
Geertz*, New York: Basic Books.
Glaser, B.G. and Strauss, A.L. (1965), 'Discovery of Substantive Theory: A Basic
Strategy Underlying Qualitative Research', *American Behavioral Scientist*, Feb:
5–12.
Glaser, B.G. and Strauss, A.L. (1967), *The Discovery of Grounded Theory*,
Chicago: Aldine.
Gonzalez, N., Moll, L. and Amanti, C. eds (2005), *Funds of Knowledge: Theorizing
Practices in Households, Communities and Classrooms*, New York: Routledge.
Graddol, D., Cheshire, J. and Swann, J. (1994), *Describing Language*, 2nd edn,
Buckingham: Open University Press.
Green, J. and Bloome, D. (1997), 'Ethnography and Ethnographers of and in
Education: A Situated Perspective', in J. Flood, S.B. Heath and D. Lapp (eds), *A
Handbook of Research on Teaching Literacy through the Communicative and
Visual Arts*, 181–202, New York: Simon and Shuster/Macmillan.
Heath, S.B. (1983), *Ways with Words: Life and Work in Communities and
Classrooms*, Cambridge: Cambridge University Press.
Heller, M. ed. (2007), *Bilingualism: A Social Approach*, New York: Palgrave
Macmillan.
Holland, D. and Lave, J. eds (2001), *History in Person: Enduring Struggles,
Contentious Practice, Intimate Identities* (Advanced Seminar Series), Santa Fe:
School of American Research.
Hymes, D.H. (1981a), 'Ethnographic Monitoring', in H.T. Trueba, G.P. Guthrie
and K.H. Au (eds), *Culture and the Bilingual Classroom: Studies in Classroom
Ethnography*, 56–68, Rowley, MA: Newbury House.
Hymes, D.H. (and others) (1981b), *Ethnographic Monitoring of Children's
Acquisition of Reading/Language Arts Skills in and out of the Classroom*, vols.
1–3: Final Report. Graduate School of Education, Philadelphia, PA: University
of Philadelphia.
Jeffrey, B. and Troman, G. (2004), 'Time for Ethnography', *British Educational
Research Journal*, 30(4): 535–548.
Kramsch, C. (2002), 'From Practice to Theory and Back Again', *Language, Culture
and Curriculum*, 15(3): 196–209.
Labov, W. (1972), *Sociolinguistic Patterns*, Philadelphia: University of Pennsylvania.
Lassiter, L. and Campbell, E. (2010), 'What Will We Have Ethnography
Do?'*Qualitative Inquiry*, 16(9): 757–767.
Lefstein, A. and Israeli, M. (2015), 'Applying Linguistic Ethnography to
Educational Practice: Notes on the Interaction of Academic Research and

Professional Sensibilities', in J. Snell, S. Shaw and F. Copland (eds), *Linguistic Ethnography: Interdisciplinary Explorations*, 187–206, London: Palgrave Macmillan.

Mehan, H. (1981), 'Ethnography of Bilingual Education', in H.T. Trueba, G.P. Guthrie and K.H. Au (eds), *Culture and the Bilingual Classroom: Studies in Classroom Ethnography*, 36–55, Rowley, MA: Newbury House.

Mercer, J. (2007), 'The Challengers of Insider Research in Educational Institutions: Wielding a Double-Edged Sword and Resolving Delicate Dilemmas', *Oxford Review of Education*, 33(1): 1–17.

Mishler, E.G. (1990), 'Validation in Inquiry-Guided Research: The Role of Exemplars in Narrative Studies', *Harvard Educational Review*, 60(4): 415–442.

National Association for Language Development in the Curriculum (NALDIC) (2013), EAL Pupils in Schools: The Latest Statistics about EAL Learners in our Schools. Available at: http://www.naldic.org.uk/research-and-information/eal -statistics/eal-pupils/ (accessed 29 December 2016).

Ochs, E. (1979), 'Transcription as Theory', in E. Ochs and B.B. Schefflin (eds), *Developmental Pragmatics*, 43–72, New York: Academic Press.

Ogbu, J.U. (1981), 'School Ethnography: A Multilevel Approach', *Anthropology and Education Quarterly*, 12(1): 3–29.

Peshkin, A. (1982), 'The Researcher and Subjectivity: Reflections on an Ethnography of School and Community', in G. Spindler (ed), *Doing the Ethnography of Schooling*, 49–67, New York: Holt.

Peshkin, A. (1988), 'In Search of Subjectivity – One's Own', *Educational Researcher*, Oct: 17–22.

Piller, I. (2016), *Linguistic Diversity and Social Justice: An Introduction to Applied Sociolinguistics*, Oxford: Oxford University Process.

Rampton, B., Maybin, J. and Roberts, C. (2015), 'Theory and Method in Linguistic Ethnography', in J. Snell, S. Shaw and F. Copland (eds), *Linguistic Ethnography: Interdisciplinary Explorations*, 14–50, London: Palgrave Macmillan.

Richards, K. (2003), *Qualitative Inquiry in TESOL*, Basingstoke: Palgrave Macmillan.

Sevigny, M.J. (1981), 'Triangulated Inquiry – A Methodology for the Analysis of Classroom Interaction', in J. Green and C. Wallat (eds), *Ethnography and Language in Educational Settings*, 65–85, Norwood, NJ: Ablex.

Shah, S. (2004), 'The Researcher/interviewer in Intercultural Context: A Social Intruder!', *British Educational Research Journal*, 30(4): 549–575.

Spradley, J.P. (1979), *The Ethnographic Interview*, Belmont, CA: Wadsworth (Reissued Long Grove, IL: Waveland Press, 2016).

Torrance, H. (2012), 'Triangulation, Respondent Validation, and Democratic Participation in Mixed Methods', *Research Journal of Mixed Methods Research*, 6(2): 111–123.

Trueba, H.T., Guthrie, G.P. and Au, K.H. eds (1981), *Culture and the Bilingual Classroom: Studies in Classroom Ethnography*, Rowley, MA: Newbury House.

Van der Aa, J. and Blommaert, J. (2011), 'Ethnographic Monitoring: Hymes's Unfinished Business in Educational Research', *Anthropology and Education Review*, 42(4): 319–334.

PART ONE

Looking Forward – Getting into the Research

I begin this part by introducing its three chapters. Then I briefly discuss each chapter in relation to two generic methodological themes, showing the ways in which each of the three authors exemplifies them in their own work:

- making the familiar strange
- constructing the process as praxis.

Introducing the chapters

The starting points for PhD research in education are often problems that practitioners face in real-world social contexts, which then need to be shaped into a viable research project theoretically, methodologically and practically, as well as in relation to the substantive issues embedded in the questions. The three projects featured in this part of the book are all examples of this. They all deal with large-scale, ongoing issues related to social justice in education (and beyond) for groups of people who can be defined as belonging to linguistic and cultural 'minorities': Tibetan-Chinese bilinguals in China, British Asian Muslims in the United Kingdom and young people from poor rural communities in Sindh, Pakistan. All these groups have been categorized in different ways as 'disadvantaged', but their disadvantages have been constructed by forces largely outside their control and not through their own actions. Thus, the nature of the issues which need to be understood is not just personal, but cultural, political and historical and – I suggest – philosophical, ethical and moral. Through fine-grained analysis of a small number of individual cases, the three studies all explore large questions, identifying the ways in which they have profound effects on the lives of their participants. They show, among other things, how the origins and causes of the problems are – for the most part – outside of the immediate experiences of their participants. Despite their wide origins, the studies are all very specific to particular communities. They cannot be generalized or replicated, but, in the spirit of Mishler's notions of validation (1990), they can – as I suggest in Chapter 1 (p. 10) – illuminate similar contexts and similar issues for other researchers and practitioners.

The three contributors, Yixi, Nasir and Ambreen, are all themselves members of the communities they researched, and so began their research journeys very much as insiders to the contexts they studied. All had direct personal experience of the problems they identified in their research. They all show awareness in their theses of the point that this is a methodological issue, as well as one of method, and so it needs to be considered in both theoretical and practical ways. In their chapters in this book, they all reflect on this aspect of their research: in other words, they show how they made 'the familiar strange' as part of the broader processes of framing and shaping their studies. Making the familiar strange is not an activity restricted just to the initial stages of the project, to the decisions that are made about research sites, participants, access and so on. It is an ongoing process, one that Mercer (2007) describes as engaging with the 'delicate dilemmas' that surround the establishing and maintaining of insider/outsider roles, to do with issues of 'access, intrusiveness, familiarity and **rapport**' (p. 6). Mercer argues that insider/outsider positions are not binary, but a continuum that needs to be mediated with balance and delicacy. The chapters in this part illustrate in practical ways what this mediation looks like. It is interesting, though, that in Mercer's arguments about the risks of insider research, her register shifts and she characterizes insiderness as a 'double-edged sword' (p. 5), a somewhat risky and dangerous, and potentially destructive research tool. In this way, she indicates the dangers inherent in insider research that does not recognize the complexities of positionality.

Mercer also alludes to the important epistemological point that insider research conceptualizes knowledge as constructed and 'participative' (p. 11).

This aligns with the way I argue for the theorization and construction of knowledge in ethnographic research in Chapter 1 (p. 11). Again, this view can be seen in the chapters in this part: Yixi, Nasir and Ambreen all entered their research sites with personal knowledge of the issues they were investigating, which helped them in understanding the perspectives of their participants. It can be argued that, at the same time as they were researching the experiences of their participants, they were also coming to a deeper understanding of themselves. They all mention how, at different points in their research, they were re-encountering times and situations where they had had to face up to difficult issues in their own lives. In this way, the three authors all show in their work the importance of recognizing and engaging with the research process as praxis, of theorizing personal knowledge and experience in order to develop a broader theory as part of the process of understanding the personal and social experiences of others. Nasir's chapter illustrates this particularly well in the way he explains his journey through the literature, showing how it helped him to understand the words of his participants.

Making the familiar strange and developing praxis

At the beginning of an EdD or PhD study, there are many ways in which you can position yourself in relation to the problem you have identified, and many different stances you can take as a researcher. The three authors in this part illustrate different facets of this and show how they justified their decisions and choices. Yixi positions herself in relation to her research in very personal ways; Nasir's positioning is closely linked to his aim of developing a strong, sustained theoretical argument to link his own experiences to his questions and his data; and finally, Ambreen takes a more detached, reflexive position in her chapter. She links her work to **phenomenography** (Francis 1993) to consider some of the ethical issues she faced in interviewing participants who recognized the differences in status between themselves and the researcher.

As Yixi shows in her chapter, she was born into the community that she proposed to research, a community that has suffered great oppression over the years. There is absolutely no way that she could be considered neutral, nor did she want to be – from the start, her motivation and desire were to find ways to make things better for the future of her community and its members. Throughout her chapter, Yixi makes her insider status in her research very clear. She is transparent about her own history in her research contexts, including the relationships she already had with the people who became her participants. Her accounts of returning to China and meeting them as a researcher are infused with warmth and emotional engagement.

As she indicates, she found that her physical distance from her participants while studying in Leeds over two years was important in developing an outsider position to her questions. While she was in Leeds, learning how to be a researcher, developing the contextual sections of her thesis, planning her fieldwork and reading and writing endlessly, she was coming to understand fully the complexity of the researcher role. A key realization during her planning stage that was very valuable in understanding her role as an outsider was that she could frame her research as a historical study. Her eldest participant, the first she recruited, the professor, was in his 70s. Her youngest, Jampa, was thirteen years old. Between them, they spanned over fifty years of change in relation to language education in China. This helped Yixi to see that the personal experiences of her participants needed to be contextualized within the wider themes of change in language and education policy in China and in the theorization of bilingualism and bilingual education. She also realized that both themes were strongly influenced by the political and cultural changes of their times. So, in Yixi's case, it can be argued that a key element in developing an outsider perspective was in the way she developed her research design.

In the second chapter in this part, Nasir begins by recounting his discomfort and anger at the experiences faced by the students he worked with in secondary schools in a multilingual city in the north of England. A member of a well-established Pakistani-heritage community for whom maintaining links with the 'homeland' is very important, he had not lived in England very long at the time he began his research, and the rawness of his experience was still very apparent. At the same time, meeting him when he was in the process of applying to do a PhD at Leeds, my first impression of Nasir was of a somewhat reserved, scholarly person, who already had an impressive grasp of the ideas that came to form the theoretical framework to his study. These ideas clearly fascinated him, and sometimes – it can be said – they ran away with him as he was working on his transfer materials and struggling to shape his own arguments, grounded in his extensive reading. What seemed to help was when he began to generate some data, and he came to recognize how the ideas he was reading about were embodied in the words of his participants. So, in many ways, Nasir's process of making the familiar strange was a cyclical one; from the theoretical ideas into the processes of data collection, which took him back into the lived situations he knew so well both personally and through the engagement with his participants, and then out again into the theoretical framework he was developing for his analysis. Unlike Yixi, Nasir changed his project design in response to emerging themes in his data: for example, he began to notice that gender was a more salient factor than he had first anticipated and decided to follow it through. This entailed the need to recruit more women participants in his study. Like Yixi, he accessed the people who became his participants through personal contacts. He maintained his outsider position through the theoretical rigour of his research design, which fed into the construction of his interview processes, as well as his transcription and analysis.

In the third chapter in this part, Ambreen gives a more reflexive perspective on her study, focusing on her research design and her methodology, which – like Yixi's – combined ethnographic principles with life history interview. Though her participants shared a common linguistic and sociocultural background, the study was not an ethnography in the established sense of the word; instead, it used an ethnographic approach to explore and give voice to individual people, focusing on their specific contextual peculiarities, rather than studying a particular group in its social context. Though her methodological approach was very similar to Yixi's, the two differ in the questions they were asking and the purposes which each researcher had for their data. While Yixi was exploring her participants' experiences in order to understand systemic issues from national and historical perspectives, Ambreen's purpose was to explore the motivations of her participants as individuals from their own understandings of the situations in which they found themselves. She wanted to see them as individuals who had lived through painful experiences, with influences on their lives which they may never have articulated before. To do this, Ambreen explains how she adopted Hazel Francis's concept of phenomenography so that she could 'have the interviewee thematize the phenomenon of interest and make the thinking explicit' (1993: 70). In this way, she was able to see the experiences of each of her participants as distinctive, and the participants themselves as individuals, not simply members of a linguistic and cultural group.

In his account of how phenomenography gave him the tools he needed for his own life history research, Kearney (2003: 59) reminds us how, in ethnographic research, the tools we use 'are not neutral or innocent', and so must be chosen and handled with care. He describes the delicate and subtle processes of life history interviewing in a way that sums up the importance of nurturing trusting and empowering relationships between the researcher and the researched in ethnographic research:

[A]s my interventions became less and less sure and articulate, the interviewees became more sure and fluent. I also realized that, through my reading and previous experience in this area, I have access to information the interviewees do not. They on the other hand have a lifetime of lived experience and deep and often painful reflections upon what it means to negotiate complex networks of people and signs, within layers of history and, sometimes conflicting, traditions. Where we connect is where we are trying to unriddle these complex processes of cultural change we are living through. What concerns me here is how we, as researchers, can engage in a fruitful dialogue in which we neither overplay our knowledge and stifle the conversation nor underplay it and miss opportunities to widen the parameters of the picture.

Reflection and discussion points for Part 1

In this part of the book, you will read accounts of three PhD studies which show you different ways of thinking about the initial shaping of the project. They show clearly that there is no one right way to do this. Whatever way you choose, the process depends heavily on the theoretical, methodological and practical decisions you make, and how you construct your own role as a researcher. While these decisions need to be well justified from the literature and so will have some things in common with other projects, they will be unique to your study and to you as a researcher. Here are some questions to help you reflect on how you are shaping your own PhD project, as you read Chapters 2, 3 and 4. You may also find them useful as discussion points with your peers:

- What are your personal and/or professional links with your own research questions and contexts, and how might these impinge on your planning and carrying out your fieldwork? What ethical issues may arise because of these links?

- From what you can discern from the chapters, how did the three authors 'make the familiar strange' in their projects? What issues do you think you might face in making the familiar strange in your own study?

- What have you learned so far about analyzing data from this part of the book? What questions do you have about analysis as you continue to read Parts 2 and 3?

References

Francis, H. (1993), 'Advancing Phenomenography: Questions of Method', *Nordisk Pedagogik*, 2: 68–75.

Kearney, C. (2003), *The Monkey's Mask: Identity, Memory, Narrative and Voice*, Stroke-on-Trent: Trentham Books.

Mercer, J. (2007), 'The Challenges of Insider Research in Educational Institutions: Wielding a Double-Edged Sword', *Oxford Review of Education*, 33(1): 1–17.

Mishler, E.G. (1990), 'Validation in Inquiry-Guided Research: The Role of Exemplars in Narrative Studies', *Harvard Educational Review*, 60(4): 415–442.

CHAPTER TWO

Stories of Becoming Bilingual in Complex Contexts

Yi XiLaMuCuo

Guiding questions

1 The main theme in Yixi's chapter about her research into Chinese-Tibetan bilingualism is the way she accessed the participants. Are there any similarities with the processes you used to access suitable participants for your own research? What might you take from Yixi's account to inform your own processes of accessing participants?

2 In her chapter, Yixi outlines three strategies that she used in her interviews to elicit her participants' narratives. What were they, and how useful might they be for your own research?

Introduction

The aim of my study was to understand the experiences of Tibetan people becoming bilingual in the Tibetan areas of China. I had five participants in my research: my five participants belonged to four different generations from 1950 to the present day and their educational experiences took place at four points in time during that period. I intended to gain a deep understanding of how the processes of becoming bilingual in Tibet have been affected by the changing of society, especially with regard to how the changes of policy towards the Tibetan language have been implemented in schools and have impacted on bilingual development for individual Tibetans since 1950.

My research sought to understand how these individuals' learning experiences had been influenced by this context, which had been brought about by the changing national policies towards minority languages in China. This research did not intend to seek truth; rather it intended to understand how individuals reflect on their developing bilingualism in a certain time and in a particular context. I used ethnographic principles to underpin my research approach.

My connection with the ethnographic approach

Madden (2010: 16) notes that

> the term 'ethnography' comes from Greek and broadly means 'writing about people', but that, in a qualitative research context, it has a narrow meaning of writing about particular groups of people, that is to say 'ethnically, culturally or socially defined groups'.

Ethnography is a form of qualitative research always conducted in real settings, involving the study of the daily lived experiences of a particular group (Stewart 1998) or an approach to study 'a way of life' of groups of people (Wolcott 2008: 188). There are several key features of ethnography:

- Studying human behaviour in natural settings;

- Pursuing real understanding rather than attempting to find truth;

- Discovery through seeking **thick description** and explanation.

My interest in this topic initially came from the life I had experienced. My bilingual experiences had been strongly affected by the changing of policy and society in China. My early educational experience in a Han city where the school did not value my first language made me gradually lose my first language and my Tibetan identity. Moreover, this was the period of the Cultural Revolution (1966–1976) when the Tibetan language was regarded as an inferior language. Goldstein states that during this time, 'Tibetans were pushed into the larger Han Chinese linguistic world' (Goldstein 1999: 184). In the early period of the Cultural Revolution, Han people directly told my parents: 'Do not speak black language.' There are lots of implications in that term of black language. It implies a bad language, a barbarian language and a banned language. My first language was devalued by both school and society during my formative years. The negative attitudes towards my first language led me to feel ashamed to be a Tibetan. I remember my refusal to speak Tibetan when my parents spoke with me; I even hid myself whenever my father came to my school because I was embarrassed by his appearance.

The turning point came when I entered college. The Cultural Revolution had ended, and minority languages had started to revive in China. I was enrolled at one of the minority universities in China, where I selected Tibetan literature as my major. I studied for four years in this university, during which time I met my wonderful Tibetan teacher, *A ke Kunchok Tsden*: we called him Ake (this means uncle in Tibetan). This is our cultural way to name someone we like very much. Ake was a monk before the Liberation (in 1949), and he had been a Tibetan teacher in my university before the Cultural Revolution. During the Cultural Revolution no Tibetan classes were offered, so most of the Tibetan teachers including Ake went back to their home towns and became farmers. He returned to the university after the Cultural Revolution. I still remember the first time I met him in his tiny dark room. During that time, China was undeveloped and people didn't have their own flats. Ake was allotted two rooms in a building belonging to our university, the building had a very long corridor leading to Ake's rooms. The corridor was dim, even in day time. Ake's room was simple: the only furniture he had was a desk, a few chairs, and a bed. It was his study room, as well as his bedroom. I was taken to his rooms by my father, who happened to be Ake's friend. He chatted with me in Tibetan, I just responded to him in Chinese. I understood what he was saying but was unable to answer him in Tibetan. That night he said something like: 'Oh, poor girl, you have just forgotten your Tibetan language. However, I will teach you.' He always gave extra classes to any of us who had a desire to learn Tibetan. Every night from Monday to Sunday his small room (which was only 15 square metres) was full of students. It was so crowded that the students just sat on the floor to listen in his class. For me it was my time for the rediscovery of Tibetan. I grew a sense of pride in being a Tibetan during this time through learning, reading and writing in Tibetan. Just as losing my first language related to a particular period of national policy, so regaining my first language was also closely related to the changing of policy towards minority languages in China during this time.

Monolingual people might ask members of minority groups: if it is so difficult to become bilingual, why not just simply remain monolingual in the dominant language? I always ask myself this question: do I have a choice not to become bilingual? The answer always is 'No'. I have asked this question to my mother and sister and many Tibetans whom I have encountered every day, and their answers were the same as mine: 'No'. Safe Alladina (1995: 19) argues that, 'early experience of love, pleasure, joy and the things that are important to children happen in the home languages'. Losing your first language means losing your tie with your home. For me my first language evokes the warmth of the relationship with my grandmother. I was raised by her; she was the one who always cared about me. I remember, every time I went back to my home town, she would always come to the bus station to wait for me. Sometimes she would spend several hours waiting there. When I got there, the first sentence she always said was, 'my precious one has come.' I remember during the time I studied Tibetan as my major in college, my grandmother was so proud of this, and she would tell everyone, 'my precious one is studying Tibetan in a college.' And the others would say, 'we thought your granddaughter could not speak Tibetan.' My grandmother would always say, 'she can even read Tibetan books.'

My personal experience as a bilingual and how it became the starting point of my research illustrates my relationship with the ethnographic approach as a researcher. The significance of personal experience in ethnographic research is that an ethnographer 'uses a self to learn about the other' (Ryan et al. 2000: 741).

Narrative in ethnography

I designed my study to gain understanding of the diverse language learning experiences of individual Tibetans through listening to their stories. The method I chose to collect my data was narrative. Bruner (1986: 264) indicates that

> ethnographies are guided by an implicit narrative structure, by a story we tell about the people we study. We are familiar with the stories people tell about themselves in life history and psychiatric interviews, in myth and ritual, in history books and Balinese cockfights. I wish to extend this notion to ethnography as discourse, as a genre of storytelling.

He further states that ethnographers acted as 'a material body through whom a narrative structure unfolds' (Bruner 1986: 274). My research started from my own story of developing as a bilingual; furthermore, it was inspired through interaction with other people in my daily life. For example, the decision for me to select my youngest participant resulted from hearing his story from my sister. The stories are always there and what I have done by going back to the field is to act as a 'material body' to encourage my participants to unfold their stories to me. This is how ethnographic research manifested in my study.

The features of narrative method are:

- Stories are the distinctive outcomes, as well as the substance of narrative method.

- Exploring an individual's experience is a key feature of narrative method.

- Narrative is representing the part in a whole and the whole in a part. It illustrates the relationship between the self and the society. The stories of self always happen in a particular place; they are about the self in the context.

Narrative in the field – being there

Narrative exists within ethnography. I would say that my narrative in the field was an example of this. In this section I show the process of how, as an ethnographer, I acted as 'a material body' (Bruner 1986) to unfold the existing narrative. The first place I visited was the university where I had worked for more than sixteen years, where I met most of my participants in this research. All of the stories of meeting my participants occurred in the Tibetan department.

The Tibetan Department of this university is one of the largest Tibetan departments in the whole of China. It recruits Tibetan high school graduates from all the Tibetan areas in China, which include Gansu, Qinghai, Yunnan, Sichuan and the Tibet Autonomous Region. The city in which the university is located is predominantly Han Chinese: you will see few Tibetans on the streets. However, soon after entering one of the three gates of this university, you can see many Tibetan students, some wearing Tibetan outfits but most others simply wearing ordinary clothes. Located in front of a small mountain, the university campus is surrounded by a wall, which separates it from the Han Chinese-dominated city. I had lived in this city long enough to know how little the society outside of the university walls knows about Tibetans and how they view them. As soon as I entered the gate of the university, I felt connected to my participants. I had studied, worked and lived there for many years. I carried out most of my interviews on this campus. Every time I entered the gate during my fieldwork, I met many students who said *bdemo* to me ('Hi' in Tibetan). Former students from my classes would approach me and ask me what I was studying in the United Kingdom and what it was like.

The university was like a Tibetan community where I met many people. I visited my second participant many times before conducting the interviews with her. The visits afforded opportunities for her to know and understand more about my research. She would ask me why I wanted to do this research and I would explain to her what I felt like when I could first read Tibetan and how I felt when I was criticized by my Tibetan students because of my poor Tibetan. Moreover, I told her how bilingualism had become a global issue, as many people in this world need two languages in their lives. After many visits, she changed from being a passive participant. She arranged a dinner to welcome me in a very good restaurant. She sent a text to everyone she invited for this dinner, which said, 'I am very impressed by Yixi's courage to go to England to study for a PhD. I think she will make a great contribution to our nation. I am proud of her. I invite all of you to join me to have a special dinner to honour her.' I was touched by this text. Later, she arranged a trip for me to go with her to her husband's home town, a small Tibetan village.

Establishing connection with my participants

My relationship with my third and fourth participants began as teacher and student. I was requested by the Tibetan department to provide some help to students in English during the time when I was doing my fieldwork. I gave a group of students some help twice a week. There was a girl who was very active in my English class, but I was told she was very quiet in her Tibetan classes. Her silence in Tibetan class aroused my interest to learn the story behind it, and later she told me she did not get any opportunities to learn Tibetan in her village primary school. It surprised me because I had learned from all the official documents that bilingual schools had been set up from the 1980s in Tibetan areas, and she was born after 1990, so should have benefited from this. However her village did not have a bilingual school when she was of school age. The result was that her Tibetan was much weaker than her Chinese. Her differing attitudes in classes and her weakness in Tibetan drove me to attempt to understand her bilingual learning experiences. Therefore, I decided to invite her to be one of my participants and she gave consent. We spent lots of time together, going to the park, drinking tea and talking. All of the time I spent with her was for her to get to know me and my research, and learn to trust me. The trust gradually built up when she learned that my Chinese is much stronger than my Tibetan. Moreover, when she learned I have been struggling to speak better Tibetan all my life, she knew I understood her feelings towards the difficulties of majoring in Tibetan in university. That began the connection I had with her.

However, there was another girl who had caught my attention during my interaction with her in English class. She was very active in the Tibetan class, the Chinese class and the English class. Most of the time she only spoke Tibetan to me, but she also spoke fluent Chinese. Her abilities in languages were very different from her classmate. This difference led me to inquire why the language abilities among people from the younger generation vary so drastically under the same national policy implemented in Tibetan areas. It led me to decide to select her as one of my participants in the third **case study** of my research. She gave her consent as soon as I asked her. I was not surprised by this. In our culture, students are expected to honour their teachers, so it would hardly occur to her as a student to reject her teacher's research request. However, I knew her consent did not mean she trusted me, and if she did not trust me I would not be able to get her story from her. Again it was the issue of entering the participant's world, as well as that of building a positive relationship. I decided to turn our first relationship of teacher-student into a researcher-participant relationship. She did not really have any choice about her participation at the beginning because she was obligated to respect my wishes as her teacher, but to truly gain her trust, I needed to wait for the opportunity to move our relationship in the research from researcher-participant to narrator and listener. I believed this was the only access to get truthworthy data in the narrative method. Moreover, I believed this process of encouraging the narrative to unfold was up to me as an ethnographer. The breakthrough moment happened one morning when we were having our class, and we were talking about famous Tibetan contemporary poets. She shared with me one of her favourite poems written by Yidan Cairong, the famous Tibetan poet who passed away in 2004. She recited it to me in English (several of Yidan Cairong's poems have been translated into English). I told her it is one of my favourite poems as well, and then I told her Yidan Cairong was my father. Suddenly I saw tears in her eyes, and I felt my eyes were moist as well. At that moment I saw a sparkle in her eyes. I realized this formed the connection between us.

I found that I shared similar experiences with my participants, which gave us an immediate connection that went beyond our shared culture and identities. I found common ground with my third participants simply because we had both started to learn the written form of Tibetan at university. Similarly, my oldest participant told me when I was interviewing him that, like me, most of his Tibetan teachers when he started to learn Tibetan in college were Chinese. He had known me since I was a little girl, and he said in his interview, 'Just like your experience, most of my Tibetan teachers were Chinese as well'. I would say my oldest participant knew my connection with him more deeply than I myself did, which was the reason he was so open with me. Our shared experiences, culture, identity and even love for a particular person were all elements which determined how deep and detailed the stories I could elicit from my participants would be. That is how I was involved in their real world in order to get trustworthy data.

Robert Park insists that his students 'go get the seat of your pants dirty in real research' (cited in Brewer 2000: 13). He thinks fieldwork is very important and regards it as 'the first hand observation' in qualitative research. Furthermore, Park also indicates that 'what sociologists most need to know is what goes on behind the faces of men' (cited in Gubrium and Holstein 1997: 6). I would say that my own narrative in the field was the process through which I got to know more about my participants and their stories. I regarded it as the opportunity to know 'what goes behind the faces of men'.

Research tool: Life history interview

Ethnographic research focuses on the life experiences of individuals. Life history is one of the ethnographer's tools to study the lived experience of individuals. A life history interview starts from the lived experience of the participants. The term *life story* has more of a home in folklore (Titon 1980) and focuses on how the storyteller sees her or his life and what is significant for them (Atkinson 1998: 4). The term 'story' arouses memories for me of the nights when I was a little girl sitting on my grand mum's traditional Tibetan carpet listening to her sister telling stories of going to Lhasa on foot with a pilgrim group. This story held great significance for us as we considered the holy city of Lhasa to be the ultimate pilgrim destination for all Tibetans. How we all longed to go there as well!

Biesta et al. (2005) indicate that life history research aims to understand those stories against the background of the wider sociopolitical and historical context in processes (cited in Bathmaker and Harnett 2010: 4). Through life history interviews, we gain a deeper understanding about ourselves, about others, about our surroundings and about how events influence us as human beings. The form of a life interview is that of biography (Tierney 2000; Creswell 2011). However, it is not actually a biography. A biography intends to put 'the narrative more in the voice of the researcher', but in a life story, the researcher tends to 'retain the voice of the storyteller, often in its entirety' (Titon 1980). A person's story is always heard in the voice of the first person in the life history interview, capturing the subjectivities in their stories.

How I carried out the life history interview: Strategies for inviting stories

The purpose of a life history interview is to elicit first-person stories in order to seek an understanding of how the self evolves over time. Now I would like to discuss what I did in my interviews to get personal stories of developing bilingualism in different periods of time in the Tibetan areas, using the three strategies highlighted in Figure 2.1.

FIGURE 2.1 *Strategies used for inviting stories*

Sharing my stories

The life history interview is a form of first-person interview. As a researcher, everything I tried to do in my interview was to invite stories. Chase (2005: 661) refers to inviting stories as 'inviting interviewees to become narrators'. Stories in my interviews always began with personal memories. Stories are memory. I remembered my second participant frequently told me, 'I feel like I had forgotten everything which happened in primary school', during the interview or even before I started the interview. This was the time that I shared my personal feelings for the first time about learning Tibetan as a college student. Through this she started to recall her own story that had happened in a village primary school. She even remembered the first day she went to primary school, how all of her peers in her class laughed at her because of her wearing a Tibetan outfit. That was the moment I asked her, 'Why did pupils laugh at you? Was not this primary school located in a small Tibetan town just five or six miles away from your village?' She said, 'Yes, but as far as I remember most of the pupils in my class were Chinese.' That was the moment when she saw herself as a Tibetan child going to school in a Tibetan area and being laughed at because of her Tibetan outfit. And at this moment we both shared the power of a life story interview; it enabled us to see the meaning behind the laughter. It is through the story that we gain context and recognize meaning made in a particular time within a particular setting. It would be understandable if this laughter had been in a Chinese town: however, it happened in a Tibetan area. It shows the 'history hidden in a memory'. Her memory is very specific: a Tibetan outfit which she was wearing on her first day to school. I did not ask if they were new clothes, but I would imagine they were nice and most likely the ones she liked very much because she was wearing them on the first day of school. Her memory is in the people – she was laughed at by her classmates. Her memory is in a place – it happened in the school in her hometown. This illustrates that history is the discovery of patterns, place and people (Tierney 2000: 544). Moreover, the memory of the first day at school shows the memory and history are 'conjoined in mutual construction' (Tierney 2000: 545). What I did by sharing my personal experiences was not only to stimulate memory, but I also put myself into my own research, thereby showing that we 'as researchers … are participants in the creating of the data' (Tierney 2000: 543). It further shows how co-constructed memories happened in life history interview between researcher and participant.

Becoming a listener in interviews

In the life history interview, the centre of research is the narrator, the interviewee. The purpose of life history is to hear the narrator's own voice.

Based on my fieldwork, conducting the life history interview is a lesson in learning how to let interviewees to become the narrator in an interview.

I designed my questions chronologically from primary school, to middle school, to high school and university. However, in some cases my interviewees did not follow this time line. For instance, in the first interview with one of my young participants, I asked about her childhood language experiences in her village, but she started talking about the activities of the mother tongue protection organization in her village and did not talk about her own language learning experience. At first I was puzzled, but I did not stop her. Later on I understood how her image of a Tibetan had been influenced by this organization, as well as how her pure spoken Tibetan had been influenced through it ('pure' here means she did not mix Tibetan with Chinese words in her speaking). Furthermore, all the years of hard study in learning Tibetan initially came from the influence of this organization. Her interview started with talking about this organization and finished with talking about it as well. During the interview, I really became a listener and my participant became a narrator whose talk I enjoyed very much. My interview with my young participant was very similar to Debray's interview (1984, cited in Tierney 2000: 540) with Rigoberta. She said:

> As we continued, Rigoberta made more and more digressions, introduced descriptions of cultural practices into her story and generally upset my chronology.... I became what I really was: Rigoberta's listener. I allowed her to speak and then became her instrument, her double, by allowing her to make the transition from the spoken to the written word.

The importance of 'What' and 'How' questions in interviews

I used an open-ended interview. Chase (2005: 661) points out that 'the open ended interview offers the opportunity for an authentic gaze into the soul of another'. I prepared questions for every interview, but tried not to interrupt if my interviewee moved off the given topic. I remember the interviews I conducted with my oldest participant. As soon as I gave the leading question, he would start talking. In every interview I had a feeling he was waiting to share his life with me. He had memorized everything in detail and sometimes I was amazed how he could construct in memory the dialogue he had with an individual. For instance, he was telling me about a conversation he had with a Chinese leader who had worked in the Tibetan areas for many years and who, even though he himself had not bothered to learn the Tibetan language, was laughing at a young Tibetan teacher who did not understand his Chinese. While my oldest participant was recalling his argument with that Chinese leader, he constructed the dialogue sentence by sentence in a very detailed form. It was not generalized but in specific detail. It was his story in the details of everyday dialogue. This supports the idea that the life history interview is talking about life in everyday form (Atkinson 1998). It is not general and abstract but rather detailed, based on everyday experiences. Chase (2005) suggests if we ask 'sociological questions the interview would easily end up with generalities about interviewees and the others' experiences'. Sack (1989: 88) defines 'sociological questions' as 'questions that are organized around the researcher's interest in general social processes' (cited in Chase 2005: 661). Czarniawska (cited in Chase 2005: 661) indicates that researchers prefer to ask interviewees in the field 'to compare, to abstract, to generalize'. Sack (also cited in Chase 2005: 661) refers to these questions as 'social-logical questions'. For example, questions like 'Can you compare?' 'What is the most…?' are the kinds of questions which encourage the interviewee to draw generalizations and comparisons from their experiences. Chase (1995) further suggests that by avoiding sociological language in our questions but rather framing questions in simple, everyday language which focus on participants' experiences, thoughts and feelings, we can 'gather data thick enough to shed light on our sociological problems'. The questions we ask and the relationships that we form with our interviewees will affect the quality of the information we collect and the responses we obtain.

With other interviewees I needed to ask *How* and *What* questions to invite more detailed stories. Atkinson (1998: 31) indicates that sometimes asking directly what you want to know is the best approach. When I was conducting the interview with my youngest participant (aged thirteen years), he was not able to talk a lot. I asked, 'How did you feel when you could not understand Chinese in class? What language did your teacher speak in Chinese class? How did you feel when your teacher in nursery asked you how to play a Tibetan game?' Through asking all of these *What, How* and *Why* questions, I was able to draw the story out in detail. Sack (1989) recalls how *Why* and *What* questions invited stories in her research instead of sociological questions (cited in Chase 2005). Gubrium and Holstein (1997) elaborate on how, for qualitative research, the *What* questions address the meaning in context and the *How* questions typically emphasize the production of meaning. They further point out that to answer *What* questions, one must focus on people and settings, looking for the meanings that exist in, emerge from, and are consequential for, those settings. Researchers seeking answers to constitutive *How* questions temporarily set meaning as they identify meaning-making practices (Gubrium and Holstein 1997: 14).

In my research, by asking *What* questions, I tried to find out the way my participants interacted with two languages in school and home. Moreover, I also asked lots of *Why* questions in my research. This helped me to identify the meanings hidden in the stories. Moreover, the example I cited with one of my oldest participants (see p. 58) shows how *Why, How* and *What* questions evoke interviewees to be 'fully aware, fully conscious, of our own lives through the process of putting them together in story form' (Atkinson 1998: 7). Nevertheless, Josselson and Lieblich (1995: 3) state that if we want to hear stories rather than reports, then our task as interviewers is to *invite* others to tell stories, to encourage them to take responsibility for the meaning of their talk.

The journey from insider to outsider in research

My research was a journey for me, beginning as an insider and gradually becoming more and more of an outsider. My long-term experience of working as an educator in Tibetan areas gave me a unique perspective on what exactly it means for Tibetan individuals to become bilingual in Tibetan and Chinese. In my research, I am bilingual in Tibetan and in Chinese, and my five participants are also bilingual in Tibetan and in Chinese. This experience afforded certain advantages as an insider sharing the same culture and language.

However, there is a potential disadvantage to being an insider. I had to mediate my insider bias and be aware that my research was an opportunity for the world to hear the authentic voices of Tibetan individuals. One means of doing it is through using unfamiliar methodology and theoretical frames, which are new to me and which I discovered through my PhD study. By doing this I became an outsider. Moreover, I realize that the process of gaining new knowledge from my participants also showed me how to be an outsider to the participants. For instance, my interviews always started in Tibetan, but often moved into other languages. This occurrence of language shift from Tibetan to Chinese and (sometimes) English that happened in the interviews was unexpected. It seemed that the frequency of my five participants' shifts from one language to another varied because of the range of their abilities in the different languages, their bilingual learning experiences and the subjects they were talking about. This was part of the new knowledge I learned from my participants. From this I realized that I had become an outsider through my research. Furthermore, the outward and inward travelling between the United Kingdom and China over the four years of study also led me to become more and more of an outsider in my own context. Finally, in the data analysis, I focused on participants' voices rather than my own. I was always conscious of my insider biases and the need to recognize their influences on my five participants' stories.

References

Alladina, S. (1995), *Being Bilingual: A Guide for Parents, Teachers and Young People on Mother Tongue Heritage*, London: Trentham Books.

Atkinson, R. (1998), *The Life Story Interview*, London: Sage Publications.

Bathmaker, A. (2010), 'Introduction', in A. Bathmaker and P. Harentt (eds), *Exploring Learning, Identity and Power through Life History and Narrative Research*, 1–10, London: Routledge.

Brewer, J. (2000), *Ethnography*, Buckingham: Open University Press.

Bruner, E.M. (1986), 'Ethnography as Narrative', in V.W. Turner and E.M. Bruner (eds), *The Anthropology of Experience*, 139–155, Chicago: University of Illinois Press.

Chase, S.E. (2005), 'Narrative Inquiry: Multiple Lenses, Approaches, Voices', in N. Denzin and Y. Lincoln (eds) *The Sage Handbook of Qualitative Research*, 651–679, London: Sage Publications.

Creswell, J.W. (2011), *Educational Research: Planning, Conducting, and Evaluating Quantitative and Qualitative Research*, 4th edn, Chicago: Prentice Hall.

Goldstein, M. (1999), *The Snow Lion and the Dragon: China, Tibet, and the Dalai Lama*, London: University of California Press. Ltd.

Gubrium, J.F. and Holstein, J.A. (1997), *The New Language of Qualitative Method*, Oxford: Oxford University Press.

Josselson, R. and Lieblich, A. (1995), 'Introduction', in R. Josselson and A. Lieblich (eds) *Interpreting Experience: The Narrative Study of Lives*, x–xii, London: Sage Publications.

Madden, R. (2010), *Being Ethnographic: A Guide to the Theory and Practice of Ethnography*, London: Sage Publications.

Ryan, G.W., Bernard, H.R., Denzin, N. and Lincoln, Y. (2000), *Handbook of Qualitative Research*, London: Sage Publications.

Stewart, A. (1998), *The Ethnographer's Method*, London: Sage Publications.

Tierney, W.G. (2000), 'Undaunted Courage: Life History and the Postmodern Challenge', in N.K. Denzin and Y.S. Lincoln (eds), *Handbook of Qualitative Research*, 2nd edn, 537–553, London: Sage Publications.

Titon, J.T. (1980),'The Life Story', *Journal of American Folklore*, 93: 276–292.

Wolcott, H.F. (2008), *Ethnography: A Way of Seeing*, 2nd edn, Oxford: AltaMira Press.

CHAPTER THREE

Misrecognition Performances of Multilingual Social Consciousness in the Lives of British-Pakistani Muslim Teachers

Nasir Mahmood

Guiding questions

1 In his chapter, Nasir traces the way he developed the theoretical concept of 'misrecognition' from his reading in order to explain his data. Can you identify the key ideas contributed by the following authors, according to Nasir's argument:

   Thompson and Majid, Taylor, Honneth, Parekh, Fanon, Said, DuBois

2 After reading the chapter, think about your own project, and see if you can identify the key strands in your own theoretical arguments, related to the substantive issues you are researching, and the texts that mediate them. List the authors and texts and write a brief commentary about each.

Introduction

In this chapter, I outline the way I developed a theoretical framework suited to my research questions. My PhD study is about the educational and social experiences of British-Pakistani Muslim teachers based on life history case studies, which critically explore their identities, agency and belonging. I show how the theory of misrecognition illuminates the narratives of my participants, revealing how they evoke **doubleness** and multicultural liberal subjectivities. I argue that my participants' own narratives about their lives raise challenges to the racialized boundary-making attitudes that are often embedded in popular discourses surrounding British-Pakistani Muslims, which are infused with notions of segregation, monolithic identity and – more recently – disloyalty. My four participants (two men and two women) were all British-Pakistani adults who had been educated in the mainstream system in the United Kingdom. They were accessed through personal contact and the data were generated using four iterative 'problem centred' interviews with each of them (Witzel and Reiter 2012). I transcribed the interviews myself and shared the transcriptions before the subsequent interview with each participant individually. I invited feedback in order to make participants' voices more democratically and ethically accessible (Bucholtz 2000).

The context of misrecognition

My initial awareness of the 'problem' of Muslim identities, agency and belonging came from my own experiences working as an English as an Additional Language (EAL) tutor. During my six years in a secondary school between 2007 and 2013, I came across deficit school practices towards British-Pakistani Muslim pupils and ethnic minority pupils more broadly. I experienced the effects of post 9/11 and 7/7 politics from a personal and professional viewpoint when my pupils started coming to my room to pass their lunchtimes. They said that they felt vulnerable as the atmosphere outside was hostile. I noticed that the school diversity agenda was increasingly being influenced by counter-terrorism policies (Thomas 2011) as the senior management team began to think about implementing the 'Prevent counterextremism' strategy. Despite the fact that the school had only a limited number of Black Ethnic Minority and British Muslim pupils (10 per cent), their exclusion rate was much higher, compared to the students from White backgrounds (Osler and Starkey 2005). The school ethos and policies were shifting from a positive multicultural orientation, and the British-Pakistani pupils increasingly faced experiences of racism (Rhamie et al. 2012). The provision and funding for many initiatives to support students, such as one-to-one language support lessons, self-esteem listening sessions and homework catch-up provision came to a sharp end. Cultural festival celebration assemblies and study support links with community groups were terminated (NALDIC 2011). Teachers' own pedagogic knowledge and attitudes towards students' cultural diversity were increasingly influenced by and filtered through largely negative broader cultural-political and media discourses (Keddie 2014).

I want to recount my memory of a history lesson to make my point clear. It was October 2010, and I was supporting Year Nine students. It was a lesson about the civil rights movement in the United States. The learning objectives were to understand the contributions of major civil rights activists and the meaning of the word 'ideology'. The teacher introduced the lesson with images of Martin Luther King and Malcolm X. He told the students that one was Christian, and the other was a Muslim convert, and that each had a different set of ideologies; one believed in peace and the other believed in violence. Then he asked the students which one they thought believed in peace and they pointed to Martin Luther King. At that point, it was obvious which one – according to the teacher – believed in violence. There was banter in the class about recent media coverage of Muslims' connections with terrorist groups. The teacher tried to stop it. He wanted to develop a critical examination of Malcolm X's choices and his political orientations, but it was too late. The Muslim pupils were completely silent, and one of them had her head bent down. As the bell rang for the next lesson, she was the first one to leave.

Such moments in classrooms formed an initial 'horizon of experience' (Jauss 1982) for me as a teacher researcher. They affected me personally and created a powerful urge in me to seek social justice for my students. I recognized the need to understand the changing nature of inclusion/ exclusion for British-Pakistani Muslim pupils, and, through my Master's course, started to probe deeper into the wider cultural-political and historical layers of the problem. I opted to study the Prevent counter-terrorism strategy for my dissertation. I found that the policy was constructed in a pathological integrationist way to squeeze and marginalize cultural freedoms and the public expression of Muslim pupils' identities (Mahmood 2011). I disseminated the findings and some implications of my research to my school, and I think this contributed to the school dropping the idea of going further with Prevent.

After I completed my Master's, I continued reading about theory and policy. My observation of the ways that British-Pakistani Muslim consciousness was mediated politically in England provoked me to study critically the phenomenon of the politicization of their identities, agency and belonging. I came to understand that British-Asian Muslims had been continually at the centre of political, media and educational policy debates since the 1980s (Halstead 1988; Basit 1997; Shain 2011). In these debates, questions about the reasonableness/unreasonableness of British-Asian Muslim consciousness are positioned in relation to the larger questions and debates about issues such as Britishness, liberalism, secularism, religion and multiculturalism (Taylor-Gooby and Waite 2013). Since 2010, there have been big policy debates about the 'malaise' of multiculturalism and British Muslim consciousness, such as David Cameron's muscular liberalism, the Prevent counter-terrorism strategy, the Trojan Horse narrativization and the articulation of British values (Thomas 2011; Latour 2012; Miah 2014). I also observed in the literature the historical continuity of the socioeconomic disadvantage discourse for individuals from British-Pakistani ethnicity related to housing, higher educational opportunities, jobs and career progression (Khattab and Johnston 2013).

I was beginning to realize that the established theoretical perspectives on the voices from British Muslim communities did not conceptualize their agency, identities and belonging in ways that made sense to me as a member of those communities (Meer and Modood 2013). By that time, I was developing a perspective on the problem which deconstructed the master narrativization of British-Pakistani Muslim consciousness. My search led me to explore critical race and critical feminist theories (Butler 1990; Gillborn 2006), which were helpful in illuminating questions of racial and socio-structural privilege and in revealing the situatedness of the political performance of identities, and so the importance of studying the issues in context. But these approaches lacked methodological coherence for researching questions of racial equality and respect hierarchies around ethno-religious identities related to citizenship (Meer and Modood 2013; Meer and Nayak 2013). During this time, I read Thompson and Majid (2011), who situated misrecognition language in the multicultural recognition politics of Charles Taylor and Axel Honneth. They also brought into focus the postcolonial emancipation agenda through reference to DuBois's ideas of doubleness. I found this intervention fresh and useful. It brought into focus DuBois's ideas on double consciousness and racialized veiling. It helped me to see that the politicization of British-Pakistani Muslim consciousness was a misrecognition critical case. In the next section, I briefly present my revised version of misrecognition theory.

Misrecognition normativity

As I said above, misrecognition theory is historically situated in the multicultural recognition tradition. More recently, theorists have explored misrecognition normativity in the postcolonial domain, mainly focusing on DuBois's ideas of double consciousness. I realized that the ideas of Frantz Fanon, Homi K. Bhabha and Edward Said further illuminated the struggles of my participants as they are performed in their life history narratives, and I saw the need to include them in my model of misrecognition. Philosophers in the recognition tradition, such as Taylor and Honneth, treat misrecognition as an inverse form of recognition. They take as a premise that recognition is essential for the formation of selfhood and true self-consciousness in a multicultural society. Taylor (1992) sees recognition as a vital human need.

He proposes the notion of 'equality of dignity' to suggest that everybody is equal in terms of legal status and its implementation in social practice; and 'equality of respect' to mean that individuals and groups are also equal in terms of respect statuses, that is, in the ways respect should be accorded them. Honneth (1995) considers the demands of recognition as a social-psychological need. He regards the recognition of love, respect and self-esteem as essential drivers for the mobilization of personhood in private, public and social spheres. By 'love', he means the secure and sympathetic conditions of bonding and belonging that help individuals to grow. By 'respect', he means the right bearing of individuals in the state for the functioning of legal or public personhood. Finally, he sees 'recognition of self-esteem' as the acknowledgement by society of the contributions of individuals. According to Honneth, the denial of these three basic needs places individuals in the state of inequality and with a reduced sense of belonging. Both Taylor and Honneth reject the idea of the construction of group identities through the mobilization of religion. In my view, their position is unhelpful because there can be many ways of motivating group identity, provided the mobilization remains peaceful in character. Other misrecognition theorists have mobilized the concept of groupness and race in a dynamic sense (Meer et al. 2012). Furthermore, although Taylor and Honneth construct misrecognition as the inverse of recognition, they do not effectively displace it from the recognition tradition. According to Meer et al. (2012: 133) this perspective addresses 'the effects of lack of recognition' without fully exploring the complexity of the misrecognition theoretical space.

Ideas about diversity and doubleness have the capacity to advance the misrecognition agenda by enriching its conceptual vocabulary. I will show this by referring to the work of Parekh, Fanon and DuBois. In the domain of moral diversity, Parekh's ideas are particularly useful. He sees the Western European moral philosophy scene as a case of 'moral monism' (Parekh 1996). He argues that, historically, European moral philosophy has not engaged with the non-European and non-Christian moral diversities. Rather, it has tried to answer the questions of diversity from the position of European exclusivism. Historically, this led to liberal and missionary projects of colonialism in the marginalized global south, along with deficit and reduced modes of identity formation and belonging for ethnic and non-Christian diasporas in the European centre (Parekh 1995). However with ever-increasing globalization, moral and cultural diversities have become normal. Moral orientation to life needs to be cross-culturally constructed. Misrecognition in the Parekhian sense can be interpreted as the imposition of 'moral monism' and exclusivism that implies prejudice against negotiations of the self which are based on 'multicultural perspectives' (Parekh 2002).

Fanon and DuBois focus on misrecognition in the doubleness domain. Fanon's ideas on existential doubleness and humanism are extremely important.

According to him (2008), individuals and 'races' have to be existentially equal in relation to each other before they can have any meaningful conversation and realize intersubjective personhood. Misrecognition in the Fanonian sense can be interpreted as the denial of equality in interpreting individualism and racial justice in the world. DuBois (2007), like Fanon, is of the view that there can be no true being through 'looking at oneself through the eyes of other'. For DuBois and Fanon, accepting a sense of degraded Black self leads to a colonizing of the mind, leaving little room for minority consciousness to bring any cultural originality and creativity to the world (Black 2007). However, DuBois further argues that true self-consciousness cannot be attained by being trapped within one's cultural perspective and by holding a sense of victimhood and marginalization, demanding either revenge or pity. For DuBois (1969), the sense of political self-consciousness can only exist in its 'doubleness'. By this he means that the identity and belonging formation spaces between minorities and majorities should be about connection, integration and creative synthesizing. In this way, it becomes possible to realize identities as multiple and fluid, and to connect diverse histories, trends and cultures. Thus, the 'doubleness' sense of identities brings the best of both worlds, mixing them to transform the belonging binaries in order to reach a richer sense of inclusive humanity (Du Bois 2007). In the DuBoisian sense, we can understand misrecognition as the rejection of existential, political, creative and integrated plural forms of self-consciousness.

Still in the doubleness domain, Homi Bhabha's (1994) ideas of **liminality** and hyphenation resonate with those of DuBois and Fanon. Bhabha maps the importance of cultural location in self-making by means of its situatedness, and also in terms of displacement and dislocation. In the processes of identity formation, there is the desire to articulate cultural situatedness within different social worlds (Bhabha 1992, 1994). So in Bhabha's terms, misrecognition can be understood as reification, determinacy, hegemonic naivety and dominance, which close down the possibilities of hybridity, and of transforming spaces to offer new ways of belonging. Finally, Said's contribution is to address the misrecognition of cosmopolitan spaces in self-making. According to Said, civilizations need to be seen as inherently plural and in connection with each other, not in opposition. He argues that cosmopolitan moral orientation draws on compassionate cross-cultural enquiry, 'contrapuntal reading' based on the principles of humanism, pluralism and democratic criticism, in such a way as to reimagine the secular as having room for all types of progressive humanisms, whether religious or nonreligious (Said 1997, 2004). Thus, in Said's sense, misrecognition can be interpreted as ideologies and practices of cultural imperialism, clash of civilizations, a narrow sense of civic orientation, disaffection and practices of superficial learning that impair any possibilities of cosmopolitan self-making.

I see the ideas discussed above as feeding into my argument for the misrecognition case of the politicization of British-Pakistani Muslim consciousness. In the following sections, after briefly explaining how my data were collected, coded and thematized, I show how I elicited misrecognition from my participants' narratives. Finally, in the light of my analysis, I present my alternative framing of misrecognition: misrecognition of multilingual social consciousness.

Methodology and analysis

The data were collected through a series of four iterative life history interviews with each of my four participants. The interviews were conducted using 'problem centred' interview typology (Witzel and Reiter 2012), and were enriched by including insights from complexity-based 'strong emergence' (Osberg and Biesta 2007) and 'active interview' conversations (Gubrium and Holstein 2004), video-based provocation and projection conversations (Haw and Hadfield 2011). In carrying out the interviews, instead of a formal question and answer exchange, I tried to develop theoretically informed 'reflexive and restructured conversations' with my participants (Conteh and Toyoshima 2005; May 2011: 125). After transcribing the interviews, I looked for narratives (Maxwell 2012), containing the theoretical categories of identity, agency and belonging as I had identified them from the literature. From this 'theoretically descriptive' analysis, I moved to 'theoretically substantive' themes (Maxwell and Miller 2008). Each set of interviews was separately coded, and the theoretical links I had identified at the start helped me to see the thematic connections across all four cases.

In this way, the interview data were analyzed as discourse, searching for themes that could be theoretically related to the concept of misrecognition. In addition, I applied three main rhetorical analytical strategies: 'problem setting', 'stance taking' and 'provocation and projection' strategies (Finlayson 2006; Baynham 2011; Hadfield and Haw 2012). In stance-taking performance, participants manifest their 'stance taking' by strategically 'aligning and positioning' themselves in the discourse, marking how the political performance of their subjectivities is made publically visible (Baynham 2011).

According to Finlayson, social actors speak about problems in a rhetorical way, thus getting their representative positions recognized both in arguing a case and also in contesting the socially prevalent problems. In this way, they reset and redefine problems from particular cultural-political positions (Finlayson 2006). In doing so, they offer situated reasoning, demystify the problem context and creatively mobilize traditions and metaphors from various cultural positions to give a new narrativization of the problem (Finlayson 2006). In provocation modality, participants deliberately invoke social misrepresentations in their discourse in order to self-contest them. In this way, they make their subjectivities publicly visible and their voices 'persistent and difficult' to ignore. In the projection mode, participants challenge cultural-political normalization and give their reaction in a strategically self-selected context. The purpose of this is to perform their personal and cultural positions (Hadfield and Haw 2012).

Below are the 'theoretically substantive' themes which emerged from my data:

How have female participants read misrecognition (M) problem formulation?

● M1 Contesting self-segregated and divided selves

● M2 Contesting the framing of over-determined and oppressed selves

● M3 Contesting the framing of passive, unrealistic, less abled and educationally less aspirational cultural consciousness

How have male participants read misrecognition (M) problem formulation?

● M1 Contesting the virulent selves

● M2 Contesting effeminate masculinities

● M3 Contesting the framing of disloyal, monolithic and segregated masculinities

Misrecognition data categories common in both male and female data

● M4 Contesting structural and socioeconomic inequalities

● M5 Contesting media representations

It is beyond the scope of this chapter to discuss even briefly the data against all tropes. To illustrate how my theoretical position on misrecognition is illuminated in my data, I will touch on trope M3 from the male data. I will first briefly refer to the literature on this trope before showing an example of one of my participant's counter-performance narratives.

The framing of disloyal, monolithic and segregated masculinities

Following the Rushdie affair and the 'northern riots' of 2001, British-Asian Muslim boys' and men's masculinities have increasingly been positioned in public and social discourse as self-segregation, hot-headedness and disloyalty (Alexander 2004; Farrar 2012). Their loyalties to Britain have been questioned, for example, on the myth of return, the game of cricket, the Iraq War and over the terrorist acts of the 7/7 London Bombings (Dwyer et al. 2008; Werbner 2012; Bolognani 2015). Their identities and political consciousness have been described as culturally monolithic, socially non-cohesive, staid and noncreative (Hopkins 2009). These discursive and political constructs have led to racially gendered experiences for British-Asian Muslim males which ignore the complexity of their consciousness and suppress cultural-political and social discourses (Shain 2011).

In their interviews, both my male participants contested the misrecognition of disloyal, monolithic and segregated selves. Because of space, I can only talk about Majid's performance. I use stance taking, problem setting and provocation and projection discourse analysis strategies to deconstruct two of his narratives, and show how he performs his personal and communal subjectivities in relation to the framing of disloyal, monolithic and segregated masculinities.

Majid's Performance: 1

01	Interviewer:	Hmm, pop culture you talking about!
	Majid:	Yeah, so…eh…I have got one of my friends, he is from Pathan background
	Interviewer:	Hmm
05	Majid:	He is born in this country, he is proper Yorkshire man
	Interviewer:	Hmm
	Majid:	and in regards to his knowledge on history, UK history and regards to eh the actual culture of the 80s; 90s; he can name you every single hit or song or whatever
10	Interviewer:	Hmm
	Majid:	and that's kind a baffle a lot of the people that's oh bloody hell we didn't realize it (Interviewer: Hmm)…and this is a guy that has got beard, he has got beard and once you have beard traditionally you know! [laugh]
15	Majid:	They like oh we realize then
	Interviewer:	So were you guys into it, into the pop culture when you were doing?
	Majid:	Back in the days when we were youngsters yeah you get influenced by that side
20	Interviewer:	Hmm
	Majid:	Eh so for that our sort of experience has been that we have, our general feeling is we are trying to integrate or that's what they be using as much as possible
	Interviewer:	Hmm
25	Majid:	Eh and unfortunately that's not always been positive from the other side.

In the narrative above, the interviewer adopts positioned probing (line 01) in actively exploring Majid's earlier performance on popular music culture in the 1990s. Majid shows immediate alignment with his previous performance and manifests his affirmative stance ('Yeah'...line 2). He then sustains the rhetorical performance of his stance taking in the projection mode by selecting his friend's fondness for popular music. The projection of his friend's belonging is further stretched to show liminal displacement and hybridity of his identities in terms of Pakistani, British and 'proper Yorkshire man' (lines 2–5). Majid positions his friend's deep knowledge of local history and passion for music as manifesting the stance that they are active performers of local cosmopolitan culture (lines 7–9). At this point, Majid performs provocation-projection rhetorical strategy by self-invoking his friend's beard as a marker of a practising Muslim. At the same time, he positions his selfhood as fluid and permeable in terms of negotiating the religious and secular (line 13). Majid's comments displace the notion that judging Muslims on merely outward appearance serves as 'conveyor belt' approach suggesting that every bearded man has monolithic and segregated identity. In fact, at the subtext level, Majid suggests that if there are deep secular influences in the conception and practice of practising Muslims, then non-practising Muslim youth's identities are even more fluid (lines 11–14). The interviewer at this points makes another probe to explore whether this influence was more generic for the British-Pakistani Muslim community ('So were you guys into it'...lines 16–17). Majid answers positively (lines 18–19), affirming that they were indeed influenced. However, the problem setting is rhetorically directed outward by Majid through his allusion to the nonacceptance and misrecognition of the British-Pakistani Muslim community's integration in the United Kingdom when he performs (we are trying to integrate...and unfortunately that's not always been positive from the other side, lines 25).

Majid's Performance: 2

01	Interviewer:	In the last couple of minutes now eh if I ask you how do you see your identities and belonging in reflexive mode about your life story
	Majid:	as I said to you before I see myself as a British Muslim...eh. ...
05		further down...eh... a Yorkshire man; I see myself that because I am proud of that, however experiences of the recent years by the so called indigenous population is they will never see me on that light
	Interviewer:	Hmm
10	Majid:	You know no matter what I do; you can't go more than fighting for Queen and country
	Interviewer:	Hmm

	Majid:	You gone through, you done that; you risked your life for your country
15	Interviewer:	Hmm
	Majid:	and people perceive you as not one of them!
	Interviewer:	Hmm, hmm. Thank you very much for your conversation and really had a nice time all your time and energy and thank you
20	Majid:	No, no much appreciated thank you very much

In the narrative above, Majid performs problem setting by rejecting the racializing common sense arguments that see his masculinity from the Muslim position as disloyal. In line 4, he argues the case by situating his identities and belonging in terms of doubleness ('I see myself as a British Muslim'), but also in line 5, articulates it through deep localism ('further down eh a Yorkshire man'). The national and local senses of integrative doubleness are then contrasted in lines 7–8 with the racializing understanding that sees him and by extension his community as not integrating ('so called indigenous population is they will never see me on that light'). The organizing narrative perspective is delivered in resetting the problem rhetoric on disloyal selves (that is, 'you can't go more than fighting for Queen and country'). The purpose of this is to engage the wider social audience in rhetorically provoking in line 16 that even when life is risked at the frontline, 'people' still raise racializing question marks about his Britishness and Muslimness.

Misrecognition theorization

Majid's identity orientations can be understood by drawing directly on misrecognition ideas. In Taylor and Honneth's sense, Majid has performed against the social misrecognition of 'respect', interpreted as not acknowledging the community's creative contribution in pluralizing the national and local multicultures and in advancing the social justice agenda in society. In the ways he performs self-making, his performance also invokes Fanon, DuBois, Bhabha and Said's senses of existential, integrative, liminal and cosmopolitan double consciousness. There is both connection with his own culture and religion, and also the sense of displacement and beyondness that makes him 'flexible', 'open' and enthusiastic to find new spaces for belonging performance. So Majid's understandings of religion and his culture show his capacity for synthesizing Britishness with Muslimness, importing secular and popular influences, mediating local identities and performing the active voice of his community in resisting racial unbelonging. He also shows how his civic, local and public identities are liminally patriotic and integrative. So, being a soldier and fighting for the Queen, taking pride as a Yorkshire man and being a British Muslim are not at odds with each other, and the sense of political double consciousness enables Majid to navigate his plural, civic and political senses of the self.

In the 1980s and 1990s, most research into identities and masculinities was carried out through studying British African-Caribbean pupils' experiences in schools and popular urban subcultures. In these studies, the researchers claimed that British African-Caribbean youth identities were cosmopolitan in character (Back 1996). Similarly, Stuart Hall (1992: 258) proposed the 'New Ethnicities' paradigm, arguing that ethnic identities were subject to constant change through what he described as 'the process of unsettling, recombination, hybridization, and cut-and-mix'. Modood et al. (1994) in their national survey on ethnic identities found that Asian and Muslim identities had some of these characteristics which they described 'changing ethnic identities'. My study shows how British-Asian Muslim identities, even in the past, can be understood under such secular, popular, national and local multicultural influences. In the decades since the 1990s, researchers have noted these trends more richly and more widely (Mythen 2012; Herding 2013). As the data above show, my study indicates there is progressive politicization around religion among the participants in my research. They show that they understand such politicization in terms of humanism, hybridity, doubleness and social justice. Researchers have noted there is a continued lack of theoretical understanding in making sense of the politicization of British-Asian Muslimness, related to how religious and secular practices are subject to permeability, fusion and 'overlapping consensus' (Modood and Ahmad 2007; Panjwani 2016). My study rearticulates this thesis and shows how my participants have displaced the dominant Western mode of thinking that sees religion as a mere belief and as impractical, irrational and segregating. Indeed, the theoretical-empirical argument of this study further enriches the existing evidence on the elasticity, hybridity, multicultural liberal existentialism and manifestation of 'dynamic consciousness' from the British-Pakistani Muslim perspective (Modood and Ahmad 2007; Meer 2012; Mythen 2012).

Conclusion: The need for new multicultural discourses to contribute to change

Taylor (2016) argues that the function of multicultural discourse is to create possibilities for political action in terms of registering newness, liminality and negotiation for social change:

> In addition, in multicultural societies, the boundary conditions of certain registers may be no longer so clear as they were in earlier hierarchical societies; register has to be frequently re-negotiated, which in fact leads

to change. Rules are creatively broken. The system is constantly in some degree of flux. (p. 330)

Thus, he suggests, in order to develop possibilities for new social meanings, it is important to develop new ways of talking and writing about race, ethnicity, gender, religion and so on. He points to the ways in which we need to challenge some of the established hierarchical social language registers through a process of multicultural communicative renegotiation. Social registers are no longer as clear and straightforward as they once were. We need to think differently about concepts that previously were constructed and embedded in discourses in a monocultural way. I suggest that we can consider concepts such as race, ethnicity, gender religion and nation as languages, which have the potential to help us all to move to understanding the world in new, syncretic ways as we learn to live side by side. Discourses around religion and secularism are represented extensively in my research. My participants challenge the strong Western view which understands religion only as belief. In terms of religion, they understand that their own positions as British-Asian Muslims involve culture and practice, as well as belief. In addition, they are very much imbued with historical, contextual, fluid and fusional senses of identities.

Taylor's work (2016) points to some of the ways in which we need to challenge the established hierarchical discourses that prevail in British society. He argues for the importance of 'multicultural' social discourses. In such discourses, actors acquire and critically sharpen their rich cultural repertoires. In the process, they reveal hybrid, multicultural and multilingual identities. I argue that the British-Pakistani Muslims adults in my study show how this happens in their conversations, and in my thesis I described this as 'multilingual social consciousness'. When I say that my participants perform the misrecognition of multilingual social consciousness, I mean that, in positive and hopeful ways, through their narratives they have performed critical multicultural interaction, re-negotiation and integration. In other words, they are leading the way in performing doubleness in languages of existential resistance, fusion, creativity and social change.

References

Alexander, C. (2004), 'Imagining the Asian Gang: Ethnicity, Masculinity and Youth after "the riots"', *Critical Social Policy*, 24 (4): 526–549.

Back, L. (1996), *New Ethnicities and Urban Cult: Racism and Multiculture in Young Lives*, Abingdon: Routledge.

Basit, T. (1997), *Eastern Values; Western Milieu: Identities and Aspirations of Adolescent British Muslim Girls*, Abingdon: Routledge.

Baynham, M. (2011), 'Stance, Positioning, and Alignment in Narratives of Professional Experience', *Language in Society*, 40 (1): 63–74.

Bhabha, H.K. (1992), 'Freedom's Basis in the Indeterminate', *October*, 61: 46–57.

Bhabha, H.K. (1994), *The Location of Culture*, Abingdon: Routledge.

Black, M. (2007), 'Fanon and DuBoisian Double Consciousness', *Human Architecture: Journal of the Sociology of Self-knowledge*, 5 (3): 393–404.

Bolognani, M. (2015), 'From Myth of Return to Return Fantasy: A Psychosocial Interpretation of Migration Imaginaries', *Identities*, 23 (2): 193–209.

Bucholtz, M. (2000), 'The Politics of Transcription', *Journal of Pragmatics*, 32 (10): 1439–1465.

Butler, J. (1990), 'Gender Trouble, Feminist Theory, and Psychoanalytic Discourse', in L.J. Nicholson (ed), *Feminism/Postmodernism*, 324–340, New York: Routledge.

Conteh, J. and Toyoshima, S. (2005), 'Researching Teaching and Learning: Roles, Identities and Interview Processes', *English Teaching: Practice and Critique*, 4 (2): 23–34.

Du Bois, W.E.B. (1969), *The Conservation of Races*, New York: Arno Press.

Du Bois, W.E.B. (1903/2007), *The Souls of Black Folk*, Oxford: Oxford University Press.

Dwyer, C., Shah, B. and Sanghera, G. (2008), '"From Cricket Lover to Terror Suspect" – Challenging Representations of Young British Muslim Men', *Gender, Place and Culture*, 15 (2): 117–136.

Fanon, F. (2008), *Black Skin, White Masks*, London: Pluto Press.

Farrar, M. (2012), 'Multiculturalism in the UK: A Contested Discourse', in S. Robinson and P. Wetherly (eds), *Islam in the West: Key Issues in Multiculturalism*, 7–23, London: Palgrave Macmillan.

Finlayson, A. (2006) '"What's the Problem?": Political Theory, Rhetoric and Problem-setting', *Critical Review of International Social and Political Philosophy*, 9 (4): 541–557.

Gillborn, D. (2006), 'Critical Race Theory and Education: Racism and Anti-racism in Educational Theory and Praxis', *Discourse: Studies in the Cultural Politics of Education*, 27 (1): 11–32.

Gubrium, J. and Holstein, A. (2004), 'Active Interviewing', in D. Silverman (ed) *Qualitative Research: Theory, Method and Practice*, 2nd edn, 140–161, London: Sage Publications.

Hadfield, M. and Haw, K. (2012), 'Video: Modalities and Methodologies', *International Journal of Research and Method in Education*, 35 (3): 311–324.

Hall, S. (1992), 'New Ethnicities', in J.D.A. Rattansi (ed), *Race, Culture and Difference*, 252–259, London: Sage Publications.

Halstead, M. (1988), *Education, Justice, and Cultural Diversity: An Examination of the Honeyford Affair, 1984–85*, London: Falmer Press.

Haw, K. and Hadfield, M. (2011), *Video in Social Science Research*, London: Taylor and Francis.

Herding, M. (2013), *Inventing Muslim Cool*, Bielefeld: Transcript verlag.

Honneth, A. (1995), *The Struggle for Recognition: The Moral Grammar of Social Struggles*, Cambridge: Polity.

Hopkins, P.E. (2009), 'Responding to the "Crisis of Masculinity": The Perspectives of Young Muslim Men from Glasgow and Edinburgh, Scotland', *Gender, Place and Culture*, 16 (3): 299–312.

Jauss, H. (1982), *Toward an Aesthetic of Reception*, Minneapolis: University of Minnesota Press.

Keddie, A. (2014), 'The Politics of Britishness: Multiculturalism, Schooling and Social Cohesion', *British Educational Research Journal*, 40 (3): 539–554.

Khattab, N. and Johnston, R. (2013), 'Ethnic and Religious Penalties in a Changing British Labour Market from 2002 to 2010: The Case of Unemployment', *Environment and Planning A (Environment and Planning)*, 45 (6): 1358–1371.

Latour, V. (2012), '"Muscular Liberalism": Surviving Multiculturalism? A Historical and Political Contextualisation of David Cameron's Munich Speech', *Observatoire de la Société Britannique. La Revue*, (12): 199–216.

Mahmood, N. (2011), 'A Critique of Multiculturalism in England's Contemporary Policy and Practice: Preventing Violent Extremism and Multicultural Tensions', (Unpublished MA Thesis, University of Sheffield).

Maxwell, J.A. (2012), *Qualitative Research Design: An Interactive Approach*, London: Sage Publications.

Maxwell, J.A. and Miller, B.A. (2008), 'Categorizing and Connecting Strategies in Qualitative Data Analysis', in S.N. Hesse-Biber and P. Leavy (eds), *Handbook of Emergent Methods*, 461–477, New York: Guilford Press.

May T. (2011), *Social Research: Issues, Methods and Research*, McGraw-Hill International.

Meer, N. (2012), 'Misrecognizing Muslim Consciousness in Europe', *Ethnicities*, 12 (2): 178–196.

Meer, N., Martineau, W. and Thompson, S. (2012), 'Misrecognition and Ethno-religious Diversity', *Ethnicities*, 12 (2): 131–141.

Meer, N. and Modood, T. (2013), 'Beyond "Methodological Islamism"? A Thematic Discussion of Muslim Minorities in Europe', *Advances in Applied Sociology*, 7 (3): 307–313.

Meer, N. and Nayak, A. (2013), 'Race Ends Where? Race, Racism and Contemporary', Available at: http://soc.sagepub.com/content /early/2013/11/15/0038038513501943.full (accessed 1 December 2016).

Miah, S. (2014), 'Trojan Horse, Ofsted and the "Prevent"ing of Education', Discover Society. [Online]. (10). Available at: http://discoversociety .org/2014/07/01/trojan-horse-ofsted-and-the-preventing-of-education/ (accessed 29 November 2016).

Modood, T. and Ahmad, F. (2007), 'British Muslim Perspectives on Multiculturalism', *Theory, Culture and Society*, 24 (2): 187–213.

Modood, T., Beishon, S. and Virdee, S. (1994), *Changing Ethnic Identities*, London: Policy Studies Institute.

Mythen, G. (2012), 'Identities in the Third Space? Solidity, Elasticity and Resilience amongst Young British Pakistani Muslims', *The British Journal of Sociology*, 63 (3): 393–411.

NALDIC (2011), Ethnic Minority Achievement. Available at: http://www.naldic .org.uk/Resources/NALDIC/Research and Information/Documents/EMAG _Survey_Report.pdf (accessed 29 November 2016).

Osberg, D. and Biesta, G.J. (2007), 'Beyond Presence: Epistemological and Pedagogical Implications of "strong" emergence', *Interchange*, 38 (1): 31–51.

Osler, A. and Starkey, H. (2005), 'Violence in Schools and Representations of Young People: A Critique of Government Policies in France and England', *Oxford Review of Education*, 31 (2): 195–215.

Panjwani, F. (2016), 'Towards an Overlapping Consensus: Muslim Teachers' Views on Fundamental British Values', *Journal of Education for Teaching*, 42 (3): 329–340.

Parekh, B. (1995), 'Liberalism and Colonialism: A Critique of Locke and Mill', in J.N. Pieterse and B. Parekh (eds), *Decolonization of Imagination: Culture, Knowledge and Power*, 81–98, London: Zed Books.

Parekh, B. (1996), 'Moral Philosophy and Its Anti-pluralist Bias', *Royal Institute of Philosophy Supplement*, 40: 117–134.

Parekh, B. (2002), *Rethinking Multiculturalism: Cultural Diversity and Political Theory*, Boston: Harvard University Press.

Rhamie, J., Bhopal, K., and Bhatti, G. (2012), 'Stick to Your Own Kind: Pupils' Experiences of Identity and Diversity in Secondary Schools', *British Journal of Educational Studies*, 60 (2): 171–191.

Said, E. (1997), *Covering Islam: How the Media and the Experts Determine How We See the Rest of the World*, London: Vintage.

Said, E. (2004), *Humanism and Democratic Criticism*, Columbia: Columbia University Press.

Shain, F. (2011), *The New Folk Devils: Muslim Boys and Education in England*, Stoke-on-Trent: Trentham Books.

Taylor, C. (1992), 'The Politics of Recognition', in A. Gutmann (ed), *Multiculturalism: Examining the Politics of Recognition*, 25–74, Princeton, NJ: Princeton University Press.

Taylor, C. (2016), *The Language Animal: The Full Shape of the Human Linguistic Capacity*, Harvard: The Belknap Press of Harvard University.

Taylor-Gooby, P. and Waite, E. (2013), 'Toward a More Pragmatic Multiculturalism? How the UK Policy Community Sees the Future of Ethnic Diversity Policies', *Governance*, 27 (2): 267–289.

Thomas, P. (2011), *Youth, Multiculturalism and Community Cohesion*, London: Palgrave Macmillan.

Thompson, S. and Majid, Y. (2011), *The Politics of Misrecognition*, Farnham, Surrey: Ashgate Publishing Ltd.

Werbner, P. (2012), 'Folk Devils and Racist Imaginaries in a Global Prism: Islamophobia and anti-Semitism in the Twenty-first Century', *Ethnic and Racial Studies*, 36 (3): 450–467.

Witzel, A. and Reiter, H. (2012), *The Problem-centred Interview*, London: Sage Publications.

CHAPTER FOUR

An Ethnographic Study of Young People from Poor Rural Sindh, Pakistan

Ambreen Shahriar

Guiding questions

1 In Chapter 1 (p. 17), I propose two main criteria which ethnographic research needs to meet. Briefly, these are:

- Make the familiar strange: recognize the significance of the researcher's role
- Strive to understand the local in the global and the global in the local

How does Ambreen meet these criteria in her chapter?

2 Heath and Street (2008) say, 'Every ethnographer must always be on guard against letting one's own beliefs about what *should* overcome the accuracy of what *is*'. How does Ambreen illustrate this in her chapter? In what ways do you need to guard against letting 'what should be' overcome 'what is' in your own research?

Introduction

This chapter discusses methodological choices I made in the process of my PhD study. I conducted my research in Pakistan with young men and women from deprived backgrounds – financially, educationally, linguistically – who aspire to better lives and respected positions in society. Though my participants share a common sociocultural background, the study is not intended as research on a particular cultural group. Therefore it is not ethnography in the established sense of the word, but it uses an ethnographic approach to explore and give voice to people, focusing on their individual contextual peculiarities rather than studying a particular group in its context. The participants of the study belong to a multilingual Pakistani context. This can be considered a minority language context as their first language, Sindhi, is considered inferior to Urdu and English. The research focuses on the perspectives and concerns of the participants due to their being both economically and socially weak, having a comparatively inferior language in a multilingual context.

In the chapter, I explain how I understood my big question related to my theoretical choices. I also discuss the methodological issues that were considered during the initial stages of my research. It begins with a short overview of my research context. Then, the main body of the chapter presents my research theory, explaining and arguing around my choices of research approach, methodology and tools. The chapter also highlights my decisions on my position as a researcher; I have the same linguistic and ethnic background as my participants, but a better social standing due to my education and job. My theoretical considerations, in terms of methodology, are the focus of the discussion throughout this chapter. I then present the role of **reflexivity** in my study before concluding the chapter.

Social science research explores the perceptions of the social actors (see Miller and Glassner 2004; Charmaz 1995). Therefore, my research tries to capture the meanings that my participants from poor rural backgrounds attribute to the events and incidents in their lives; I wanted to understand the ways they see the world they live in. Through in-depth life story interviews I learn about the views and ideas of my participants and give voice to them. I try to present reality *as seen by the interviewees* 'with depth and detail' (Fowler 1996; Bourdieu 1999). Such sociocultural perspectives of reality have great significance for my participants, for me as a researcher and for the social world where this reality belongs.

Research context

The research focuses on the people of rural areas of the province of Sindh (see Shahriar 2013; Shahriar et al. 2014, for detailed discussion).

In this section, I explain the broader context for my Western readers. Rind (2012: 50) notes:

> In the context of Pakistan (and particularly in the Sindh), rurality and village life are associated with poverty (Baluch 2002), poor education (Sawada and Lokshin 1999; *The Daily Observer* 2009), and a lack of facilities and resources (Freeman 1982). More importantly, rurality is characterized by the class divisions of the feudal landlord vs. the agricultural labourers (Naimullah 2003)…the Zamidars [*waderos* or landowners] have blocked any attempts to improve the quality of education provision in the rural villages of the Sindh (Qazi 2004). Being rural in the Sindh is therefore characterized by a low socio-economic status, being poorly educated, oppressed and lacking confidence.

The participants for my study belong to different villages in Sindh. Their stories show that living conditions can be different in different villages. Some villages have, and others don't have, basic facilities like electricity, gas, clean drinking water or a non-asphalted road leading to the nearest town which makes motorbike, rickshaw or bus transport possible. Likewise some villages have separate primary and even secondary schools for both boys and girls; others have one and some have none. Thus in some villages (e.g. Farwa's village; see Shahriar 2013, for all references to the research participants) the education of girls is common but in others even that of boys is rare (e.g. Ahmar's village). It is clear from every interview I conducted that boys are given better treatment than girls whenever there is a matter of choice or priority.

During the discussion with my participants, I also noticed that the social atmosphere in different villages could vary greatly. In some villages, people live in harmony with each other, helping each other in times of need; in others you find jealousy (Ahmar's story), family feuds (Shabana's story), quarrels among villagers (Ahmar's story) and the issues of safety and security (Abdur Razzak's story). Some villages have an education-friendly environment. Some give a fair amount of freedom to their girls and allow them to play with boys in the street (Farhana's and Farwa's stories), go to school and take decisions on their own.

The family system is more or less the same in all the villages. It is a joint family system where several nuclear families live in the same compound. Even if siblings after getting married no longer live under the same roof, they share a very close bond. Men and women have distinct roles: the husband is the breadwinner and deals with affairs outside the home and the wife takes care of the household and children. The parents of my participants all followed this pattern. For my participants themselves, and especially for the women, these roles were beginning to change.

Theoretical considerations

My research studies the lives of five young men and women. My study cannot be called 'an ethnography', which has been defined as 'a detailed study of the life and activities of a group of people' (Feagin et al. 1991: 4). I am not looking at a group but at *individuals* from a group and how they are, or try to be, different. My study can therefore be called 'a study of multiple cases', or 'a case study that is ethnographic in nature', since the big question deals with issues of culture, and these are usually addressed through ethnographic studies. Within this framework, my research methodology is case study and life stories provide the data for these case studies. Through this research I attempt to explore the lives of my participants, with the following being my big question:

> How do some people from poor rural backgrounds in Sindh try to progress to a higher standard of living?

Mine is an interpretive study, which attempts to understand the meanings participants assign to the various social phenomena in the context. Consequently, my research seeks to answer the following questions:

1   How do their familial and social backgrounds affect the life of the participants?
2   How far is continuing without quitting important?
3   Why is it important for the participants to improve their social status?

Although the importance of the established social structures in the world around my participants is undeniable, an exploration of their daily interactions helps us to understand their disadvantageous social position within the wider social structures. It was important to understand the influence of these wider structures on their lives. The next important issue was the agency that my participants could exercise and what personal choices they could make to forge their path and fortune. And most importantly, why do they want it to be in this way? I used case study as a methodology to better understand the research problem and answer my research questions. Life story interviews are my research tool as 'the case study needs to present people as complex creatures. Biographies offer the researcher provocative models' (Stake 1995: 97). I discuss the theoretical issues related to my methodological choices in the following sections.

Research methodology: Ethnographic approaches

The ethnographic approach suits my project because I focus on the uniqueness of my participants and their situations, and not on generalization. Moreover ethnography starts with a big question by identifying a problem in the field, as I did in the case of my study. I started my research by identifying a practical problem, which I discovered during my teaching career in Sindh. Because of my shared background, I largely share, and sympathize with the perspective of my participants (Conteh et al. 2005: xxi). Davies (2008) agrees with Kristmundsdóttir (2006) that an ethnographer's personal history, job experience and sociocultural environment all affect their selection of issues and population to be researched; this is certainly true in my case. The origins of my research go back to the three years I spent teaching at the University of Sindh from 2004. After doing an MA in English Literature, I taught English language and literature, first in a private school for a year and then at the university at which I had studied. My experience of teaching at the university where nearly half the students came from rural areas led me to this research. In Pakistan, the students from rural areas with Sindhi (also Balochi, Siraiki, Pashto, Punjabi) speaking families come to cities for higher education, where Urdu is a common language of communication and English is the medium of instruction in higher education. Education in university is especially difficult due to this issue of multilingualism, and my research participants discuss this extensively.

Following Davies's (2008) view that ethnographic research should use qualitative techniques based on the lives of the researched (see Fig. 4.1), I conducted life story interviews with my participants. My data comprise whatever useful information I could gather through the interviews (Hammersley and Atkinson 1983).

Edwards and Talbot (1994: 49) describe ethnography as a 'progressive focusing design' and say that ethnographic study requires special knowledge of sociological conditions since individuals are observed in interaction with the environment in which they belong. Through their

---

- Empirical data systematically selected for the purpose
- Real world context (no experimental conditions produced by researcher)
- Informal conversation
- Open approach to data collection
- A small number of participants
- Data analysis involves interpretation, description and explanation of human action or words

Adapted from Hammersley, M. (1993)

FIGURE 4.1 *Ethnographic traits in my research*

stories I study my participants' interaction with their social contexts. Thus rich and readable data are produced. Edwards and Talbot (1994) further point out that, in the course of examining the data, the focus of the research is continually refined. Successive study of different cases therefore leads to progressive focusing. My study is based on the cases of five different participants, and each helps to define and redefine the information gathered from the others.

Nader (1993: 7; cited in Altheide and Johnson 1998) quotes the objective of ethnographic research from Malinowski as, 'to grasp the native's point of view, his relation to life, to realize his vision of the world'. The goals of my study are to give voice to my participants from rural Sindh and to understand, interpret and discuss their stories so that more people know about their journey towards a better life. My research also fits Hammersley's (1993) idea of three features of ethnographic thinking:

1 *Naturalism:* My research is based on natural knowledge and understanding of actual social situations. This knowledge and understanding developed out of knowing what people do in real-life situations through the life story interviews. Data gathered explain events with reference to the context.

2 *Discovery:* I am doing this research due to my personal interest in the social setting and the problem under research in this thesis. I began research with minimal assumptions so that I would be able to see the world through the perspective of my participants, without it being overshadowed or blurred by any already existing hypotheses or assumptions. I continuously narrowed down and sharpened the focus of this research, which, in turn, changed it substantially, as it proceeded.

3 *Understanding:* My data explain human actions and behaviour, with reference to cultural perspective. I carry the knowledge of the culture of the group under study, in many ways; I belong to the same culture and, therefore, have experienced their way of life in my own life. That is why I attempt to produce a valid explanation of its behaviour.

The suitability of an ethnographic approach for research on human behaviour is accepted widely (Bruyn 1966; Blumer 1969; Harre and Secord 1973, all cited in Hammersley 1993). It can give us a profound understanding of behaviour, of the complexity of relations, of power relations, of the complexities of everyday life, for many significant trivialities *seem* so insignificant that they are hardly ever noticed (see Fig. 4.2, on the next page for details).

The study of cultures is mainly the domain of ethnography. My study is only partly ethnographic, namely inasmuch as it takes culture into

- Its participants have a common culture or world view (Alasuutari 1998, Hammersley 1993).
- It seeks to understand human behaviour from participant's point of view (Fetterman 1998, Clifford 1988, Kamil, Langer and Shanahan 1985).
- It identifies and describes phenomena from beginning to end across cycles. (Edwards and Talbot 1994, Kamil, Langer and Shanahan 1985).
- It develops hypotheses grounded in the event and driven by the conceptual framework of the study (Hammersley 1993, Kamil, Langer and Shanahan 1985).
- It presents a vivid picture of another culture to its readers. (Alasuutari 1998, Geertz 1988).
- It provides emic – insider's or native's – perspectives (Robson 2002, Fetterman 1998, Hammersley 1993, Nader 1993).

FIGURE 4.2 *Ethnographic nature of my study*

consideration. But it focuses on *individuals*, inasmuch as they are trying to improve their standard of living. It is not trying to describe the culture for its own sake.

Research methodology: Case study

As well as having strong ethnographic elements, my research can be called a case study as it includes the study of five different cases, whom I would prefer to call 'my participants'. Case study research has the case as a unit of analysis. 'Case studies are undertaken to make the case understandable' (Stake 1995: 85). Case study research investigates an existing problem in a real-life setting. I set out to explore the 'how' and 'why' questions in my field (Yin 1989). Feagin et al. (1991: 9) regard case study as a holistic approach and note that it 'can permit the researcher to examine not only the complex life in which people are implicated but also the impact on beliefs and decisions of the complex web of social interaction'. For my research field, case study is advantageous as it can provide fundamental insights, detailed analysis and rich and in-depth description (Feagin et al. 1991; Sjoberg et al. 1991). Mine is a 'descriptive multiple-case study' which 'presents a complete description of the phenomenon within its context' (Yin 2003: 5).

Some cases are studied for the sake of generalizing. Others, like mine, have significance of their own and the interest in their generalization is negligible (Stake 1995) (see Fig. 4.3, on the next page).

My study focuses on young people:

- from rural and economically weak areas of Sindh, Pakistan;
- from deprived and less educated families;
- from monolingual setting, they move to multilingual setting.

My study comprises 5 different cases: 3 females and 2 males. In order to understand their path towards better life, I expect to find out:

- the impact of their native field, capital and *habitus* on their achievements in life;
- the impact of day-to-day interaction with other individuals.

FIGURE 4.3 *My case study design*

Research tool: Life story interview

My research is based on the life stories of five young men and women from rural and economically weak backgrounds in the province of Sindh, Pakistan. I chose life story interviews as the research tool within a narrative research framework, expecting that it will help me gather the type of data I want. Though narrative research has fewer participants than any other form of research, I have been able to gather a large amount of data by having five participants. They were all eager to talk about themselves. I was really moved when, at the end of his interview, Abdur Razzak (a male participant) said that nobody had ever listened to him for so long with so much interest. These words revealed to me an important aspect of his life. Every narrative I collected was very personal and provided rich autobiographical accounts (Lieblich et al. 1998). Agreeing with Davies (2008), I studied the lives of my participants in order to understand the social and cultural issues existing in their world, but I did not expect their stories to be entirely representative. Some of their experiences will be entirely personal, and the fact that this is possible is interesting in itself.

One important reason behind choosing life story as a research method is that it would be difficult for the Western public to imagine the life and culture of my participants. However, their specific narratives will be much easier to understand since

we may not be able fully to comprehend specific thought patterns of another culture, but we have…less difficulty *understanding* a story coming from another culture, however exotic that culture may appear to us. (White 1981: 1, original emphasis)

Telling, and listening to, stories is common in everyday life. Narrative 'is international, trans-historical, trans-cultural: it is simply there, like life itself' (Barthes 1977: 79). The translatability of narrative is accepted by Barthes (1977), Lejeune (1989), Mishler (1986), Rosen (1998) and White (1981).

When we use any qualitative method, participants are expected to respond by telling stories. During the interviews, whenever I put a question to Shabana, a female participant, she started her reply with, 'Oh, that is another story…' and then described the incident. Everyone can, when given a chance, narrate their life story, as all of us have a sketch of our biography in our minds (Lejeune 1989; Rosen 1998). All of my participants were quite comfortable narrating their life stories though, unlike the rest, Ahmar brought some jotted notes to the interview which were to remind him of the incidents he wanted to share.

There is a reciprocal relationship between life stories and life: life provides raw material for the stories; life stories provide meaning and understanding to life. Life stories are an act not only of expressing oneself but also of understanding oneself. Time and again my participants said that narrating their stories gave them a chance to see their lives all over again, and sometimes even from a different perspective. Kearney summarizes this idea in Fig. 4.4.

Narratives cannot be taken as accurately reflecting reality, rather they are personal to their narrators and creative in nature (Lieblich et al. 1998). Different persons can give different accounts of the same incident. What is remembered and how it is narrated has special significance for an ethnographer (Davies 2008). Life stories are valuable even if they are not verifiable because they reveal the understanding and perception of the participants, their ways of looking at events and the world in general (Fetterman 1998). Fetterman accepts incompleteness in autobiographical accounts due to memory failure and so on but, for him and for me, narratives still express whatever is important for the participants because that is what they remember, and choose to tell. However, it is also possible

---

Not a private act of self writing but a cultural act of self reading

Understanding:

- oneself/self-reflective
- One's perspective of the surroundings
- Relationships between individual and society

Adapted from Kearney (2001)

FIGURE 4.4 *Autobiography*

that some very disturbing and painful, and therefore important, incidents have been 'repressed' and forgotten. Nietzsche and Freud, among others, have pointed this out. The interviews I gathered show the interviewees' own understanding about the incidents they choose to relate (see also Denzin 1991, cited in Miller and Glassner 2004).

I chose life stories because I wanted to explore those aspects which more positivist research usually avoids or misses out – subjectivity, exceptions, contradictions, complexities and most importantly the general messiness of ideas and points of view gathered through this type of research. Using life stories as a research tool has allowed me to focus on individuals and emphasize subjectivity. I preferred life stories to other research tools because I want to see my participants as individuals in their social circle with their real-life family problems, along with their typical identity, style and mental make-up. I wanted to see them as they see themselves or as they want me to see them. I also wanted to understand how they portray themselves when they act in adverse circumstances. I do not want to categorize individuals only by their social or economic or educational circumstances, neither do I want to study only those circumstances and draw my results from them alone. Individuals are not simply either their social persona or their educated persona. Individuals are a combination of these personae, and that combination makes them the unique person they are. My research gathers all incidents and aspects and circumstances of the lives of my participants that they wanted to share with me. In this way, my research explores and interprets their lives with their uniqueness, triviality, individuality, predictability and commonness, heroic acts and failures. Classical German poet Friedrich Schiller (1759–1805), talking about the dramatic arts, makes a very similar point. He puts it like this:

Mit allen seinen Tiefen, seinen Höhen,	With all its depths and all its summits
Roll' ich das Leben ab vor deinem Blick.	I unroll life before your eyes.
Wenn du das große Spiel der Welt gesehen,	When you have seen the world's great game,
So kehrst du reicher in dich selbst zurück.	You will return enriched into your self.

(From Schiller: Huldigung dr Künste [Homage of the Arts]).

I have used Francis's (1993) phenomenographic approach to qualitative interviewing (see also Kearney 2001 for an application of Francis's approach), which affords greater significance to individuals' reflection on an experience than to the events themselves. Not only the interview, but also the experience and processes of interviewing themselves are important: how it is conducted and where the interviewee reveals some specific emotions and expressions, how the interviewer feels at the time when different incidents are narrated are no less important than the events narrated. By using Francis's (1993) approach of 'unstructured' interviews in the form of a conversation, I handed the reins of the entire conversation to my participants, with me asking questions only when clarification or explanations were needed. Such interviews yielded rich data. 'The aim of the interview is to have the interviewee thematize the phenomenon of interest and make the thinking explicit' (Francis 1993: 70). During these interviews no schedule of questions was used, and I had no expectations of what the participants would say. The participants thought aloud about their own lives and in this way increased their awareness of them, exactly what Marton (1981, cited in Francis 1993) expected to happen. This proved very helpful in the analysis stage.

Fetterman (1998: 52) notes that life stories provide invaluable depth 'in putting the pieces of the puzzle together'. The data gathered through the life stories of my participants helped me to understand the context better and answer my research questions. My participants provided me with their experiences and predominantly painful reflections, accumulated during their lives. Their accounts were embedded within layers of history and in sometimes conflicting cultural and social traditions. My participants, politically oppressed, socially ignored, economically deprived and linguistically rejected, revealed in their interviews their rich home culture and the blend of complex networks of people around them. They all had fascinating stories to tell.

Reflexivity in qualitative research

Research in the social world is affected by the physical presence of the researcher (Bourdieu 1977; Clifford 1986; Kenway and McLeod 2004). Research on human subjects can never be completely objective. Believing in complete objectivity is denying the presence of the researcher herself/himself and their relationship with the research participants, and the choices they make during the research process. It is also denying the identities and individualities of all those involved in the research. However, research on human subjects cannot be completely subjective either. Adopting a completely subjective approach would be ignoring the objective realities like race, colour, language, social status, chance happenings, etc., all of which exist beyond the will and effort of human agents.

According to Davies (2008), ethnography emerges from the ethnographer's personal areas of concern or interest. He suggests that these need to be acknowledged at all points, as I have done throughout this chapter and in my research (Shahriar 2013). Davies goes on to say that the ethnographer's views on the field also affect her interpretation of what the informant is trying to say. Therefore, we need to heed the warning from Heath and Street (2008: 37) that, 'every ethnographer must always be on guard against letting one's own beliefs about what *should be* overcome the accuracy of what *is*' [original emphasis].

Edwards and Talbot (1994: 45–46) note that while doing a case study 'the very labeling of an event or phenomenon as a case and your presence as an observer of the case will in fact change it', since being a 'participant covert observer' is unethical in research. They suggest that the researcher needs to 'accept that you will disturb the case, name it and note it'. Therefore I did not try to eliminate any influence I might have on the data but decided to be aware of it, to acknowledge it and to consider its influence on the data (Hammersley and Atkinson 1983; Miller and Glassner 2004; Davies 2008). As my participants and my readers expect me to be aware of, and open about, my role in relation to my data, I write not only about my participants but also about my own background and previous experiences, and how these and my presence during the interviews might have affected my findings. 'How people respond to the presence of the researcher may be as informative as how they react to other situations' (Hammersley and Atkinson 1983: 15).

Nowadays many researchers recognize the importance of their own biographical details as part of qualitative research. They draw attention to the fact that the results are not objective (so not absolute), were obtained by a specific researcher with specific life experiences and would not have been obtained in the same way by a different researcher with different life experiences, even if conducting the research in very similar circumstances and with the same participants (Woods 1999). Qualitative writers prefer to write in the active rather than the passive voice and the first person ('I understood', rather than 'It was understood'). Davies (1982, cited in Woods 1999), for example, refers to herself in her book by 'I' instead of by 'the author'. She declares thereby that she was significant during data collection and that she herself is part of her data. Wherever necessary I have pointed out the influence of my prior knowledge or my physical presence on my data and findings, due to my having the same ethnic and linguistic background as my participants.

The question of power relations (Miller and Glassner 2004) is also worth mentioning here. Edwards and Talbot (1994) advise that while collecting the data, the researcher must always ask herself, 'Am I taking undue advantage of my position to gain information?' In my case, though I was not intentionally taking advantage, it seems to me that I have an undue advantage due to my position as a university teacher in Pakistan, a researcher and above all a PhD student from the United Kingdom. My position as an interviewer was one of authority, particularly in the cultural setting in which my research took place. I was motivated by the desire to find out as much as possible about the lives of my participants, but I must admit that presumably they accepted to be interviewed more out of respect for me than because of a desire to *give* as much information as possible about their lives. I used phenomenographic interviews (which I consider in the next section) to compensate for the problems of power relations. Phenomenography tries to obtain reliable insights into a person's perception of the external world. These insights should be new to the researcher and not be influenced by his preconceptions. (See also Marton 1981, cited in Francis 1993.)

Ali and Kelly (2004: 124) concurring with Code (1991) say:

> objectivity and ethics in research are linked in a complex relationship which requires us to question who can know, and what they can know.

If the interviewee knows in advance what the researcher is likely to think, the interviewee is likely to think and talk about the events from the researcher's point of view instead of his own (Francis 1993). I therefore did not tell the participants what I was expecting from them. Even though they asked me repeatedly about my area of interest, my only reply was, 'I want to know about your entire life, everything that you want to share.' I therefore expected to get more valid first-hand knowledge by using a phenomenographic approach (instead of going after knowledge that was filtered by my own perceptions). Instead of asking questions and expecting my participants to reply, I let them tell me their stories as they wished, listened to them eagerly and only from time to time asked them to clarify some detail. Like Marton and Francis (Francis 1993: 70), I regarded an interviewee as a 'reporting subject' rather than 'an interrogated object'. Our 'interviews' felt more like a conversation. I tried not to ask questions in the middle of the story as I did not want to break the momentum of the narrative. I asked most of my questions at the end of their stories, usually asking them to go back to a particular incident and give me more details or reflect on a particular aspect. In order to achieve my purpose and avoid distracting my participants, I did not take any detailed notes during the interview. I only wrote a few key words while my participants narrated their story during some interviews. In fact, I was so deeply interested in the narrations that I did not want to write anything and also, I did not need to write because I knew that I could easily manage without writing questions to be reminded later.

Ethical issues emerge for all research, though they are particularly important when a researcher allows such liberty to her interviewees as I did in this case. Throughout this project I followed the accepted principles of research ethics, such as informed consent, right to privacy, confidentiality and data protection (Fontana and Frey 1998; Ali and Kelly 2004). I encouraged my participants to help with my project by telling them that I wanted to give voice to them, get the stories of their lives and make them known to the world (Couchman and Dawson 1990). I took care to treat my participants as individuals who have complete control over what they want to share. I am grateful to them.

As my interviews were informal, unfocused and uncontrolled, I had to be particularly mindful of privacy and confidentiality during the data analysis (Fetterman 1998). I ensured privacy by using pseudonyms for my participants. During the analysis I did not discuss anything the participants told me after the recorder was turned off, except with their explicit permission. I wanted to keep my participants safe and make sure that my research could in no way disturb their personal lives.

Conclusion

This chapter has reflected on the choices I made that contributed to the methodological processes of my doctoral research. I said that my study is not ethnography in the established sense of the word as, though my participants shared a common sociocultural background, the study was not intended as research on a particular cultural group. Instead, it *uses* an ethnographic approach. I have discussed this in detail in the section on the ethnographic approach. I then discussed case study as my research methodology design. I used five participants for my main study and two for the pilot study. They would help me to understand my big question. I wanted to know why *individuals* want a better life and improve their position in the pecking order of society, and what happened to them later in life. Life story interviews helped me achieve this aim. However, I did not make statements about the group. With these decisions at the early stage of my research, I moved ahead into the field. Being clear on my basic methodological stance helped me later during data collection and analysis and the research itself did not face any serious problems.

References

Alasuutari, P. (1998), *An Invitation to Social Research*, London: Sage Publications.

Ali, S. and Kelly, M. (2004), 'Ethics and Social Research', in C. Seale (ed), *Researching Society and Culture*, 2nd edn, 115–128, London: Sage Publications.

Altheide, D.L. and Johnson, J.M. (1998), 'Criteria for Assessing Interpretive Validity in Qualitative Research', in N.K. Denzin and Y.S. Lincoln (eds), *Collecting and Interpreting Qualitative Materials*, 283–312, Thousand Oaks, CA: Sage Publications.

Baluch, B. (2002), 'Being Poor and Becoming Poor: Poverty Status and Poverty Transitions in Rural Pakistan', *Journal of Asian and African Studies*, 37(2): 168–185.

Barthes, R. (1977), *Image, Music, Text* (Translated by Stephen Heath), New York: Hill and Wang.

Blumer, H. (1969), *Symbolic Interactionism: Perspective and Method*, Englewood Cliffs, NJ: Prentice-Hall.

Bourdieu, P. (1977), *Outline of a Theory of Practice*, Cambridge: CUP.

Bourdieu, P. (1999), *The Weight of the World: Social Suffering in Contemporary Society*, Cambridge: Polity Press.

Bruyn, S.T. (1966), *The Human Perspective in Sociology: The Methodology of Participant Observation*, Englewood Cliffs, NJ: Prentice-Hall, Inc.

Charmaz, K. (1995), 'Between Positivism and Postmodernism: Implications for Methods', *Studies in Symbolic Interaction*, 17: 43–47.

Clifford, J. (1986), *Writing Culture: The Poetics and Politics of Ethnography*, Berkeley: University of California Press.

Clifford, J. (1988), *The Predicament of Culture: Twentieth-Century Ethnography, Literature, and Art*, London: Harvard University Press.

Code, L. (1991), *What Can She Know? Feminist Theory and the Construction of Knowledge*. Ithaca, NY: Cornell University Press.

Conteh, J., Gregory, E., Kearney, C. and Mor-Sommerfeld, A. (2005), *On Writing Educational Ethnographies: The Art of Collusion*, Stoke on Trent: Trentham Books.

Couchman, W. and Dawson, J. (1994), *Nursing and Health Care Research*, London: Scutari Press.

Davies, B. (1982), *Life in the Classroom and Playground*, London: Routledge and Kegan Paul.

Davies, C.A. (2008), *Reflexive Ethnographies: A Guide to Researching Selves and Others*, London: Routledge.

Denzin, N.K. (1991), 'Representing Lived Experiences in Ethnographic Texts', *Studies in Symbolic Interaction*, 12: 59–70.

Edwards, A. and Talbot, R. (1994), *The Hard-pressed Researcher: A Research Handbook for the Caring Professions*, London, New York: Longman.

Feagin, J.R., Orum, A.M. and Sjoberg, G. (1991), 'Introduction', in J.R. Feagin, A.M. Orum and G. Sjoberg (eds), *A Case for the Case Study*, 1–26, Chapel Hill and London: The University of North Carolina Press.

Fetterman, D.M. (1998), *Ethnography: Step by Step*, Thousand Oaks, CA: Sage Publications.

Fontana, A. and Frey, J.H. (1998), 'Interviewing: The Art of Science', in N.K. Denzin, J. Maybin and Y.S. Lincoln (eds), *Collecting and Interpreting Qualitative Materials*, 47–78, Thousand Oaks, CA: Sage Publications.

Fowler, B. (1996), 'An Introduction to Pierre Bourdieu's "Understanding"', *Theory, Culture and Society*, 13(2): 1–16.

Francis, H. (1993), 'Advancing Phenomenography: Questions of Method', *Nordisk Pedagogik*, 2: 68–75.

Freeman, D.M. (1982), 'Power Distribution and Adoption of Agricultural Innovations: A Structural Analysis of Villages in Pakistan', *Rural Sociology*, 47(1): 68–80.

Geertz, C. (1988), *Works and Lives: The Anthropologist as Author*, Stanford, CA: Stanford University Press.

Hammersley, M. (1993), 'Introducing Ethnography', in G. Graddol, J. Maybin and B. Stierer (eds), *Researching Language and Literacy in Social Context: A Reader*, 1–17, Clevedon: Multilingual Matters.

Hammersley, M. and Atkinson, P.A. (1983), *Ethnography: Principles in Practice*, London: Routledge.

Harre, R, and Secord, P.F. (1973), *The Explanation of Social Behavior*, Totowa, NJ: Littlefield, Adams.

Heath, S.B. and Street, B.V. (2008), *On Ethnography: Approaches to Language and Literacy Research*, New York: Teachers College Press.

Kamil, M.L., Langer, J.A., and Shanahan, T. (1985), *Understanding Research in Reading and Writing*, Boston, MA: Allyn and Bacon.

Kearney, C. (2001), *The Monkey's Mask: Identity, Memory, Narrative, Voice* [PhD Thesis] submitted to Goldsmith's, University of London.

Kenway, J. and McLeod, J. (2004), 'Bourdieu's Reflexive Sociology and "Spaces of Points of View": Whose Reflexivity, Which Perspective?', *British Journal of Sociology of Education*, 25(4): 525–544.

Kristmundsdóttir, S.D. (2006), 'Far from the Trobriands? Biography as Field', in S. Coleman and P. Collins (eds), *Locating the Field: Space, Place and Context in Anthropology*, X163–178, Oxford: Berg Publishers.

Lejeune, P. (1989), *On Autobiography*, Minneapolis: University of Minnesota Press.

Lieblich, A., Tuval-Mashiach, R. and Zilber, T. (1998), *Narrative Research: Reading, Analysis and Interpretation*, Thousand Oaks, CA: Sage Publications.

Marton, F. (1981), 'Phenomenography: Describing Conceptions of the World Around Us', *Instructional Science*, 10: 177–200.

Miller, J. and Glassner, B. (2004), 'The "Inside" and the "Outside": Finding Realities in Interviews', in D. Silverman (ed), *Qualitative Research: Theory, Method and Practice*, 2nd edn, 125–139, London: Sage Publications.

Mishler, E. G. (1986), *Research Interviewing Context and Narrative*, Cambridge, MA: Harvard University Press.

Nader, L. (1993), 'Paradigm Busting and Vertical Linkage', *Contemporary Sociology*, 33: 6–7.

Naimullah, M. (2003), *Pakistan under the Stranglehold of Feudalism: A Nation Under the Agony of Fundamentalism*, Lahore: Rehmat Publications.

Qazi, N. (2004), 'Feudalism Keeps Sindh Backward' [Online] Published in *Dawn* on 07th June 2004. Available at: http://www.dawn.com/news/361022/feudalism-keeps-sindh-backward (accessed 11 April 2016).

Rind, I.A. (2012), 'Investigating Students' Experiences of Learning English as a Second Language at the University of Sindh, Jamshoro, Pakistan' [PhD Thesis] submitted to University of Sussex.

Robson, C. (2002), *Real World Research: A Resource for Social Scientists and Practitioner-Researchers*, 2nd edn, Oxford: Blackwell Publishers.

Rosen, H. (1998), *Speaking from Memory: The Study of Autobiographical Discourse*, Stoke on Trent: Trentham Books.

Sawada, Y. and Lokshin, M. (1999), 'Household Schooling Decisions in Rural Pakistan', *World Bank Policy Research Working Paper No. 2541*. Available at: http://papers.ssrn.com/sol3/papers.cfm?abstract_id=632608 (accessed 30 April 2016).

Shahriar, A. (2013), 'Making a Better Life: Stories of People from Poor Rural Sindh Pakistan', (PhD Thesis submitted to Goldsmiths, University of London).

Shahriar, A., Baloch, S. and Bughio, F. (2014), 'Restraints on Language and Culture of Sindh: An Historical Perspective', *Grassroots*, 48(1): 29–42.

Sjoberg, G., Williams, N., Vaughan, T.R. and Sjoberg, A.F. (1991), 'The Case Study Approach in Social Research: Basic Methodological Issues', in J.R. Feagin, A.M. Orum and G. Sjoberg (eds), *A Case for the Case Study*, 27–79, Chapel Hill and London: The University of North Carolina Press.

Stake, R. (1995), *The Art of Case Study*, Thousand Oaks, CA: Sage Publications.

The Daily Observer (2009), 'Private Jails in Sindh', Published on 17th October.
Available at: http://pakobserver.net/201110/17/detailnews.asp?id=120194
(accessed 01 November 2012).

White, H. (1981), 'The Value of Narrativity in the Representation of Reality', in
W.J.T. Mitchell (ed), *On Narrative*, 1–24, Chicago: The University of Chicago
Press.

Woods, P. (1999), *Successful Writing for Qualitative Researchers*, London; New
York: Routledge.

Yin, R.K. (1989), *Case Study Research: Design and Methods*, London: Sage
Publications.

Yin, R.K. (2003), *Applications of Case Study Research*, 2nd edn, Thousand
Oaks: Sage Publications.

PART TWO

Developing the Research Processes

The chapters in this part take us into the processes of fieldwork in ethnographic research. In this introductory section, after briefly introducing each chapter, I consider two methodological themes that are significant in all the chapters, and show how the four authors addressed them in their projects:

- Positionality
- Researching multilingually

Introducing the chapters

All the chapters in this part have particular methodological issues as their central focus, whether broader concerns such as design, choice of research site and access or the ongoing processes that demand detailed, iterative decision-making, such as building relationships with participants and developing appropriate strategies to generate and collect data. These aspects of a research project are often grouped together and known as the 'methods', that is, the ways of doing things that follow from the epistemological and methodological decisions made at the start. The important thing is to see everything as part of a whole process, and to understand that the decisions you make in one area always have implications for the project as a whole. The authors in this part show us the problems they faced, the decisions they made, and how those decisions played out as the research progressed. A common thread running through the chapters is the need for flexibility, whether in the research questions and designs themselves, in the research sites, the participants and the data collection strategies. As Chisato reminds us in Chapter 5 and Jessica shows in Chapter 8, the need to be flexible does not mean that there is no need for a carefully thought-out plan from the start. Indeed, the uncertainties ahead make this even more important.

The communities that are the focus of the research projects you read about in Part 2 are not linguistic or 'ethnic minority' groups in the same way as the communities in Part 1, though the young migrant students in Robert Sharples' study could, in some ways, be said to be a minority group in their school as well as being members of minority ethnic and linguistic communities in their lives outside school. Although the communities being researched may not have been facing the same kinds of systemic disadvantage as those we met in Part 1, they were still encountering social injustice in different ways. The link they have is that they were all moving into new social, cultural and political contexts, facing change of sometimes complex and difficult kinds, and trying to find ways to adjust to the demands of living in societies that did not recognize their experiences, skills and agency.

The first two chapters in Part 2 have many parallels. Chisato Danjo and Indu Meddegama both worked with families with whom they shared some cultural and sociolinguistic experience and knowledge, and both were seeking to understand those families' language practices across the generations. But the aims of the studies were different. Chisato's project, which she describes as a sociolinguistic study, focused on the families' language practices in relation to official discourses about language maintenance emanating from the Japanese government-sponsored complementary school (the *Hoshuko*) which the children attended. Indu's interest, in contrast, was more in the ways in which the families' multilingual practices indexed status and power relationships within and across the generations within the family. For both, interviewing was the main data collection strategy. In Chapter 5, Chisato describes how she worked with the Japanese/British intermarriage families she accessed in the northeast of England to explore how they negotiated their multilingual practices in the contexts of family, home and complementary school. With Japanese as a first language and experience as a primary teacher in Japan, one would have expected Chisato to be an unquestioned insider in the contexts she was researching, but this was not entirely the case. The main focus in her chapter is on her role and the negotiation of her positionality as a multilingual researcher, who is in some ways an insider to her research contexts and in other, significant, ways an outsider.

Following this, in Chapter 6, Indu reveals to us the interview processes she developed in exploring family relationships in the Malayali community she was researching, whose cultural backgrounds were in some ways similar to her own. This was a first-generation 'immigrant' community in a small city in Yorkshire. Her research shows, among other things, how it is very easy to make assumptions about people, which are not always borne out when we get to know them better. Her chapter focuses on the actual processes of interviewing and sketches the ways in which her interviews were guided iteratively by emergent themes, which identified areas for further enquiry. Her sensitivity to the perspectives of her participants allowed her to strengthen the data analysis process and ultimately the credibility of the research findings.

The second two chapters in Part 2, by Robert Sharples and Jessica Bradley, report studies from very different contexts, but have some clear parallels in design and process. For both, their research methodology and data collection developed through close collaboration with the research participants, who became more like co-researchers. Robert's chapter, Chapter 7, is the only classroom-based study in this part of the book and takes us into the 'international department' in a South London secondary school to meet a very diverse group of learners. He wanted to understand the ways in which these students made sense of their experiences as 'EAL (English as an additional language) learners' in a mainstream education system that does not recognize or value multilingualism in any meaningful way. His work began as an 'ethnographically informed' project that aimed to capture the range of language that the young migrants were exposed to during their studies. Over two years of fieldwork he amassed a significantly larger, richer and more complex body of data than he anticipated, that incorporated field notes, photographs, interviews and documents. The focus of his study also shifted as the students' voices emerged more and more strongly through the data, and he began to realize that what was significant for their success in the system into which they had been introduced was what had happened and was happening to them outside the classroom, much more than in it, in many ways.

Jessica's project arose from a combination of her own professional experience in arts and languages and the conditions of a very large, externally funded research project, which aimed to explore translanguaging in cities (TLang 2014), to which her studentship was attached. Attesting to the fact that there is a huge difference between producing a research proposal which is coherent, neat and is presented with a clear, linear progression, and doing a 'real' project, Jessica's chapter explores the ways her research project moved from West Yorkshire to Slovenia as she followed in the footsteps of a grassroots community arts organization. She documented the ways they developed, planned and carried out street performance involving traditional story and visual arts. Drawing from her empirical data which included field notes, audio recordings, photographs and video collected in the United Kingdom and Slovenia, she explores in her chapter how 'liquid' settings, characterized by fluidity and unpredictability, require 'liquid' methodologies (Bauman 2000).

Positionality and researching multilingually

None of the authors in this part have the same, direct kind of insider status in the communities they were studying, as do the three authors in Part 1. On the surface, it would appear that Chisato had perhaps the greatest claim to be an insider, as she shared linguistic and cultural experiences with many of her participants. But, as she was to discover in the processes of gaining access to and winning the trust of her young participants and their parents, she lacked one big qualification that she had not anticipated – she did not have a child of her own. She had to work out how to prove her own worthiness to 'join the club' of the mothers whose experiences she was keen to investigate, and language proved to be a key factor in this. She recognized that her multilingualism, particularly her expertise in Japanese, was a key factor for her participants, and I discuss this further below. Similar to Chisato, Indu had some strong cultural connections with her chosen participants, but also significant differences. She describes herself at the start delicately as an 'acquaintance' of the Malayali community whose intergenerational language practices and language choices she studied, and claims that by the end of the research they were 'close friends'. This attests to the quality of the relationships that developed through the course of her research. Her own cultural upbringing in a South Asian context meant that many aspects of their lives were familiar to her, but she found some surprising differences, especially in intra-family relationships. In an interesting twist on the insider/outsider dilemmas, she also sensitively points out how her cultural knowledge meant that she could recognize that the interviewing processes themselves with their enquiring into family life were part of her outsider identity in the eyes of the families. One significant clue in her chapter, that shows Indu clearly overcame such obstacles, can be discerned in her use of pronouns. She naturally and seamlessly uses 'we' to include herself and her participants together in the processes of interviewing and making meaning of the families' experiences.

Both Robert and Jessica brought relevant professional and personal experiences to the role of researcher in their projects; Robert had been a TEFL teacher and had experience as a voluntary youth worker and Jessica had trained as a translator and as an educational engagement practitioner. These experiences contributed to their insider roles in relation to their questions and research design. But they also limited their opportunities to construct appropriate relationships with their participants, particularly in relation to the mediation of power in their interactions. Indeed, Robert suggests that it was not possible to achieve a fully emic position with his participants, arguing that the demands of the research and its presentation in conventional written forms entailed the need to stand back from the contexts being researched. The best that can be achieved, he suggests, is to become a 'legitimate outsider', which is good enough to report what you have found. This resonates with Indu's point that the interviewer role in itself places the researcher outside the participants' communities and cannot be reduced to nothing. It also raises an interesting general problem about positionality as a PhD or EdD researcher. Perhaps, becoming a full insider in a complex context marked by disadvantage and low status while meeting the demands, as a novice researcher, of being a student in the academy (particularly in the more elite 'ivory towers' institutions) simply represents too great a gap to fill. And on top of this are the demands of producing a text which meets the highest academic criteria that exist. Perhaps the insiderness can only be fully realized after the thesis itself is completed and you can then speak and write with authority on what you have learnt about the communities you have researched. This is when you can begin to fulfil effectively the responsibilities of advocacy and activism that researching for social justice entails.

Issues around working as a researcher in multilingual settings are clearly linked to positionality and the mediation of outsider/insider status, as Chisato highlights in Chapter 5 (p. 105). Despite the fact that so many EdD and PhD students are themselves multilingual and also that there have been several large, funded projects around researching multilingually (e.g. AHRC 2014, TLang 2014), it is perhaps surprising that there is still little attention given in methodological texts to issues around the topic. One key aspect to consider is the ways in which different languages are valued and recognized in projects and among all participants in the research, and the power differentials entailed. In a seminal paper from 1998, Martin et al. outline the 'complex issues surrounding working in a research team in a bilingual research project' (p. 121) and point out there are always 'structural constraints' which encourage 'inequalities and power asymmetries'. This may be considered inevitable in funded projects but, as a doctoral researcher, you have more freedom to negotiate roles and strategies. The first point to make is that if you don't share the languages spoken by the participants in your research, ways need to be found to develop appropriate rapport through other shared factors. Following this, you need to work out how you will mediate the complexities of accessing the data in the languages that you do not share and then meeting the requirements of the doctoral thesis by reporting the findings in English. In Chapter 7, Robert shares his struggles with 'writing outwards' to produce the right kind of text for the PhD, while at the same time doing justice to the generosity of his participants. As I have said elsewhere (p. 9), the demands of the academy cannot be avoided. But once they are met, opportunities for presenting your ideas multilingually and to a wide range of audiences will open up.

Issues around translation will arise in any multilingual project, not just because researchers and researched may not share the same language repertoires. There is also the need to disseminate your work for an English-speaking audience. In the same volume as the chapter by Martin et al. cited above, Bassnett argues against the 'universality' of any translation, reminding us that the translator 'is a product of his or her time, culture, gender, society, which means that a translation is always embedded in a context' (1998: 4). In my own research with multilingual teachers, my quest for a transcript that did justice to the ways the teachers used their language repertoires in their teaching, and also one that could be published in appropriate journals, often led to the need to harmonize dissonant translations offered by different co-researchers (e.g. Conteh 2007). My strategy was to be as transparent as possible about the processes of interpretation and analysis. In this respect, in Part 2, Robert's and Jessica's chapters are perhaps the most revealing of the strategies used by the researchers to capture the multilingual practices of the participants as transparently as possible. Robert shows us how he carefully noted his participants' translanguaging texts using his iPad, and points out how illuminating they were of their **'funds of knowledge'**, often showing us how the students themselves interpreted their own words. In her chapter, Jessica also uses a translanguaging lens to capture the fluidity and contingency of the multilingual practices of her participants. This plays well into the quest for social justice by equally valuing all the means of expression of their participants, in line with the way I theorized language in Chapter 1 (p. 23–26).

As multilingual researchers, both Indu and Chisato show acute awareness of this aspect of their identities as researchers, and reveal how they developed strategies which, in different ways, enabled them to research multilingually. Indu did not share the language repertoires of her participants, but she did – largely – share the cultural repertoires, and so she was able to use the language skills of her participants, at times, to translate each other's words. That they were entirely trustworthy in this shows the quality of the rapport she developed. Chisato's multilingualism, particularly her skills in Japanese, on the other hand, was a significant factor in the growing trust her participants had in her, and in negotiating access to the family homes. Both Chisato and Indu write about these facets of their research in illuminating ways. I suggest that such writing needs to have a more prominent place in PhD writing, revealing as it does the author's understanding of the research process. In working with one of my own students, a Japanese teacher of English who was interviewing other Japanese teachers, we discussed at great length the ways she could use her multilingualism in generating, interpreting and analyzing her data. Her decision to do all the interviewing, transcribing and as much of the analyzing as possible in Japanese led to a richness and depth of outcomes that significantly improved the quality of her thesis. Shortly afterwards, we wrote about this together (Conteh and Toyoshima 2005).

Reflection and discussion points for Part 2

The four PhD studies in this part of the book all feature multilingual individuals in communities undergoing change and experiencing uncertainty, even while the processes of the research are ongoing. In revealing the detail of their fieldwork, the contributors all show clearly the need for flexibility and close collaboration with their research participants. But these always need to be grounded in the theoretical and methodological frameworks of the thesis, developed through engagement with the literature and related directly to the research questions. These are the first principles of the research. As you proceed, you may become aware of the need to return to them and to make changes, and this always needs to be done with an awareness of the implications for the project as a whole.

As you read Chapters 5, 6, 7 and 8, here are some questions to help you reflect on your own PhD project. You may also find them useful as discussion points with your peers:

● What differences can you discern in the ways the four contributors developed and mediated their positionalities in their chapters? What changes to positionality occurred in the course of their projects?

● In what ways did the contributors in this part consider language as a key factor in their research? How do their views resonate with the arguments I present about language as data in Chapter 1?

● What understandings about the role and processes of writing in a PhD thesis following ethnographic principles do you gain from the chapters?

References

AHRC (2014), *Researching Multilingually at the Borders of Language, the Body, Law and the State*, AHRC Grant Ref: AH/L006936/1. Available at: http://researching-multilingually-at-borders.com (accessed 30 December 2016).

Bassnett, S. (1998), 'Translating across Cultures', in S. Hunston (ed), *Language at Work, Selected Papers from the Annual Meeting of the British Association for Applied Linguistics (BAAL)*, University of Birmingham, September 1997, 72–85, Clevedon: British Association for Applied Linguistics.

Bauman, Z. (2000), *Liquid Modernity*, Cambridge: Polity.

Conteh, J. (2007), 'Opening Doors to Success in Multilingual Classrooms: Bilingualism, Codeswitching and the Professional Identities of "Ethnic Minority" Primary Teachers', *Language and Education*, 21(6): 457–472.

Conteh, J. and Toyoshima, S. (2005), 'Researching Teaching and Learning: Roles, Identities and Interview Processes', *English Teaching Practice and Critique*, 4 (2): 23–34. Available at: http://education.waikato.ac.nz/research/journal/view .php?article=true&id=91&p=1 (accessed 30 December 2016).

Martin, D., Stuart-Smith, J. and Dhesi, K.K. (1998), 'Insiders and Outsiders: Translating in a Bilingual Research Project', in S. Hunston (ed), *Language at Work, Selected Papers from the Annual Meeting of the British Association for Applied Linguistics (BAAL)*, University of Birmingham, September 1997, 109–122, Clevedon: British Association for Applied Linguistics.

TLang (2014), *Translation and Translanguaging: Investigating Linguistic and Cultural Transformations in Superdiverse Wards in Four UK Cities.* Available at: http://www.birmingham.ac.uk/generic/tlang/index.aspx (accessed 30 December 2016).

CHAPTER FIVE

Reflecting on My Positionality as a Multilingual Researcher

Chisato Danjo

Guiding questions

1 Chisato describes in some detail the processes she underwent in order to gain initial access to her chosen research site, and then goes on to discuss the importance of being 'initiated', leading to the sense of being 'in'. What does she mean by this? What factors were important to her 'initiation' into the community she was researching?

2 As a multilingual researcher who shares a similar linguistic background with her research participants, Chisato argues that 'language' is an important factor in the processes of negotiating and maintaining her positionality in her research. Can you identify some of the ways in which she manages interactions to do this?

Introduction

In autumn 2011, I visited for the first time the site where I was planning to conduct ethnographic research. This was, in fact, the first time that I conducted ethnographic fieldwork. I had only recently embarked on a doctoral programme following a year of Master's studies in the United Kingdom, which had interrupted my career as a primary school teacher in Japan. Keen, however, to connect the practical experience I gained as a teacher with my newfound interest in sociolinguistics, I conceived a project that would examine the multilingual practices of pre- and early-school age children born to Japanese-English intermarriage parents in the United Kingdom across two field sites: a Japanese Saturday complementary school and at home. An investigation of linguistic phenomena in a 'natural' setting meant that whatever utterances would eventually constitute the data to be analyzed, these would originate from real-life interactions – among the children, between children and teachers, children and parents, or between myself as a researcher and my participants. Sharing the broader interests of 'linguistic ethnography' in understanding social and political contexts and the nature of power relationships through the analysis of linguistic interaction (Creese 2007; Rampton 2007; Tusting and Maybin 2007; Blackledge 2011), I was thus interested in observing and understanding both *practices* – i.e. the way multilinguals use language – and *perceptions* of language use – i.e. how they think they use language.

My fieldwork eventually lasted for sixteen months, and consisted of fortnightly visits to the complementary school and monthly visits to the family homes of a number of selected 'core' participants. During the fieldwork, I collected a variety of different data from different sources: field notes from ethnographic observations, audio recordings of naturally occurring linguistic interactions, interviews with teachers and parents, e-mail and diary exchanges, and institutional policy documents. These data were dominated by one conspicuous presence, that of myself as a 'participating' researcher. It is this 'presence' that I wish to elucidate in this chapter by understanding my positionality and role during the fieldwork, not only from my own perspective, but also from that of my research participants.

Such concerns, of course, did not, and should not, emerge just at the end of my research project. As I will show in the following, one's position as a researcher and the way this position is perceived by participants has great influence on almost all aspects of the research, and as such, active reflection on these issues must follow each stage of the project. Especially in ethnographic research, where data analysis often runs alongside data collection (Spradley 1979), it is of utmost importance to understand how your presence as a researcher, and the participants' perceptions of you, may have influenced – or may still be influencing – the quality and significance of your data. Before I begin to set out my own experiences and reflections on my positionality from the very first encounter with 'the field', I will provide a brief theoretical context to the main concepts at the centre of my current analysis.

Positionality and reflexivity: An overview

Ethnography, as a social scientific method, emerged in early-twentieth-century anthropology as a preferred approach to describing and understanding societies of which little was known. It required – as it still does – that the researcher become fully immersed in the everyday life of a given community in order to be able to give an account of that community from the perspective of 'the researched'. By participating in social life, experiencing what the 'natives' did and felt, the researcher was expected to gain a holistic emic understanding of the examined people. Despite the depth of understanding conferred by research in this tradition, early ethnographers, maybe under the influence of the then prevailing positivistic and reductionist approaches to the study of social life, rarely considered critically the impact of their own participation on the communities they studied and on their findings.

A self-reflexive interest in the researcher's role emerged in the second half of the twentieth century, but often with the aim of compiling rigorous categorizations of the researcher's roles, so that she/he could clearly acknowledge their position. For example, taking into consideration the researcher's distance from participants, Gold (1958) proposed four roles that researchers could assume as observers: (1) a complete-observer; (2) an observer-as-participant; (3) a participant-as-observer and (4) a complete-participant. Similarly, based on the researcher's involvement in activities in the field, Spradley (1980) differentiated between (1) non-participation, (2) passive participation, (3) moderate participation, (4) active participation and (5) complete participation. While these taxonomic exercises did little to foster a better understanding of how different levels of involvement and positionalities affect the data, emerging debates around insider/outsider statuses and their respective benefits and drawbacks moved these questions centre stage (e.g. Schatzman and Strauss 1973).

Awareness of these issues became more conspicuous with the so-called 'reflexive turn' in anthropology, the discipline most closely associated with participant-observation (Rabinow 1977; Ruby 1982; Clifford and Marcus 1986; Hymes 1999). The concept of *reflexivity* facilitates researchers' continuing awareness and assessment of their own position in the social world and its impact on their research process, project design, data collection, data analysis and the consequent findings (Finlay and Gough 2003). Importantly, *reflexivity* requires a 'critical' reflection on the researcher's situated position, involving the researcher's own social and cultural assumptions and practices underpinned in the research process.

Questions regarding the 'positionality' of the researcher can be traced back at least to postwar inquiries in sociological **epistemology**, which broadly asked whether 'insiders' or 'outsiders' ('natives' or 'strangers') have better access to culturally coded information (Nash 1963; Agassi

1969; Merton 1972). The question originated in the surge of social psychological interest in concepts like 'strangeness' or 'foreignness' and the social construction of these categories, as social scientists were trying to explain the origins of the radical ethnocentrism and xenophobia which dominated the first half of the twentieth century to devastating effects (Berger and Luckmann 1967; Schütz 1944). Stemming from this line of inquiry, perceptions of racial and ethnic distance have remained dominant categories in the analyzes of researcher positionality and effectiveness (e.g. De Andrade 2000; DeVault 1995; Hawkins 2010); but the palette of social factors of possible significance has broadened considerably to include, among others, religion, language, class, profession, age, gender, motherhood and marital or relationship status (Freedman 1986; Bolak 1996; Naples 1996; Adams 1999; Ceglowski 2000; Sherif 2001; Winchatz 2006; 2010; Ergun and Erdemir 2010; Chen 2011). Together with the diversification and fragmentation of the attributes to be critically reflected upon, there is an increasing realization that the insider/outsider dichotomy is itself much richer in complexity, with various intermediary positions.

These changes were driven not only by the postmodern paradigm shift, but also by ethnographers' intensified interest in their own (sub)cultures or societies. Despite the expectation that the latter would ultimately resolve the insider/outsider dilemma, the question of 'how native is a "native"' researcher' – as pertinently posed by Narayan (1993) – is still a valid one in ethnographic research. It is broadly this question to which the present chapter aims to provide a subjective answer by reflecting on my own ethnographic experience (Danjo 2015). During my fieldwork, I found myself sharing ethnic, cultural and linguistic ties with the research participants, factors which I considered essential for the success of a project investigating multilingual practices. Yet, as Narayan (1993: 680) pointed out:

> given the multiplex nature of identity, there will inevitably be certain facets of self that join us up with the people we study, other facets that emphasize our difference.

Given the nature of my research, I will focus in particular on the role of language in my discussion of the 'multiplexity' of researcher positionality. Taking forward the idea that when reflecting on our positionality as ethnographers, instead of presuming rigid insider/outsider juxtapositions, we should view ourselves 'in terms of shifting identifications amid a field of interpenetrating communities and power relations' (Narayan 1993: 671). I shall thus focus on the ongoing and moment-to-moment negotiations of positionality as a multilingual researcher, and discuss what impact these issues have had on my data collection procedure.

Negotiating positionality beyond the insider/ outsider dichotomy

Martin et al. (1998: 110) define an insider as

> someone who identifies themselves as a member of the community and is in turn recognized as a member by the community [who shares] the community's culture which at a surface level manifests as, for example, skin colour, language, dress, knowledge, neighbourhood, as well as at a more fundamental level, such as consciousness, belief and value systems.

By this definition my ethnic, linguistic, cultural and national identities would have granted me an 'insider' position in the field. Furthermore, my experience as a primary school teacher in Japan would have been a clear advantage when negotiating access to the field, especially in the complementary school context. However, while in certain contexts these attributes did in fact take primacy, in others they were trumped by 'other facets of self' (Narayan 1993: 680).

Negotiating access

On my first visit to the complementary school, I was equipped not only with an initial research idea, but also with an awareness of Japanese social norms which are notorious in permeating interpersonal relations at all levels. The Japanese 'community' in the part of England where I was planning to conduct my research was rather small and enclosed, but I also enjoyed the privilege of having a friend, from another area of life, who was acquainted with a member of the school, who on her part could introduce me to an influential member of the community. This initial contact was crucial, as it was through him that I was then introduced to one of the chairs of the school and could make a formal appointment for an 'interview' to clarify my status and aims.

My 'insider' knowledge also helped at this 'interview'. Although the complementary school was based in the United Kingdom, the documents I was required to bring with me for the interview were a curriculum vitae and a personal statement in standard Japanese business format, significantly different from the ones used in the United Kingdom. We started the interview by exchanging our business cards, and the conversation took place entirely in Japanese. The interview felt rather like a test of my 'Japaneseness' than of my 'researcher qualities', and it required an understanding of norms of verbal and nonverbal politeness expected of formal job interviews in Japan. While for the interviewer it may have felt like the most natural encounter, for myself as the interviewee it was rather like a quaint social masquerade.

Although it seemed to me that my 'educationist' experience was making a good impression, and that the interview itself would generate trust in my research aims, the negotiation did not succeed on that occasion. The school chair told me that they would be happy to offer me a position as 'a teacher', but not as 'a researcher'. There seemed to be a group of people who felt uncomfortable with the idea of being 'researched' and opposed my presence in that particular role. That a stranger would be observing their actions and making detailed notes on them was understandably an unsettling feeling for them. For me, on the other hand, it was a realization that my 'insider' qualities could only take me that far, and that I was still a stranger, an outsider, in that world.

Although the first answer from the school was negative, and I was contemplating the prospect of having to radically rethink my research, subsequent email exchanges with the school led me to believe that there may still be an entry point. I continued to attend the school's open public events in order to meet with members of the community face to face and start building relationships with individual families and potential gatekeepers. I had a positive progress in this process as I became close with a few families, some of whom showed an interest in participating in my research. This slow negotiation process lasted for six months, and finally another opportunity arose when the school offered me an assistant teacher position in the nursery, and allowed me to present my research project to the parents. At the following parent meeting, I obtained permission from both the parents and the teachers to conduct my fieldwork at the school.

It is widely acknowledged by ethnographers that gaining access to a setting or community is probably one of the hardest tasks in their trade (e.g. Hammersley and Atkinson 2007). Once gained, however, access is not unconditional and final. I was aware that the school community only 'kindly' offered me permission to conduct my research at this stage, but this did not mean that I gained their firm trust. During my research, therefore, I had to be careful to minimize my interference with the normal flow of events at the school and further develop my interpersonal relationship with members of the community. The process of access negotiation made me aware of how much of an outsider a female student without a child is in the context of the complementary school.

Initiation as process: The parents' case

It is commonplace in the ethnographic literature that in order to obtain access to the 'insider' view on things, the researcher must undergo an 'initiation' process, whose length and terms may often remain unknown to the researcher. Once passed, however, '[y]ou have crossed, somehow, some moral or metaphysical shadow line' (Geertz 1973: 413). In Clifford Geertz's famous account, this passage occurred rather suddenly and dramatically;

after ten days following his arrival with his wife in a Balinese village to conduct their fieldwork, during which the locals – with the only exception of their hosts and their close relatives – treated them as nonexistent, they attended an illegal cockfight. Despite the apparent conviction of the locals that the event would pass under the radar of the official government, police arrived at the scene, and the participants fled. The anthropologists escaped with the locals, finding refuge in one fugitive's courtyard. By the following day, the villagers' attitude towards the 'strangers' changes drastically, and they become the centre of attention, a sign of acceptance earned by having participated in a shared experience and proved allegiance to the villagers rather than the policemen (Geertz 1973: 412–416).

Such experiences, of course, are heavily dependent on the social context of the field, but what should be noted is that there is considerable difference between gaining initial access and obtaining an 'initiated' status by which participants accept you as a member of the community. In Bali, being accepted meant being teased by the villagers; this – as Geertz notes (1973: 416) – 'was the turning point so far as our relationship to the community was concerned, and we were quite literally "in"'. In my fieldwork, such a feeling of being 'in' arrived rather late in my fieldwork and in a much less dramatic fashion. It went, in fact, unnoticed by myself until a closer examination of my field notes towards the end of my research. By then I had somewhat accepted that not being a mother myself it would be impossible to achieve a true 'insider' status, if such status at all existed. Nevertheless, comparing excerpts from my field notes, one recorded in the first month of my fieldwork, the other after the eleventh month, shows that my position has changed considerably:

> During a break at the complementary school, I was asked by mothers about my previous profession – a primary school teacher. After a chat, one mother told me in a playful tone that it would be nice if I could baby-sit her children while teaching them Japanese, so that they could have some free time to meet up with each other.
> *(Adaptation from field note; May 2012)*

> Recently, a few mothers have often been asking me to join their private lunches and dinners. I feel much closer to the mothers nowadays.
> *(Adaptation from field note; March 2013)*

Comparing the first excerpt with the second, it becomes obvious how the relationship between myself and some of the mothers changed over time. In the beginning my 'ex-teacher' and 'student' status was emphasized, creating a certain distance between me and the 'mothers'. In the second excerpt, almost a year later, mothers seemed to accept me more as a peer. However, the advantages offered by certain aspects of my 'self' were evident from the very beginning. As an accredited and experienced teacher, I shared the same status of respectability as any other teachers at the school (in fact, my formal accreditation was often a factor pulling me into power-knowledge structures that I actively needed to evade in order to conduct my fieldwork). Yet, as a student outsider, I could perform tasks in positions that were being negotiated not only by myself, but by my participants. Having noted down the 'playful tone' in which I was asked to baby-sit, I saw that it is not only a trivial addendum, but represents the linguistic tool used in the negotiation of my positionality by the participants. It was meant to provide a safe passageway between my professional and personal statuses, and the careful acknowledgement of both is evident in that the request was not only to 'baby-sit' but also to 'teach Japanese'. At the same time, the reason given for the playful request – 'so that they could have some free time to meet up *with each other*' – spontaneously reinforced the separation between myself and *them*. The request, on the other hand, could also be interpreted as a test, as an 'invitation to the cockfight' in Geertzian terms, and one through which I could consolidate my relationship with the participants and enter the second field in which I was interested to conduct my fieldwork, that of the family home.

As we built up our relationships, mothers seemed to become more comfortable to share their time with me, and the interview data I obtained was also changing its character, becoming more emotional and personal towards the end of my research, often going beyond the scope of my original project. This also shows how certain topics that may have a significant relevance for the data only emerge after strong relationships were built between the researcher and the participant, proving the efficiency of longitudinal and immersive studies. In this section, nevertheless, I aimed to highlight how the 'initiation' process, that would ultimately grant the researcher access to such valuable emotional data, is often prolonged and unremarkable, yet clearly marked in linguistic, bodily and other forms. This 'initiation', however, still only allows entry to certain domains and participants, and as my research involved people in very different positions and relationships to one another – mothers, teachers and children – my positionality was inevitably negotiated on a moment-to-moment basis during each encounter.

Positionality beyond control: Participants' interpretations

I discussed above instances when my positionality was being 'negotiated' more or less with my active participation, and how certain aspects of the 'self' positioned me at different points on the insider-outsider continuum. In the following, I turn to examples of when my positioning takes place not only without my active involvement, but contrary to my own perceptions of my positionality as a 'multilingual' researcher. I argue that these are the processes to which we as researchers must pay careful attention, as they may go unnoticed while deeply affecting the data we collect.

Since I was interested in the language practices of multilingual children and parents across time and space, I paid careful attention to my own language use in the field. I decided not to ask my participants to use any specific language during our interactions, but that I would accommodate my language use according to theirs. While at the complementary school my observations focused on children, some of whom were bilingual children of intermarriage couples with more-or-less stable lives in England, while others were children of Japanese professional expatriates who only spent a few years on work postings outside Japan. My interests in linguistic phenomena in the family context focused more on intermarriage families.

Many intermarriage families in this study were following a One Parent One Language (OPOL) policy, which aims to help children acquire more than one language at an early age, by demanding the use of strictly one language to each parent (Park 2008). Namely, the 'Japanese' parent restricts their language use to Japanese when communicating with their children, and children are likewise required to use Japanese to that parent. This creates a similar language environment to that of the complementary school, where a Japanese-only policy is more or less enforced, but differs in that the children are required to use another language to the non-Japanese parent. Such policies, while they have their educational motivations – the usefulness of which, however, I challenged in my thesis (see details in Danjo 2015) – nevertheless created several difficulties in my research. Here I will focus only on those challenges that relate to my positionality as a researcher who shares ethnic and linguistic characteristics with my participants.

Appearance tells more than it says: The children's case

At the beginning of my fieldwork I came across an interesting phenomenon, which proved a challenge later on in my data collection. Several mothers related to me how their children tended to adapt their language use based on perceived ethnic and racial traits. Kumiko remembered how once she was conversing with a Korean friend in English in the presence of her children. Although the children witnessed the linguistic interaction between the two adults, Kumiko's four-year son addressed the Korean woman in Japanese, as unaware that she did not speak the language. Similarly, Emiko recalled how her children also chose to use Japanese to 'east-Asian-looking' women *(Adaptation from field notes, May 2012)*.

These observations by Kumiko and Emiko highlight how children construct ethnic and gendered perceptions of their interlocutors and adjust their language choice according to these. The gendered nature of these mental constructions was reinforced by the One Parent One Language

(OPOL) policy, since in most of the intermarriage families in my study it was the mothers who were the Japanese speakers to whom children were expected to use Japanese.

Consequently, my child-participants, almost without exception, used Japanese language to me – an East-Asian looking woman – during my fieldwork, and it was very difficult to challenge such 'routine' language practices that my participants had already developed in their daily lives. Thus, the 'insider' characteristics which were supposed to ease my data collection proved to be at times actually working against my research aims to collect data on naturally occurring 'multilingual' practices. Chances were that what I was observing was not 'natural' behaviour at all, but one shaped by my ethnic appearance. A clear indication of this was when one of my child-participants disciplined her younger brother that he should use Japanese to me after he addressed me in English several times *(field note, November 2012)*.

The above examples suggest that it is essential for researchers to first understand the research participants' 'routine' language practices before attempting to predetermine their own position. I am not arguing that participants' interpretations of my positionality are definite and fixed; rather, as you will see below, their interpretations are dynamic and fluid, changing throughout the fieldwork period. However, it is important to be aware that a researcher's predetermined position in the research planning process can be easily challenged if it does not comply with participants' routine practices. This also vividly highlights that certain social categories in which the researcher may find herself could have more significance than others, and it is the participants who will ultimately determine the researcher's position in different situations.

The researcher as a Japanese language resource: The parents' perception

I also observed similar attitudes and practices on the part of parent participants. During the fieldwork, it became evident how the Japanese mothers were desperately seeking Japanese resources (e.g. Japanese-speaking persons and communities, Japanese media and teaching materials) in an English-speaking society. Parents actively created opportunities for their children to be exposed to Japanese language through, for instance, local Japanese communities (e.g. toddlers' groups, story-telling and reading groups, complementary schools) and regular visits to Japan. In family contexts where access to Japanese language is fairly difficult, my status of 'Japanese' and my home visits were often perceived and welcomed by parents as a Japanese language development opportunity for their children. As such, parents often expected me to serve as a Japanese linguistic resource.

The mothers often told me enthusiastically that their children seemed to enjoy my visits very much, and that they tended to use Japanese more often following my visits. Some parents even instructed their children to use Japanese to me, despite the fact that I had informed them about the nature of my research, and asked them not to do so.

It is also noteworthy that during my home visits, I was rarely provided with the opportunity to engage with the English-speaking parent – mostly the fathers – and a distance was maintained between myself and them. One reason may be, as mentioned above, that my presence was regarded as a Japanese linguistic resource. Some Japanese mothers tended to arrange my visits while the English-speaking father was absent, so that the language spoken in the household during my visits would be only Japanese. On the other hand, non-Japanese-speaking fathers may themselves feel uncomfortable being at home during my visits, which appeared to increase Japanese language interaction among the family members, thus excluding them.

As the above examples show, the way in which both parents and children perceived my position and role had an impact on my research. Which dimensions of identification have significance on practices depends on each participant's routine practices, and therefore, it is impossible to plan comprehensively in advance. Participants have the liberty to perceive the researcher very differently from what the researcher's self-assumed position is thought to be, and sharing a number of traits with the participants often makes discerning the disjunction between the two perceptions even harder to recognize. I would argue, however, that paying attention to such issues not only helps avoid inaccurate interpretations of your data, but also brings up broader questions that are increasingly the focus of ethnographic investigations. Through identifying and trying to elicit 'routine' practices, we can gain a deeper understanding of participants' values and beliefs. This argument is similar to those advocating the advantages of having an 'outsider', 'non-native' status even in linguistic research where the deepest understanding of the researched language is often preferred (Winchatz 2006, 2010; Chen 2011).

Ongoing learning from actual interactions

Compared with the complementary school context where I had a distinct and official role as an assistant teacher, my participants were less constrained by formal factors in their perceptions of my role during home visits. One example of this was their different ways of referring to me. Although some children usually called me *sensei* (teacher/Ms.) at home, just as they would at the complementary school, others adjusted their form of address. For instance, Naomi (aged seven), who usually addressed me as *sensei* in the complementary school, often called me just by my first name outside the school (e.g. in a public park or at the supermarket). Depending on the addressee, context and her intentions, she seemed to perceive me as playing a different role, and in one occasion, Naomi even introduced me as 'mum's friend' to their neighbours. The reference to me as 'mum's friend' may also imply my closeness to her Japanese mother from her perspective. Although she generally used Japanese language to me, she was more flexible on mixing Japanese and English in front of me, especially outside the home, which was another indication that she tended to see me less as a 'teacher' or enforcer of a strict language policy. Awareness of this contextual positioning was a key discovery during my research, and as a consequence I tried to create further opportunities for myself to interact with my child-participants outside the school and the family home contexts, and thus gain access to more varied data.

Some of the children in my study actively tried to understand my position in respect to language proficiency. For instance, Naomi and Tsugumi asked me directly if I understood English, in order to be able to categorize me as either a 'monolingual' or a 'multilingual' and adjust their linguistic practices accordingly. Another child, Kyoka (aged seven), asked me several months into my fieldwork if she could use English when struggling to find words in Japanese *(field note, February 2013)*. After gaining my explicit approval, she seemed more flexible in her language choice, using both Japanese and English. Although such cases when I was directly asked for permission to use a certain language were rare, many of the children in my study tried to test whether they were allowed to use English in front of me by actually using English to me. Despite the fact that Japanese mothers who strictly followed an OPOL policy would instruct them to speak in Japanese, through such actual interactions, children gradually tested my position in that respect. As I was less inclined to impose upon them the use of any one language, children gradually reverted to a more 'natural' multilingual practice in my presence, and this rapport also meant that my positioning in their respect changed from that of a 'teacher' to one they felt closer to them.

Conclusion

There is an increasing number of ethnographic studies examining the way in which 'familiar' sites are researched, in which researchers share, for example, ethnic, cultural, or linguistic background with the research participants (Martin-Jones 2012). Conducting research in such conditions has many implications for the research process, and it is generally accepted as advantageous to be highly familiar with the research language, preferably at a 'native' level. However, as I have also tried to show in this chapter, it is important to remember that such closeness to the research object has an impact on the research process, and requires an even more critical self-reflection than research in 'unfamiliar' settings.

First of all, no matter how familiar you are with the people and field where you plan to conduct your research, the entry process as a researcher inevitably casts a degree of 'outsider'-ness onto you, which will then be present in the background of all your consequent interactions from which your data emerge. On one hand, the researcher becomes part of the daily practices of their participants. In my field experience, due to my ethnic, linguistic and cultural position I have undeniably contributed to the reproduction of such 'routine' practices (e.g. extensive Japanese language use during my visits) despite my intentions. But on the other hand, the researcher and the participants are constantly constructing their relationships and the positions they occupy in respect to that through actual interactions in the field, and accordingly, the quality of the data – the way they talk about themselves – as well as their practices – the way they behave – could be in continuous flux. Notably, such ongoing negotiations usually would have already started at the access negotiation stage.

I am not arguing that there is therefore no need to 'plan' your own research carefully before the fieldwork; planning your research aims and intentions in advance enables the researcher to reflect on what is actually happening in the field, and how this differs from their initial assumptions. On the contrary, the researcher – and even more so the 'native' researcher – should actively and continually consider her position and status, and even plan in advance for ways in which such a reflexive activity would be adopted throughout the research project. An uncritical pretence of 'insider' status can do more damage to the research than the difficulties caused by being an 'outsider'. As discussed above, regardless of one's status, there usually is a process – or a clear watershed event – of initiation, which, especially in familiar settings, can go unnoticed or unreflected-upon. There is little a researcher can do in this respect, yet awareness of her position at different times and in different settings of the fieldwork can help her identify the sort of questions she can pursue at that point. Importantly, one must not assume that superficial national, ethnic, racial or linguistic characteristics we might share with the participants will overshadow the various other situated differences that make up the 'multiplexity' of our identities.

References

Adams, L.L. (1999), 'The Mascot Researcher: Identity, Power, and Knowledge in Field work', *Journal of Contemporary Ethnography*, 28(4): 331–363.

Agassi, J. (1969), 'Privileged Access', *Inquiry: An Interdisciplinary Journal of Philosophy*, 12(1–4): 420–426.

Berger, P.L. and Luckmann, T. (1967), *The Social construction of Reality: A Treatise in the Sociology of Knowledge*, New York: Allen Lane, The Penguin Press.

Blackledge, A. (2011), 'Linguistic Ethnography', in M. Grenfell (ed), *Bourdieu, Language and Linguistics*, 121–146, London: Continuum.

Bolak, H.C. (1996), 'Studying One's Own in the Middle East: Negotiating Gender and Self-other Dynamics in the Field', *Qualitative Sociology*, 19(1): 107–130.

Ceglowski, D. (2000), 'Research as Relationship', *Qualitative Inquiry*, 6(1): 88–103.

Chen, S.-H. (2011), 'Power Relations between the Researcher and the Researched: An Analysis of Native and Nonnative Ethnographic Interviews', *Field Methods*, 23(2): 119–135.

Clifford, J., and Marcus, G.E. (1986), *Writing Culture: The Poetics and Politics of Ethnography*, Berkeley: University of California Press.

Creese, A. (2007), 'Linguistic Ethnography', in K.A. King and N.H. Hornberger (eds), *Encyclopedia of Language and Education, 2nd edn, Vol. 10: Research Methods in Language and Education*, 229–241, New York: Springer.

Danjo, C. (2015), 'A Critical Ethnographic Inquiry into the Negotiation of Language Practices among Japanese Multilingual Families in the United Kingdom: Discourse, Language Use and Perceptions in the Hoshuko and the Family Home', (PhD Thesis, Northumbria University, Newcastle upon Tyne).

De Andrade, L.L. (2000), 'Negotiating from the Inside: Constructing Racial and Ethnic Identity in Qualitative Research', *Journal of Contemporary Ethnography*, 29(3): 268–290.

DeVault, M.L. (1995), 'Ethnicity and Expertise: Racial-Ethnic Knowledge in Sociological Research', *Gender and Society*, 9(5): 612–631.

Ergun, A., and Erdemir, A. (2010), 'Negotiating Insider and Outsider Identities in the Field: "Insider" in a Foreign Land; "Outsider" in One's Own Land', *Field Methods*, 22(1): 16–38.

Finlay, L., and Gough, B. (2003), *Reflexivity: A Practical Guide for Qualitative Researchers*, Oxford: Blackwell.

Freedman, D.C. (1986), *Wife, Widow, Woman: Roles of an Anthropologist in a Transylvanian Village*, 2nd edn, Berkeley: University of California Press.

Geertz, C. (1973), *Deep Play: Notes on the Balinese Cockfight*, New York: Basic Books.

Gold, R.L. (1958), 'Roles in Sociological Field Observations', *Social Forces*, 36: 217–223.

Hammersley, M. and Atkinson, P. (2007), *Ethnography: Principles in Practice*, 3rd edn, London: Routledge.

Hawkins, R.L. (2010), 'Outsider in: Race, Attraction, and Research in New Orleans', *Qualitative Inquiry*, 16(4): 249–261.

Hymes, D., ed. (1999), *Reinventing Anthropology*, new edn, Ann Arbor, MI: University of Michigan Press.

Martin, D., Stuart-Smith, J. and Dhesi, K.K. (1998), 'Insiders and Outsiders: Translating in a Bilingual Research Project, in S. Hunston (ed), *Language at Work: Selected Papers from the Annual Meeting of the British Association for Applied Linguistics (BAAL), University of Birmingham, September 1997*, 109–122, Clevedon: British Association for Applied Linguistics.

Martin-Jones, M. (2012), 'New Times, Researcher Mobility and Multilingual Research Practice: Opportunities, Innovation and Constraints', Paper presented at the conference *Explorations in Ethnography, Language and Communication:*

Analysis and impact in Linguistic Ethnography, University of Copenhagen, Denmark.

Merton, R.K. (1972), 'Insiders and Outsiders: A Chapter in the Sociology of Knowledge', *American Journal of Sociology*, 78(1): 9–47.

Naples, N.A. (1996), 'A Feminist Revisiting the Insider/outsider Debate: The "Outsider Phenomenon" in Rural Iowa', *Qualitative Sociology*, 19(1): 83–106.

Narayan, K. (1993), 'How Native Is a "Native" Anthropologist?', *American Anthropologist*, 95(3): 671–686.

Nash, D. (1963), 'The Ethnologist as Stranger: An Essay in the Sociology of Knowledge', *Southwestern Journal of Anthropology*, 19(2): 149–167.

Park, C. (2008), 'One Person-One Language (OPOL)', in J. González (ed), *Encyclopedia of Bilingual Education*, 636–638, Thousand Oaks, CA: Sage Publications.

Rabinow, P. (1977), *Reflections on Field work in Morocco*, London: University of California Press.

Rampton, B. (2007), 'Neo-Hymesian Linguistic Ethnography in the United Kingdom', *Journal of Sociolinguistics*, 11(5): 584–607.

Ruby, J. (1982), *A Crack in the Mirror: Reflexive Perspectives in Anthropology*, Philadelphia: University of Pennsylvania Press.

Schatzman, L. and Strauss, A.L. (1973), *Field Research: Strategies for a Natural Sociology*, Englewood Cliffs, NJ: Prentice-Hall.

Schütz, A. (1944), 'The Stranger: An Essay in Social Psychology', *American Journal of Sociology*, 49(6): 499–507.

Sherif, B. (2001), 'The Ambiguity of Boundaries in the Field Work Experience: Establishing Rapport and Negotiating Insider/Outsider Status', *Qualitative Inquiry*, 7(4): 436–447.

Spradley, J.P. (1979), *The Ethnographic Interview*, Belmont, CA: Wadsworth.

Spradley, J.P. (1980), *Participant Observation*, New York: Holt, Rinehart and Winston.

Tusting, K., and Maybin, J. (2007), 'Linguistic Ethnography and Interdisciplinarity: Opening the Discussion', *Journal of Sociolinguistics*, 11(5): 575–583.

Winchatz, M.R. (2006), 'Field Worker or Foreigner?: Ethnographic Interviewing in Nonnative Languages', *Field Methods*, 18(1): 83–97.

Winchatz, M.R. (2010), 'Participant Observation and the Nonnative Ethnographer: Implications of Positioning on Discourse-Centered Field work', *Field Methods*, 22(4): 340–356.

CHAPTER SIX

A Narrative on the Use of Interviews to Shape an Ethnographic Research into Family Language Practices

Indu Vibha Meddegama

Guiding questions

1 Indu uses the words *rapport* and *confidence* to describe the development of her research relationships with her participants. Can you identify the processes she uses that encourage these qualities?

2 Why do you think Indu calls her chapter a 'narrative'? In what ways can her research be considered as taking a narrative approach to her questions?

Introduction

Starting from birth, throughout the entirety of our lives, one thing that allows us to understand better the everyday phenomena that we encounter is enquiry. And so from the moment we are able to communicate – verbally, gesturally or through technological aids – we interact with others asking and answering questions of *Why* and *How* among a plethora of others. It is this process of enquiry or *interviewing*, as it is known in formal interactions, which became a key data collection instrument in my ethnographic research on three immigrant multilingual Malayali families living in the north of England.

The primary focus for my research came about from initial observations that I had come to make as an acquaintance of this Malayali community. The discrepancies that seemed to prevail across these two-generational families in relation to their proficiency in and preferences towards the use of Malayalam and English soon caught my attention. During casual conversations with them, I had begun to make a mental note of how the English-dominant children seemed to accommodate and at times disregard their parents' observed preference for using the Malayalam language. Encouraged by postulations that the authority of first-generation immigrants can be challenged by second-generation children as a result of such differences in English language proficiency (Canagarajah 2008; Hua 2008), my focus, as evinced through the research question below, fell on the manner in which the Malayali families' associated status and power structure was portrayed through their intergenerational language practices:

Research question: What are the linguistic resources that participants use in order to challenge and/or retain status and power relations?

The crux of this question lay in the language practices and the ways in which they reflected and enacted concepts of status and power. Drawing on my own cultural upbringing in a South Asian context, I presumed that the Malayali families would be based on the Indian patriarchal system within which authority and status are assigned on the basis of gender and generation (Kaul 2012). Accordingly, within a nuclear family unit in which a married heterosexual couple are of the same generation, the father would become the head of the household owing to his gender. And so, to investigate possible links between the families' everyday language practices and status and power relations pertaining to the heritage culture, data were collected from interviews, audio-recorded family conversations and observational field notes.

To address the research question and to make sense of the interconnectedness between the social constructs of status and power and language practices, I adopted a methodological framework within which the intra-family conversations were examined to identify episodes of child–parent, child–child and/or spouse–spouse disagreements. This process was guided by the assumption that such interactional segments may index how authority is exercised and received by the members of the participant families. Drawing on Hymes's (1972) ethnographic framework, the *interlocutors* of these segments and the *language practices* they adopt were then studied further, on the presupposition that interlocutors may use language strategically to maintain or challenge status and power relations. The resulting emergent themes on conformity towards and divergence from the patriarchal system were subsequently scrutinized against reported data obtained from a series of interviews with the participants.

Retrospectively speaking, the design and execution of the interviews within the research made them characteristically ethnographic in nature. In the broadest sense of the word, ethnography entails presenting a detailed account of a group of people (Agar 1996; Wolcott 1999). And this, in fact, was just what my interviews enabled me to do: to offer in-depth insights and *thick descriptions* of the Malayalis' home language use. The concept of *thick descriptions* first introduced to ethnography by Geertz (1973) and later expanded by Denzin (1989: 83) involves presenting 'detail, context, emotion and the webs of social relationships that join persons to one another'. Denzin therefore recognized that human behaviour required the examination of contextual factors, as well as the *reported* thoughts and feelings, of the individuals concerned.

The primary objective of this chapter is to narrate the manner in which interviewing helped align the emic or participant perspectives with the inevitable etic, or in this instance my own, interpretations (Agar 1996; Spradley 1980) reflected in the family conversations and the observational field notes. Although my participants and I could broadly be defined as South Asian, as the researcher, almost by definition, I arrived as an outsider or 'a foreign body' (Blommaert and Jie 2010: 26) within the research context. This, in turn, reinforces the need to refrain from allowing my prior understandings of sociocultural phenomena to impact on the data interpretation unnecessarily. Consequently, what I attempt to show in the chapter is the way in which interviewing helped strengthen the data analysis process and the credibility of the findings and ultimately to conclude the research with a sense of jubilance. However, its early stages, involving the recruitment of participants and interviewing for the first time, were riddled with the inevitable: pitfalls. This is where I would like to start this narrative.

Context and recruitment of participants

To refer to the beginnings of my research, I must necessarily refer to its context: the city of York in northern England, home to a substantial Malayali community. Among the Indians who feature at the top of non-United Kingdom-born residents in England and Wales (Office of National Statistics 2016) are the Malayalis from the south-western region of Kerala in India. The term *Malayali* traditionally refers to Keralites who speak Malayalam as their first language. However in recent years the term has been used more broadly to refer to emigrants of Malayali descent who maintain certain elements of Malayali cultural traditions (Asia Harvest 2013). York sustains such a Malayali community which statistically forms 5.5 per cent of the city's overall population (ONS 2016). As a resident of the city, I was acquainted with this community and approached two families who expressed their willingness to participate in my research straightaway. Two months later, both families migrated to Australia, apologetically explaining to me that superstitious belief had prevented them from giving me advance notice of their departure. Through sheer determination, I approached and secured the interest and consent of three other families, mere acquaintances at the time, but close friends today.

Each of the three families, referred to henceforth as A, B and C to retain their anonymity, consisted of heterosexual partners born and brought up in India and two children, some born overseas and others in the United Kingdom. The names of the family members were also replaced with pseudonyms in the interview and interactional data transcripts, and in light of this fact the participants will be referred to by their fictitious names in this chapter. The parents who were first-generation immigrants to the United Kingdom were either in the health care professions, the catering business or self-employed taxi drivers. The children fell into the age group of four to twelve years and were all attending mainstream schools locally. Among the many sociocultural aspects that allowed me to draw parallels between the participants were the linguistic resources of Malayalam and English which they had at their disposal and used to varying degrees of competence alongside other Indian languages.

The interviews themselves were scheduled at the participants' homes. As my overarching research aim was to study language practices within the home, interviewing offered me an excellent opportunity to observe the participants' verbal behaviour in the domain that I was interested in. What is more, using digital recorders provided by me, family conversations had also been recorded by the participant parents themselves in their homes. Across all three families, the mothers played a vital role in collecting the interactional data and in attending all the interviews with one or both children while the fathers made only a rare appearance due to work or other commitments.

Roles and processes

Words that immediately spring to mind when reflecting on the roles adopted by myself and the participants in the research process are *rapport* and *confidence*. They capture and characterize the progressive development of our respective roles for, as our rapport with each other strengthened, so did our confidence; mine initially as that of the one who mainly asked the questions and theirs as those who predominantly answered them. As the *respondents,* the participants answered both pre-designed and ad lib questions that were directed at them. As a deliberate attempt had been made to inform them only of the overarching aim of the project and because the preestablished questions were not shared with the participants prior to the actual day of the interviews, the reported data were taken to be spontaneous and yet in need of expansion and validation. Interviews I feel, especially when semi-structured in nature, can be free-flowing conversations where all participants feel at ease to ask, ask again, answer and reflect in silence. In hindsight, neither my participants nor I had the confidence to embrace this flexibility initially for we were constrained by lack of experience and the mere knowledge that we were part of an actual research!

Referring to the study of intra-family discourse, Mayor (2004: 2) concedes that as an inherently private domain, family life is traditionally a difficult area to explore. Once access is gained, the researcher's very presence will 'causes ripples on the surface of smooth routinized processes' (Blommaert and Jie 2010: 26), and thereby affect the family dynamics. In addition to my physical presence, the digital recorder capturing every sigh, pause and verbal utterance placed additional pressure on the participants, no doubt, and may have impacted on the interactions which were close to, yet not entirely akin to natural conversations. Time, however, was on our side – and over the weeks, months and years that ensued since the first interview, our initial fears were outweighed by a growing interest, from both parties, in the themes and areas for further enquiry which emerged in the discussions (Mason 2004) and the other pools of data. Moving on to this phase signalled that we had, together, reached a key milestone in the research process where we had become cocreators of meaning and knowledge. Another indicator that the interviews had in fact become near-naturalistic conversations were the digressions that became much more apparent and frequent over time: these ranged from unexpected visitors arriving at the door to children being cajoled by their parents into performing dance routines they had rehearsed to the latest box office Bollywood song in my presence.

And so, I too became a *participant* within the research context where my role expanded beyond that of a mere interviewer. I played with the children, watched television, exchanged recipes with the mothers and even answered questions they had for me about my background. The following excerpt indexes this very feature of interviewing, which is that it is a give-and-take process. In the opening line, as the researcher I am directing a question at Janak, the father in family A and referring to his parents both of whom were on a visit to England at the time. As I do not speak Malayalam and as the grandparents did not speak English, Janak had stepped in to translate for his parents and the conversation digresses as follows:

Indu: Since your parents are here, I have a few questions for them.
         Would you be able to translate for them please?
Janak: Yeah, yeah.

Indu: Thank you. So, what is your parents' first language?
Janak: Malayalam. You from Sri Lanka?
Indu: Yes
Janak: Which part?
Indu: Kandy, which is the hill capital of Sri Lanka.
Janak: Kandy. I never heard. And what language do you speak?
Indu: Sinhalese.
Janak: Ah, not Tamil?
Indu: No sadly, I never learnt it. So, do your parents speak Tamil or any other languages apart from Malayalam?

And thus the focus of the conversation shifted from them to me until I steered the focus back to my research, as seen in the last two lines of this excerpt. I recognized early on in the research that appreciating the participants' interest in me and my background was as important for this 'getting-to-know' stage, and only strengthened the rapport between us. What this also essentially demonstrated was that it is not always possible to neatly classify ethnographic interviews as mere 'professional conversations' (Kvale 2007: 7).

From pre-designed to ad lib: Questions and questioning

It was questions that always necessitated the scheduling of interviews with the participants: questions that arose when reading, writing, reflecting and even when watching television, while thinking, naively, that I was having a day off research! These prescripted questions, some of which I share next, allowed me to build a narrative around my participants in a much more in-depth manner.

The pre-designed questions in the preliminary round of interviews yielded: (a) participant profile information (questions 1 and 2), (b) perceptions of domain-specific (question 3), participant-specific (question 4) and situation-specific language use (question 5), (c) attitudes towards heritage language maintenance and (d) self-perceived notions on language proficiency. A select few from the questions that generated this data are the following, which are adapted from Baker and Sanderson (2000: 88):

1. For how long have you lived in the UK?
2. Why did you and your family move to the UK?
3. What language(s) did you use on a daily basis before moving to the UK?
4. In what language(s) do you speak to your relatives?
5. In what language(s) do you argue with your sister/brother?

In these two-generational families, such questions were mainly answered by one or both parents while the children interjected at irregular intervals to either assent to or disagree with what was being reported by their parents. Proving 'open-endedness' to be the essence of ethnographic interviews (Saville-Troike 2003: 100), the questions prompted narratives which evoked memories of lived experiences in the participants. For instance, Chitra, the mother of family B answers question 3 (above) by referring to the period she spent in the Middle East prior to moving to the United Kingdom and talks of the multilingual workforce she found herself to be a part of:

> Chitra: Before I came here, I was working in Saudi. So, there is only medium Arabic and English.... Not like here, but used to have English. All writing is in English.

The participants' answers, like that of Chitra offered a whole host of information that was not entirely restricted to answering *what* language was used *where*. They offered me cues on competence and attitudes to languages and created opportunities for impromptu questions. Furthermore, drawing on this data, I was able to define the participants' language practices within different geographical contexts, as well as within various domains from the home to the workplace, which proved to be significant in the analysis process.

A principal objective behind the use of interviews was to investigate how and why the participants' language practices, as well as social factors like age and gender, can create contestations of status and power. Despite being South Asian like my participants, I was very much an *outsider* to the cultural appropriateness of enquiring into family life and structure from the participant group. Furthermore, time and time again, my desire to ask questions was overpowered by a disinclination to admit to *not knowing*: something that most of us are prone to as we enter adulthood. However, having established a strong rapport with the families and having gradually developed in confidence, I was able to use the follow-up interviews to discuss topics around male-dominant households with the women. This line of questioning allowed me to understand their relationships with their spouses and in-laws back in India, and within their present context of residence in the United Kingdom. In order to enter into such discussions I chose the topic of household chores which is typically considered to be a woman-dominant domain and used the following questions:

> At home in the UK, who is responsible for the household chores?
> Was this different when you were in India?
> If so, how?

It cannot be denied that gender played a significant role in the responses I received in such follow-up interviews. As noted beforehand, while the wives were always present for the interviews, the husbands were most often at work. After months of acquaintance, the women, I felt, had begun to see me as another female friend, a confidante that they felt they could talk to, recounting the challenges and joys of a life they had left behind and the life they found themselves in, in the United Kingdom. Guided by my questions on language practices and status and power relations, their reflective accounts centred, for the most part, around their experiences of family life, aspirations for children and language use, all of which contributed to the focus of my research.

Taking its natural course in semi-structured interviews, the responses to these pre-designed questions led to the inclusion of new questions and queries as the interviews progressed. The semi-structured interviews provided the flexibility that was necessary to adapt the questions according to the different participants. As previously mentioned, my participants were of two generations and possessed varying levels of proficiency in English, the medium in which the interviews were carried out. Therefore, the questions were modified, rephrased and adjusted in a way that did not hinder the natural flow of the interview process. Unlike with the interactional data, which I had to listen to without a visual record, the interviews were conducted by me in person. Therefore, the way in which I formulated the questions and addressed them to the participants, the gaps in between questions, the digressions and interruptions, all varied from participant to participant. The interviews allowed me to observe the participants' gestures, facial expressions and interjections, and to develop a keen sense of awareness and respect for pauses, and hesitations, all of which added meaning to what was being asked, or to that which was being said by the participants. This allowed me to modify lines of enquiry and to respond to the interviewees' behaviour.

Following up for analysis

A quick reference to the interactional data obtained from the audio-recorded family conversations will be made at this point to offer a clearer picture on how they fed into the follow-up interviews in the data analysis process. Using digital recorders provided by me, the families had captured approximately seventy hours of conversations they had carried out in their homes. As the audio recordings were vital in identifying *how* the participants were using language in intra-family discourse, the bilingual conversations were transcribed and translated as an initial and mandatory step in the process of analysis. The transcriptions were completed by two members from the Malayalam-speaking community. As a non-Malayalam speaker, I was unable to check the accuracy of the transcriptions. However, playing back relevant recordings at the follow-up interviews meant that, to my relief and delight, the participants were able to vouch for the accuracy of the transcriptions.

Reading the transcripts of the interactional data, I identified conversational segments where it seemed that the status or authority of the participants was being challenged, and sought further clarification from the family members in question at the follow-up interviews. With their help, I was also able to understand better episodes of disagreement between family members as they were caught in the recordings: the absence of visuals would have made this a next to impossible task if it had not been for the participants' input. This analysis process that entailed cross-checking my interpretations of the family conversations against the interview responses will be discussed further in the ensuing paragraphs.

Clarification

On reflection, I would say that careful consideration of conversational data results from the reading and rereading of transcripts and listening and re-listening to the actual recordings themselves. To reiterate, this painstaking process only led to further interviews because they became the one data collection instrument that was used across the entire four years of my research. I will therefore explain next how the interviews offered clarification and enhanced the validity of both the primary and secondary data obtained over the course of the research.

As stated before, the focus of my research was the families' status and power relations and language practices. The transcripts of the interactional data appeared to suggest from the very start that the mothers wished to continue with a patrilineal system within their nuclear families and that this was acknowledged by the children. For instance, the following conversation between Vineeta and her daughter Anju from family C, I felt, reflected the children's acceptance of their father as the key decision-maker in the family. The English utterances in this selection and the ones to follow are in the regular font and **Bold** is used for the translated utterances from Malayalam to English.

Anju:	**Shall we take Anand brother too? He can change his books as well.**
Vineeta:	**Yeah we will take him.**
Anju:	**We will go as soon as Papa wakes up. I will beg Papa to take us.**
Vineeta:	**You will do what?**
Anju:	**I will beg Papa to him.** Ha ha Well I don't need to because Dad will let me go if you ask as well.

I noted with interest that even though Vineeta had already given her consent to Anju's request to go to the library with her brother, the daughter's words show that it is the permission of her father which ultimately matters. Wanting to know more, the following conversation took place between Vineeta and I at a follow-up interview:

Indu: When Anju wants to go to the library, she says to you that she will *beg* papa to take her – why do you think she uses the word *beg*?
Vineeta: That is the Indian system. Without asking permission from papa, we can't do anything. That's our culture, ask the Head. If Anand (*son – insertion my own*) wants to go to a friend's place, I say 'ask the dad. He's the superior. He's the decision-maker'.

And thus Vineeta's response helped with substantiating and expanding on the assumption that the patriarchal system that the first-generation participants had grown up knowing and valuing back in India was being endorsed in their own homes in a diasporic setting. So in essence, what I saw in practice in the interactional data – the practice of considering the father as the chief authority figure in the household – I was able to rationalize from the emic point-of-view as a result of the follow-up interviews.

Not just on paper: Secondary data in practice

As previously mentioned, the interviews also helped support relevant secondary data noted in the readings I carried out at the time on and about the Malayalis in diasporic settings. Such literature on the Malayalis unfailingly mentioned three things. Firstly, the remarkable 100 per cent literacy rate in Kerala and secondly, that in education, Malayali women are the most literate in the entire country (Eapon and Kodoth 2003). And that's not all, for we are told that the Malayalis are known to be the main 'export' of Kerala, a trend resulting from the women in the region migrating overseas to take up employment as nursing staff. Corroborating this secondary data, were the interview responses such as the following by Deepa, the mother of family A:

Deepa: All the house wives in India are graduates. If I go back to India I'll be illiterate because I did a diploma. If I had a plan I would have done a degree. But I wanted a job, so that's why I diverted from studies.

Like Deepa, the mothers in all the participant families were nurses at the local National Health Service and had professional qualifications and experience to work and live in the United Kingdom. However, Deepa's response in this excerpt evinced that, to them, a nursing diploma was nothing in comparison to the academic credentials of the average Keralite woman.

Thematic expansion

Complementing pertinent literature, the content of the interactional data held clues to the Malayalis' way of life in England and the roles and responsibilities they appeared to hold post migration. It was noted earlier that the Malayali families seemed to conform to a male-dominant family system and to consider the fathers as the chief authority figures in their respective families. To expand on this postulation, I began to consider the roles and responsibilities held by them and their spouses which is when I came across Percot's (2012) research on immigrant Malayali families in Ireland, the findings of which proved highly applicable to my research.

Percot (2012) writes that migration had led to a discernible role-reversal between the Malayali husbands and wives within her participant group. As the mothers in my research seemed to hold a higher socioeconomic status to that of their partners, my data appeared to echo Percot's observations. For example, in the next extract, in family A, the mother Deepa is approached by daughter Kavita about a parent's evening at her school:

Deepa: **What time do you have to go to All Saints on June 6th? Is it at 6 or 6:30?**
Kavita: **We will go at 6.**
Deepa: **Look at the paper because I have night duty that day.**
07:30 I have to return.
Kavita: Right ... 7 pm Mum.
Deepa: Is it 7 pm?

In this episode Deepa asks Kavita to confirm the time of the parent's evening. The mother has a night shift at the hospital on the same day and is keen to ensure that she can attend the meeting at her daughter's school prior to going back to work. By this stage, I had begun to see links between the parents' English language proficiency and the roles and responsibilities they held within and outside of their homes. Keen to present this as a characterizing feature or theme of these families, I met with the mothers and asked them to present their self-perceived notions of their own and their spouses' competence in English. When the women unanimously reported that they were far more fluent and competent in English than their husbands, I introduced the topic of responsibilities to the discussion:

Indu: If you think you are stronger in English, do you think you have more roles, or roles that you would not normally have had in India, now that you are in the UK?

Vineeta: Yes, I have more responsibilities. Since we came to England,
            there was a lot of applications for citizenship, so I am the one
            who took responsibility for doing that...Parent's evenings,
            he also goes with me, because he wants to know the progress.
            When making phone calls, he finds it difficult to understand
            the accent.

Vineeta, the mother from family C, cites three activities here from
completing the citizenship applications to answering the phone, to emphasize
the lead role she took or takes in official matters. She does not hesitate to
imply concurrently that her husband is as keen to fulfil his parental duties.
The women from the other families only echoed Vineeta's response citing
similar examples. I was thus able to expand on the theme that host language
competence was a determiner of the new found socioeconomic status of the
Malayali women.

Answering the 'why'

Researching the language practices of the participants necessitated
addressing the *why* question. To present their rationale for the languages
they chose to use within the family networks, I needed to consider the
participants' language ideologies or their perceptions of language including
their notions on what language can or can't do (Wei and Hua 2010: 161).
The families, as noted beforehand, all admitted to the importance of English.
They were equally or, perhaps, even more committed towards maintaining
and actively teaching the Malayalam language to the children both at
home and community level. Therefore, using interviews which are a means
of understanding the 'experiences, feelings and hopes' of the interviewee
(Kvale 2007: 1), and key to 'making sense of' their lives (Rapley 2004: 14),
I encouraged the Malayalis to discuss this topic:

Indu: Do you have British citizenship? If so, how has this affected
           your motivation to teach Malayalam to your children?
Chitra: Got it two years ago. I am still proud to be Indian, but I like to
           live here for the betterment of my children. There's a different
           style of education here. In India it's theory-based education,
           but here's it's practical education. Here, we are a bit anxious
           about the culture. But wherever we go we want to continue
           with our culture, values, relations, faith and language.

Chitra's answer was a reiteration of the responses of the other parents, all
of whom claimed that it was the education system that had attracted them
to England. It was also suggested in their explanations that despite being
permanent residents in the United Kingdom, their one wish was to make
stronger their links with the heritage culture and to continue to celebrate

their *Indianness*. In this manner, the enthusiasm of the Malayalis towards retaining the Malayalam language and transferring it to the younger generation was explained: it was the gateway to maintaining heritage cultural values, the religion and their ties with relatives in India. And thus, the interview data contributed to addressing the *why* question.

Unravelling the unsaid

One way in which I studied status and power relations was by considering *who* listened to *whom* and whose instructions were effective and whose weren't in parent-child interactions. The intra-family conversations offered me many such episodes where the children were noted to challenge the status and/or power of one or both parents. In the following excerpt from family B, five-year-old Ajith is being cajoled into opening his mouth as the parents Ashok and Chitra are concerned that their younger child may have tonsillitis:

Ashok: Let me see how your tonsillitis is. Let me see your throat. Come here where there is light.

Ajith: No, no

Ashok: Come here, let your mother see.

Chitra: I cannot see from there. Come here.

Ashok: You mother knows, she is the nurse. Open your mouth wide open.

Chitra: Say aaah

Ajith: Aaah

Chitra: Put your tongue out

Ajith: Aaah

Ajith obeys his father's instructions only when he is told that he will be checked by his mother, the nurse. Not entirely content with the possibility that Ajith's willingness to approach the mother was prompted by her profession, I encouraged Chitra to comment on this incident:

Indu: Ashok asks Ajith to open his mouth to check his tonsillitis, and Ajith says no. But when Ashok asks Ajith to show it to you, he comes. Ashok also says that you are a nurse. How would you explain this?

Chitra: Children think I'm strict, but Ashok is very soft with them all the time.

Chitra's response immediately supported my postulation that while the fathers in all the families seemed to hold a symbolic power, it was exercised in actuality by the mothers. While Chitra's profession may undoubtedly have encouraged the child to place his trust on her, it was more her approach to upbringing and disciplining the children, that resulted in the desired outcome in this episode. This was one of the many occasions where neither my field notes nor the other pools of data held the explanations for the *unsaid* – as the researcher, I was not always privy to *insider* knowledge, which in this excerpt the child Ajith has. His compliance to the instructions being given arises from his awareness of the father's soft approach as opposed to the mother's sterner methods. What is more, on careful consideration, it struck me that the father Ashok too knows his children to be more submissive to their mother's authority. This was something I was made aware of, thanks to the follow-up interviews.

The interviews, thus, lasted throughout the four years of my research and their iterative nature became an indispensable tool in the data analysis process. However, scheduling the follow-up interviews ad hoc came with the inevitable challenges. Soon after the data collection began, one of the participant families started making arrangements to relocate to a new house. Another family purchased a house, which was followed by its renovation making it impossible for them to make themselves available for the interviews. Soon afterwards, the same family had to make an unexpected visit to India due to the illness of a family member. As a researcher working 'in a real social environment and with real people' (Blommaert and Jie's 2010: 22), I had read and experienced first-hand that such trials within field work were unpreventable.

Conclusion

The ground that I attempted to cover in this chapter is primarily based on the design and implementation of interviews within my ethnographic research into family language practices. Interviewing, as I claim in the discussion, is heralded by a need for clarification, thematic expansion, context building and enhancing the validity of the findings. In the case of my research, the interactional data played a crucial role in this process, giving rise to assumptions and questions and thereby giving reason for not one but a series of follow-up interviews. These interviews afforded me and the participants the opportunity to build a narrative, to fill in gaps and to explore and explain the *Hows* and the *Whys*.

References

Agar, M.H. (1996), *The Professional Stranger: An Informal Introduction to Ethnography*, 2nd edn, London: Academic Press.
Asia Harvest (2013), *Malayali* [online]. Available at: http://asiaharvest.org/people -group-profiles/ (accessed 20 September 2016).

Baker, P. and Sanderson, A. (2000), 'Towards Obtaining Better Data on the Languages of London's Schoolchildren', in P. Baker and J. Eversley (eds), *Multilingual Capital – The Languages of London's Schoolchildren and Their Relevance to Economic, Social and Educational Policies*, 87–90, London: Battlebridge Publications.

Blommaert, J. and Jie, D. (2010), *Ethnographic Field Work: A Beginner's Guide*, Bristol: Multilingual Matters.

Canagarajah, A.S. (2008), 'Language Shift and the Family: Questions from the Sri Lankan Tamil Diaspora, *Journal of Sociolinguistics*, 12(2): 142–176.

Denzin, N.K. (1989), *Interpretive Interactionism*, Newbury Park, CA: Sage Publications.

Eapon, M. and Kodoth, P. (2003), 'Family Structure, Women's Education, and Work: Re-Examining the High Status of Women in Kerala,' in S. Mukhopahyay and R. Sudharshan (eds), *Tracking Gender Equity under Economic Reforms. Continuity and Change in South Asia*, 227–267, Ottawa: International Development Research Centre.

Geertz, C. (1973), *The Interpretation of Cultures: Selected Essays*, New York: Basic Books.

Hymes, D. (1972), 'On Communicative Competence', in J.B. Pride and I. Holmes (eds), *Sociolinguistics. Selected Readings*, 269–293, Harmondsworth: Penguin.

Kaul, A. (2012), 'Man and Woman Talk in Indian Organizations: Grammatical and Syntactical Similarities, *Journal of Business Communication*, 49(3): 254–276.

Kvale, S. (2007), *Doing Interviews*, London: Sage Publications.

Li, Wei and Zu, Hua (2010), 'Voice from the Diaspora: Changing Hierarchies and Dynamics of Chinese Multilingualism', *International Journal of the Sociology of Language*, 205: 155–171.

Mason, J. (2004), 'Semi-structured Interview,' in M. Lewis-Beck, A. Bryman and T. Liao (eds), *Encyclopaedia of Social Science Research Methods*, 1021–1022, Thousand Oaks, CA: Sage Publications.

Mayor, B. (2004), 'We're not a Team, Mum – We're Opponents!': Negotiating Adolescence Bilingually,' Symposium Proceedings. Open University. Available at: www.essarp.org.ar/bilinglatam/papers/Mayor.pdf (accessed 2 September 2016).

Office for National Statistics (ONS) (2016), *International Migrants in England and Wales* [Internet]. London: ONS. Available at: http://www.ons.gov.uk/ons /dcp171776_290335.pdf (accessed 26 August 2016).

Percot, M. (2012), *Transnational Masculinity: Indian Nurses' Husbands in Ireland*, E-migrinter. 8: 74. Available at: http://www.mshs.univ-poitiers.fr/migrinter /e-migrinter/201208/e-migrinter2012_08_074.pdf (accessed 4 September 2016).

Rapley, T. (2004), 'Interviews', in C. Seale, G. Gobo, J. Gubrium and D. Silverman (eds), *Qualitative Research Practice*, 15–33, London: Sage Publications.

Saville-Troike, M. (2003), *The Ethnography of Communication*, Malden, MA: Blackwell Publishing.

Spradley, J.P. (1980), *Participant Observation*, London: Thompson Learning.

Wolcott, H.F. (1999), *Ethnography: A Way of Seeing*, Lanham: AltaMira Press.

Zu, Hua (2008), 'Duelling Languages, Duelling Values: Code-switching in Bilingual Intergenerational Conflict Talk in Diasporic Families, *Journal of Pragmatics*, 40: 1799–1816.

CHAPTER SEVEN

Making Young People's Voices Audible in Ethnographic Research

Robert Sharples

Guiding questions

1 One of Robert's big challenges in his research was developing rapport with his participants (though it ended up, perhaps, not being as difficult as he anticipated). What are some of the ways he did this? Might any of these strategies be useful for you in your research?

2 Robert suggests that he never fully achieved an emic position with the students in his research (p. 147). Instead, he says that he became a 'legitimate outsider'. What do you think he means by this, and what, according to Robert, does it show about power relationships in ethnographic research?

Introduction

This chapter describes part of an ethnographic study conducted with young migrants at Pine Wood Academy, a south London secondary school (this is a pseudonym, as are all names in the chapter). It draws on data from the 'International Group', a full-time transition programme at the school that was aimed at newly arrived young migrants aged 14–18 years. The programme included classes at different levels to accommodate the young people's widely differing backgrounds, from those who needed to transfer their learning into a new education system to those who were taking their first steps into formal literacy. I visited the International Group weekly from December 2013 to July 2015 and worked mainly with the two groups identified as having low proficiency in English. The young people's experiences of education and migration were very different from my own and this raised practical and ethical challenges in the research. This chapter addresses those dilemmas, a process I describe as *working inwards* and *writing outwards*. They are addressed in three sections: the first offers a brief discussion of the theoretical assumptions underpinning this chapter; the second shows how the young people were active participants in the study and recognizes the complex power dynamics at play in the classroom; and the final section addresses the issues of representation raised by the writing process.

Theoretical assumptions

This section provides a brief overview of the three main theoretical assumptions that have guided the study.

Mobility, difference and change are part of everyday life for the young people in the International Group, but they are not recognized in mainstream education policy

Hamann (2016) makes a distinction between 'the settled' – the 'teachers, administrators and others who shape schools and school systems' – and the globally mobile (see also Hamann 2001). The gap between them can be difficult to bridge: the participants differ in their roles and status, in their life experiences and their expectations, and in their sense of security and rootedness. This distinction was especially marked in the International Group, which existed within the broader institutional context of the school, but where the young people were highly mobile and came from a wide range of different national, educational and cultural backgrounds. Such transition programmes can be seen as 'peripheral institutional zones' – a product, argue Xuan Wang et al. (2014: 26), of a metropolitan bias that sees the 'world through the lens of those societies that form the current centers of the world system, with the assumption that what occurs there can and should be used as a benchmark for studies elsewhere' (p. 28). Even within urban centres, the experiences of young people in transition programmes are under-researched – or 'less quickly absorbed into current scholarship' (p. 26).

The unpicking of such bias – by Canagarajah (1999, 2013), Makoni and Pennycook (2007), Blommaert (2010) and others – has shown the connection between a Western, urban focus and a privileging of settled (e.g. Valentine et al. 2009) and monolingual (e.g. Creagh 2016) perspectives. This is embedded in English education policy: in mainstream schools in England, young migrants are identified as part of a broader cohort known as 'EAL' (young people who use English as an additional language), emphasizing their need to acquire a specific range of English-language skills (Leung 2016). There is a well-attested timeline from arrival to achieving fluency (Genesee et al. 2006; Demie 2013), but very little critical analysis of the categorizations underpinning such analyzes (see Conteh 2012 for a rare example). This is a problem because the young people identified as 'EAL' are far from a homogeneous group, and their experiences of schooling are little understood except in how they diverge from the majority-language, settled norm.

Young migrants draw on multiple frames of reference to make sense of their schools

The young people in this study may have been new to schooling in the United Kingdom, but they often had wide-ranging experiences of learning in other settings. In the research literature these are often addressed separately: in complementary schools (e.g. Lytra and Martin 2010), faith settings (e.g. Gregory et al. 2013), in the family (e.g. Kenner et al. 2007) and in migration (e.g. Capstick 2016), for example. These are rarely connected at the individual level (the 'funds of knowledge' and 'history in person' approaches are notable exceptions; see Gonzalez et al. 2005; Holland and Lave 2001). It is important to recognize that young people may be engaged with different learning environments at different times of their lives, and bring those experiences with them to the classroom. This shift in perspective is one manifestation of the 'settled'/'mobile' dichotomy: these sites appear separate, but to the young people in this study they are deeply connected. Other experiences offer frames of reference through which the young migrants make sense of their schools. In my PhD thesis I use the term 'trajectory' to account for the ways that young migrants draw on earlier experiences to help understand the present, and in the sections on 'being an audience' and 'challenging assumptions' in this chapter, I offer examples of the continuing relevance of prior learning experiences, both formal and informal.

Ethnography offers a methodological framework for research in contexts of high mobility

Ethnography encourages long-term immersion as a way of understanding different viewpoints, moving, in this case, from assumptions that privilege the urban/monolingual/institutional/settled perspective to a standpoint that recognizes mobility and plurality (see e.g. Blommaert 2013; Kubota 2016). Ethnographic research emphasizes rapport-building and is often described in terms of co-construction: Conteh et al. (2005: xxiii, 132) write about 'collusion', and McDermott and Tylbor (1983: 278) about 'how members of any social order must constantly help each other to posit a particular state of affairs' (see also Chick 1996). The shifts in perspective, as I describe below, came through many interactions with the participants and emerged over time. There are risks inherent in this approach. Rampton (2003: 4) warns of the tendency for educational researchers to put 'rapport and relevance before theory development'. Success in building relationships with young people from different backgrounds can be treated as an end in itself, and their contributions to the data not subjected to appropriate scrutiny.

Ethnography is often seen in terms of Hymes's larger project: comprehensive description that emphasizes the production of generalizable findings from close observation of single cases (Hymes 1980: 104–118, see also Van der Aa and Blommaert 2011; Rampton 2011; Hornberger 2014). Writing is a central part of this process: Ellis and Bochner write about 'composing ethnography' (1996); Conteh et al. (2005) foreground the process of 'writing educational ethnographies' and Hammersley writes about the constructive process of 'reading ethnographic research' (1998), a process of 'textual construction' (Atkinson 1990). The requirements of the thesis genre require you to present yourself at your most 'settled' extent, able to stand back from the interactions that made up the research and to account for both your own activity and that of the participants, as well as the findings that resulted. This single frame of reference aligns the thesis with policy and curriculum documents – and if it is particularly successful, it may interact with and influence them – rather than the plurality of the young people's experiences. This makes representing their voices challenging, and I discuss that challenge in the third part of this chapter.

Working inwards

The process of *working inwards* was not something that I did alone or at a uniform pace. In this section I describe some of the ways in which the young people were involved with me in generating and shaping the data: acting as gatekeepers as I built rapport with the participants, positioning me as an audience for the stories they wanted to tell, and challenging the assumptions that I brought to the research.

Building rapport

In the early stages of the fieldwork I wanted to build rapport with the participants – a sense that we would get along and the precursor to more productive relationships. The literature is clear about the importance of this stage: Blommaert and Dong Jie (2010: 44) say that it is 'crucial'; Geertz (1973: 416) calls it 'that mysterious necessity of anthropological field work' (though his prescription, getting caught in a vice raid in a Balinese village, was difficult to replicate in the classroom). It is also stressful. Hammersley (1992: 199) warns of the danger of 'over-rapport' leading to bias. Peshkin (1988: 17) demands reflexivity, describing commonplaces such as 'rapport is good' as 'unexamined maxims'; and Blackledge and Creese (2010: 103–104) write of the importance of 'emotion, connection and long-term commitment', as well as 'the bigger national, cultural and religious identity markers'. I had some experience working with adolescents, but the sense that a deep personal investment was required to make a success of the project was daunting. It needn't have been.

The process of *working my way in* to the research site – developing my knowledge of the people and the practices that were normal in that setting, so that I could participate and observe – depended on a number of gatekeepers. This field note, from the first lesson I observed at the school, gives a sense of what that offered:

Field note, 6 December 2013

Siobhan's classroom is in the new building – she welcomes the dozen students as they come in and take their places. Siobhan introduces me as a researcher. We talk a little about what that means (as a class) and she gives the students an opportunity to ask me questions. I have to guess their languages and country of origin from them saying hello – Thailand, Pakistan, Brazil, Majorca, Somalia (via Germany)...she highlights some of the patterns of migration.

My initial interactions with the young people were orchestrated by the teacher, Siobhan. She welcomed me and encouraged the young people to be involved with the research project, as well as helping me to demonstrate my interest in linguistic diversity (by guessing nationalities from languages, though see Canagarajah 2013: 19–24 for a discussion of how the linking of community, place and language is problematic). She also commented on what I was seeing, pointing out students who had made particularly complex migration journeys. It was my first day, and I was grateful for her help.

As I began establishing relationships with the participants, I found that the young people also acted as gatekeepers. I was called to the front of the class fairly often and the students were asked to quiz me on the material they had covered (as a more fun way to test their knowledge). I was on display, and as we became more familiar with each other this became an opportunity for play. The following extract shows how one young person, Hugo, helped to bridge the distance between an adult, teacherly role in the classroom and the role of a legitimate, non-teacher participant that I wanted to develop:

Field note, 16 May 2015

Quite an active start to the class. The students had been learning about films (*Cutting Edge Elementary*, pages 68–69). I was called up to the front of the class to be asked questions...Hugo and I cheated where we could.

We 'cheated' by using hand signals and exaggerated facial expressions behind the teacher's back to indicate the correct answer. Hugo had taken on a gatekeeper role, engaging me in the life of the class and helping me to build rapport with the others. The data record many such examples: being brought in on jokes and catch phrases, having disagreements between peers explained, being told about the status of family members overseas. None was particularly significant by itself, but in each case an individual made a decision to include me, and this led over time to a growing sense that I was a legitimate participant in the social life of the International Group.

The process of building rapport took time, but also investment. Shared experiences helped: I got married during the field work period, and took a couple of weeks away. I talked with the students about it a lot: they made congratulatory greetings cards and I took them with me. I came back with photos of us holding the cards at the wedding as a way of showing that the young people were there with us. I was told off, humorously but insistently, by one student if I forgot to wear my new wedding ring. I also lived near the school, and would often see the young people in the street or the supermarket. At first I would be told about these encounters when I was next in school: I had been seen from the bus or from across the street. Later we would stop and chat, usually briefly and awkwardly. Now I sometimes bump into participants who have left the school, and we catch up on news. These are not replicable methodological strategies, but in hindsight they have something in common. I was asking the young people to share details of their lives – some mundane, some traumatic – and being open with small elements of my own life. The rapport that enabled the research did not emerge from a general attitude or personality, but from the accretion of small, specific acts of reciprocity.

Being an audience in the research

Some parts of the *working in* process could only be seen in retrospect. As I worked through the drafts of my thesis, revisiting data and trying to pull the individual narratives into a coherent whole, I was struck by how involved the participants had been in the process. During the field work I had focused on my own activities – an interview that I had arranged, a photograph of something I had spotted, a field note I had written or a classroom recording I had orchestrated. It was only in retrospect, when I brought these different elements together and tried to understand how they captured the environment as a whole, that the young people's influence on the study became clear.

I was particularly interested in how young people used language as a way to create space for themselves in the group. Ethnography encourages long-term participation so that you are sensitized to the 'rich points' (Agar 2009: 115 and see Chapter 1: 35), the moments when your understanding of the norms and practices of the research site take a small leap forward. To capture them I carried an iPad with me, as well as a notebook. The equipment was relatively unobtrusive and I was often able to layer different types of data: taking photographs, for example, and recording interviews with participants there and then to capture their explanations of what I saw. These could be compared with my field notes to generate a thick description (Geertz 1973) of a single incident. Here, again, rapport played an important role. I relied on the teachers to turn a blind eye when I distracted the students from the lesson, and on the young people to share their thoughts (see Rampton 2016).

The following example highlights the important role that the participants played in selecting and shaping the data. Figure 7.1 shows my name transliterated on a mini-whiteboard. It was taken in a quiet moment at the back of a Thursday morning maths lesson, as the rest of the class worked on converting between millimetres and centimetres. Eyob, Afnan, Sana and I sat quietly; the two girls (Sana from Afghanistan and Afnan from Somalia, both sixteen) wrote idly on their whiteboards. The more I showed interest, the more scripts they added to the boards.

I took a series of photographs and made brief field notes to capture the context. When Eyob (17, from Eritrea) turned to the others and said '*saboor*' I wrote that down too and asked what it meant. Afnan explained (it means 'patience') and in an interview later that day I asked them why they were reminding each other to be patient. The stories that emerged, of young people who had been to school in other countries but whose learning was not recognized in the United Kingdom, who doodled on whiteboards because the class was covering material they had studied in primary school, felt like a prize catch for the research.

FIGURE 7.1 *My name transliterated on a mini-whiteboard*

It had begun with a promising moment: a lull in the class, a researcher showing interest, a group of friends with comparable experiences, all brought together. It proceeded through many small iterations: I showed interest and another script was introduced, until a fuller picture of the young people's repertoires was made visible. Then Afnan did something unusual: she introduced a script that didn't fit with what I knew of her background and that suggested a history previously inaccessible to the adults in the school (see Figure 7.2).

The text was in Turkish, and it begins 'I love you so much'. The second line, which is partially obscured and includes non-standard syntax and lexis, can be translated as 'My friend until the last day on earth'. As she began to translate it for me, she blushed bright red and fell silent – clearly I was not the intended audience for the message, only for the script. It emerged that Afnan had spent eighteen months in Turkey after leaving Somalia (longer, in fact, than the twelve months she had spent in England at that point). I asked her teachers but nobody knew that she had lived in Turkey or had been to school before, though combing back through my field notes I found a reference to her telling a cover teacher about the subjects she had studied in Somalia. '*Saboor*' took on a new light: Afnan had need to be patient. She was now into her third school system, with much more of an education history than we had realized or were responding to.

FIGURE 7.2 *Afnan's use of Turkish*

As I began writing about this cluster of data, I realized how much it had developed reciprocally. It can be seen as a series of moments in which the young people made decisions about what to draw into the conversation and what to leave out. The most momentous decision was Afnan's, when she introduced Turkish and triggered a series of questions and retellings that would make that part of her story public, even if only within our small group. There are many examples like this in the data: young people who use the study as an opportunity to present themselves in a certain light, to test out new senses of themselves or to emphasize that the experiences they carried with them (and the different frames of reference that resulted) were still important. We often talk about participants as co-researchers in our projects, and working with these young people has shown how an important part of that collaboration comes through being an audience for the stories that participants want to be heard.

Challenging assumptions

Building rapport and being open to reciprocity were important, but it did not mean that everyone was easily convinced. One morning, in a small room attached to the teachers' office, I was interviewing a participant about the films he used to watch with his grandfather. I thought I had a new angle on my study – an example of rich literacy practices that took place outside formal schooling – when Rajaa (16, M, Somali) turned the conversation in a new direction:

Extract from interview, 26 March 2015

Rajaa: But sir can I ask you a question?
RS: Yeah, please.
Rajaa: Why are you... don't you want to go somewhere else to do your work or to get work?
RS: Like... to another country?
Rajaa: No I don't mean like another country but to get work... but this recording, it's not... I mean like... it's your job but writing is nice for you. I can't say it's bad for you. I can't see how you're trusting in stories.
RS: hmm
Rajaa: I don't know why you waste your time just with stories.

I had described the PhD as 'writing a book', trying to make the process accessible (so that the participants knew what they were involved in) while still describing the project accurately. Here, we see Rajaa speak knowledgeably about that process while challenging the rationale. He knows that the 'recording' will lead to 'writing', and that the methodology involves close attention to personal 'stories', but suggests that it is more of a pleasant pastime ('nice for you') than a rigorous approach to understanding other people's experiences. Stories cannot always be trusted, he implies, and he asks why I 'waste [my] time' with them. As the interview continues, I try to justify the approach, and he asks about the bigger issues: questions of faith and family, of what happens after we die and how we should spend our time before we do. His method is Socratic, leading me through a series of increasingly philosophical questions.

The literacy practices I wanted to learn about were part of Rajaa's migration. He had mentioned several times how he would watch and talk about films with his grandfather, and I wanted to know more about this nonschool literacy practice. It had to be done sensitively; I knew the grandfather had passed away since Rajaa had arrived at the school and I knew that he had been an important figure in Rajaa's life. I also knew a little, though not much, about Rajaa's migration. I know that after leaving Somalia he lived in Uganda with his grandparents (who had travelled with him) for four years. I also knew that he has one sibling born in Somalia and one born in Sweden. These gaps in my data were not uncommon: they hint at the different frames of reference through which the young people make sense of their school – in this case I interpreted them as the lenses of family, of purpose in an unstable world and of faith. This is in contrast to the often bare demographic details that were held in the school's records. By challenging my version of events, Rajaa gave me insight into his own perspective.

Reciprocity was not the issue here, and neither was rapport. Rajaa had been very generous with his time (in all, the interview took nearly forty minutes, most of the lunch break) and he seemed to be confident enough to ask challenging questions. Instead, it points back to the enduring gap between the settled and the mobile. What seems to have happened was that my questions missed the point. I was interested in how watching films were a form of literacy practice, thinking of it in terms of language and learning. It was an academic's view, but for Rajaa it was more relevant to see this film watching as part of an important personal relationship. He reframed my questions and, in doing so, showed how deeply rooted I was in my own experiences. I never achieved the emic perspective that the ethnography handbooks describe. Mine was always an outsider's point of view, but as I worked *inwards* I was able to see how actively the young people had helped me to understand what was important to them. One way to describe my position could be as a *legitimate outsider*, and the next stage was to share what I had learned more widely.

Writing outwards

There was writing and analysis throughout the study. Reflective interviews helped me to interpret earlier data; field notes would connect ideas; sharing drafts and conversations with peers and supervisors would help to clarify and challenge my thinking. By *writing outwards* I mean something different – the reframing of deeply involved, locally situated research activity for an academic audience. Brodkey (1987: 67–68) argues that academic publication is definitive and determines whether 'we are asked to address any of the other audiences that constitute [...] the public sphere'.

The thesis has a very specific function to fulfil, but it is also the version of record of the field work. This means that the thesis carries a particular responsibility for representing the participants – it creates a first impression that cannot easily be remade in future publications. This is the challenge of writing outwards: writing about the participants through this academic lens, finding my own academic voice, and doing so without letting go of the 'legitimate outsider' perspective that was gained from the field work.

Interpreting and presenting the data

The process of selecting and framing elements of the data can involve reconciling different ways of understanding school. The young people have often experienced several different schools (as Afnan had, in Somalia, Turkey and now the United Kingdom) and have been involved with informal, faith and community learning (as Rajaa had). These multiple frames of reference were a key part of classroom activity, as the following example shows:

Field note, 22 January 2015

Jake [the teacher] takes a few minutes to ask why measurements are important. Eyob offers two examples – if you're buying a home, you need to know the area, plus for immigration who might ask e.g. your height. Another student suggests measuring areas of countries and scale for maps [pointing to a map on the classroom wall]. Eyob comes back in with travelling, how far you will go, how long it will take and how much petrol you will 'waste'.

Here, Eyob (17, M, Ethiopian) answers the teacher's questions about measuring area, height, weight and volume in terms of his own migration experiences: moving into new accommodation, dealing with immigration officers and judging the amount of fuel needed for a long journey (his own migration involved crossing the Sahara overland). There were many such examples in the data, from young people who used informal peer networks to support their learning to those who assumed that the behavioural norms of the classroom were the same everywhere, and had trouble adjusting to the routines of their school in south London. The challenge in *writing outwards* was to reconcile these multiple frames of reference with the single frame offered by the thesis itself.

Much of this reframing was done through the structure of the thesis. I focused on a small number of participants and I organized the chapters to reflect the analytical framings that I felt were relevant to an academic audience (a chapter on policy, one on classroom interaction, one on different forms of learning and one extended study of a single young person). Across the chapters, though, I showed the participants negotiating and renegotiating their place in the school, and the resources they drew on to do so. With each chapter I sought to sensitize the (imagined) readers to the young people's mobility and to the different assumptions and beliefs that each brought to the classroom. The chapters moved from what I expected would be familiar to the reader and unfamiliar to the participants (a discussion of policy) and ended with what I hoped would be unfamiliar to the reader and very familiar to the participant (a close analysis of how a young person understood the school in terms of his migration experiences). I sought to move the readers, and myself, into nonexpert roles and to recognize the expertise of the young people – within the very settled structure of the thesis. This had important implications for the power relations embedded in the document.

Empowerment

An ethnographic thesis can be 'rooted in anger, even fury' at inequality (Gregory 2005: x). It might be motivated by feelings of 'solidarity' (Van der Aa and Blommaert 2013), or a responsibility for 'ethics', 'advocacy' and 'empowerment' (which Cameron et al. 2006: 138–145 characterize as three distinct levels of engagement). The *writing outwards* phase involves trying to account for those motivations, and how they influenced the field work, within the very 'settled' genre expectations of the thesis. Cameron et al. (2006: 133) take this very seriously: 'It would be quite irresponsible,' they argue:

> To deny the real effects of research in our disciplines or to play down the contribution they have made to maintaining and legitimating unequal social arrangements. And in this light, our hopes of 'empowering' the subjects of linguistic research might start to look at best naïve.

This was a constant challenge in the writing. The thesis is the version of record and it carries weight, but it is also written explicitly for an academic audience and is used to evaluate the writer's readiness to join that community. Part of writing outwards involved working out where to put the anger.

Barron (2013: 127) suggests that academic ethnography is uniquely placed to fuse the working in with the *writing out*. It offers

> a powerful methodological framework which accepts the contested nature of reality but which provides a means of addressing possibilities and of bringing about change where it is needed.

The academic focus of the PhD has forced me to think carefully about that methodological framework and to locate my work in relation to a body of scholarship. It is too early to speak with certainty, but what I have learned and am learning from the process of writing up the thesis is that it deepens and sharpens the criticisms I wanted to make during the field work. It pushed me to think carefully about how power relations work – and about how institutions operate, and how young people carve out space to make their voices heard. I came to realize that mine was never an emic, insider's perspective, but it can be a legitimate one nevertheless. The process of working inwards was one of learning: by developing rapport and offering reciprocity, by being challenged and offered access to personal narratives I developed a deeper – if only ever partial – understanding of the young people I worked with. By *writing outwards* I had to learn to articulate that perspective to an audience who would hold me to account. The voice I developed for the thesis came from neither the academic writing nor the field work, but from the tension between the two.

Concluding comments

In this chapter I have described some of the experience of working on an ethnographic doctoral project. I have also tried to describe some of the issues I faced in the process. Nothing about the research felt straightforward or linear, though there were some constants. The first was what motivated the project: my belief that young migrants get a rough deal in education and that we could accommodate them better if we were able to recognize more clearly what they bring to the classroom. Another was that close attention to individual voices is crucial. A third was that young people are very capable of being critical and engaging with their own education, and not just being passive recipients. I have tried to show these through the choice of examples in this chapter. Hugo, Afnan, Rajaa and many others showed that the young people engaged with the research purposefully and critically; they guided and contributed to the data in ways that I did not fully understand at the time. The ethnography was messy, complex and difficult to articulate, but it allowed me to engage with young people whose voices would not otherwise be heard, and to share those voices more widely in a way that was well grounded, consistent and robust.

References

Agar, M. (2009), 'Ethnography', in Gunter Senft, Jan-Ola Ostman and Jef Verschueren (eds), *Handbook of Pragmatics Highlights*, 110–120, Amsterdam: John Benjamins.

Atkinson, P. (1990), *The Ethnographic Imagination: Textual Constructions of Reality*, London: Routledge.

Barron, I. (2013), 'The Potential and Challenges of Critical Realist Ethnography', *International Journal of Research and Method in Education*, 36(2): 117–130.

Blackledge, A. and Creese, A. (2010), *Multilingualism*, London: Continuum.

Blommaert, J. (2010), *The Sociolinguistics of Globalization*, Cambridge: CUP.

Blommaert, J. (2013), *Chronicles of Complexity: Ethnography, Superdiversity, and Linguistic Landscapes*, Bristol: Multilingual Matters.

Blommaert, J. and Dong, Jie (2010), *Ethnographic Field Work: A Beginner's Guide*, Bristol: Multilingual Matters.

Brodkey, L. (1987), 'Writing Critical Ethnographic Narratives', *Anthropology & Education Quarterly*, 18(2): 67–76.

Cameron, D., Frazer, E., Harvey, P., Rampton, B. and Richardson, K. (2006), 'Power/Knowledge: The Politics of Social Science', in A. Jaworski and N. Coupland (eds), *The Discourse Reader*, 2nd edn, 132–145, Abingdon: Routledge.

Canagarajah, S. (1999), *Resisting Linguistic Imperialism in English Teaching*, Oxford: OUP.

Canagarajah, S. (2013), *Translingual Practice: Global Englishes and Cosmopolitan Relations*, Abingdon: Routledge.

Capstick, T. (2016), *Multilingual Literacies, Identities and Ideologies: Exploring Chain Migration from Pakistan to the UK*, Basingstoke: Palgrave Macmillan.

Chick, J.K. (1996), 'Safe-talk: Collusion in Apartheid Education', in H. Coleman (ed), *Society and the Language Classroom*, 21–39, Cambridge: CUP.

Conteh, J. (2012), 'Language Diversity and "English as an Additional Language" (EAL) in the UK: Issues for Teacher Education', in E. Winters-Ohle, B. Seipp and B. Ralle (eds), *Lehrer für Schüler mit Migrationsgeschichte: Sprachliche Kompetenz in Kintext Internationaler Konzepte der Lehrerbildung*, 130–137, Münster: Walmann.

Conteh, J., Gregory, E., Kearney C. and Mor-Sommerfield, A. (2005), *On Writing Educational Ethnographies: The Art of Collusion*, Stoke-on-Trent: Trentham Books.

Creagh, S. (2016), 'Multiple Ways of Speaking Back to the Monolingual Mindset', *Discourse: Studies in the Cultural Politics of Education*, [online first publication] 1–11. Available at: http://www.tandfonline.com/doi/full/10.1080/01596306.201 6.1163861 (accessed 04 January 2017).

Demie, F. (2013), 'English as an Additional Language Pupils: How Long Does It Take to Acquire English Fluency?, *Language and Education*, 27(1): 59–69.

Ellis, C. and Bochner, A.P. (1996), *Composing Ethnography: Alternative Forms of Qualitative Writing*, New York, NY and Oxford: AltaMira Press.

Geertz, C. (1973), *The Interpretation of Cultures: Selected Essays*, New York, NY: Basic Books.

Genesee, F., Lindholm-Leary, K., Saunders, B. and Christian, D., eds (2006), *Educating English Language Learners: A Synthesis of Research Evidence*, Cambridge: CUP.

Gonzalez, N., Moll, L.C. and Amanti, C., eds (2005), *Funds of Knowledge: Theorizing Practices in Households, Communities and Classrooms*, New York, NY: Routledge.

Gregory, E. (2005), 'Introduction: Tracing the Steps', in *On Writing Educational Ethnographies: The Art of Collusion*, ix–xxv, Stoke-on-Trent: Trentham Books.

Gregory, E., Choudhury, H., Ilankuberan, A., Kwapong, A. and Woodham, M. (2013), 'Practice, Performance and Perfection: Learning Sacred Texts in Four Faith Communities in London', *International Journal of the Sociology of Language*, 2013(220): 27–48.

Hamann, E.T. (2001), 'Theorizing the Sojourner Student (With a Sketch of Appropriate School Responsiveness)', *Faculty Publications: Department of Teaching, Learning and Teacher Education. Paper 73*. Available at: http://digitalcommons.unl.edu/teachlearnfacpub/73/ (accessed 04 January 2017).

Hamann, E.T. (2016), 'Front Matter' [book cover], in T. Catalano (ed), *Talking about Global Migration: Implications for Language Teaching*, Clevedon: Multilingual Matters.

Hammersley, M. (1992), 'Some Reflections on Ethnography and Validity', *International Journal of Qualitative Studies in Education*, 5(3): 195–203.

Hammersley, M. (1998), *Reading Ethnographic Research: A Critical Guide*, 2nd edn, London: Longman.

Holland, D. and Lave, J., eds. (2001), *History in Person: Enduring Struggles, Contentious Practice, Intimate Identities*, Oxford: James Currey.

Hornberger, N.H. (2014), 'On Not Taking Language Inequality for Granted: Hymesian Traces in Ethnographic Monitoring of South Africa's Multilingual Language Policy', *Multilingua*, 33(5–6): 623–645.

Hymes, D. (1980), *Language in Education: Ethnolinguistic Essays*, Washington, DC: Center for Applied Linguistics.

Kenner, C., Ruby, M., Jessel, J., Gregory, E. and Arju, T. (2007), 'Intergenerational Learning between Children and Grandparents in East London', *Journal of Early Childhood Research*, 5(3): 219–243.

Kubota, R. (2016), 'The Multi/Plural Turn, Postcolonial Theory, and Neoliberal Multiculturalism: Complicities and Implications for Applied Linguistics', *Applied Linguistics*, 37(4): 474–494.

Leung, C. (2016), 'English as an Additional Language – A Genealogy of Language-in-education Policies and Reflections on Research Trajectories', *Language and Education*, 30(2): 158–174.

Lytra, V. and Martin, P., eds. (2010), *Sites of Multilingualism: Complementary Schools in Britain Today*, Stoke on Trent: Trentham Books.

Makoni, S. and Pennycook, A., eds. (2007), *Disinventing and Reconstituting Languages*, Clevedon: Multilingual Matters.

McDermott, R.P. and Tylbor, H. (1983), 'On the Necessity of Collusion in Conversation', *Text*, 3 (3): 277–297.

Peshkin, A. (1988), 'In Search of Subjectivity – One's Own', *Educational Researcher*, 17(7): 17–21.

Rampton, B. (2003), 'Coming to Ethnography from a Background in Teaching', paper presented at: *Linguistic Ethnography at the Interface with Education*, UKLEF Colloquium at BAAL Annual Meeting, University of Leeds, 4–6 September.

Rampton, B. (2011), 'A Neo-Hymesian Trajectory in Applied Linguistics', *Working Papers in Urban Language and Literacies* 78, London: King's College London.

Rampton, B. (2016), 'Field work Rapport and the Positioning of Sociolinguist(ic)s', *Working Papers in Urban Language and Literacies*, 195, London: King's College London.

Valentine, G., Sporton, D. and Bang Nielsen, K. (2009), 'The Spaces of Language: The Everyday Practices of Young Somali Refugees and Asylum Seekers', in J. Collins, S. Slembrouck and M. Baynham (eds), *Globalization and Language in Contact*, 189–206, London: Continuum.

Van der Aa, J. and Blommaert, J. (2011), 'Ethnographic Monitoring: Hymes's Unfinished Business in Educational Research', *Anthropology and Education Quarterley*, 62(4): 319–334.

Van der Aa, J. and Blommaert, J. (2013), 'Ethnographic Monitoring as a Method for Observing Change', paper presented at: *Responding to Contemporary Multilingual Realities, Recasting Research Methodologies* (ESRC RDI). University of Birmingham, 25–26 March.

Xuan, Wang, Spotti, M., Juffermans, K., Cornips, L., Kroon, S. and Blommaert, J. (2014), 'Globalization in the Margins: Toward a Re-evalution of Language and Mobility', *Applied Linguistics Review*, 5(1): 23–44.

CHAPTER EIGHT

Liquid Methodologies: Researching the Ephemeral in Multilingual Street Performance

Jessica Bradley

Guiding questions

1 As you read, note what Jessica means by the concept of 'liquidity'. What did this idea mean for the development of her research processes?

2 What do you think are the main implications of the notion of a 'liquid methodology' for research design and methods? How relevant might it be for your own research?

Introduction

This chapter explores the liquid processes of conducting linguistic ethnographic research in multilingual street performance and visual arts settings with a grassroots community arts organization. Broadly, my research aims to develop understandings of how people communicate across languages and cultures. More specifically, I ask how street artists, visual artists and makers make meaning throughout the processes of putting together a street theatre production and performance. I adopt an approach which draws from linguistic ethnography (for example, Blommaert 2007; Rampton 2007; Blackledge and Creese 2010; Maybin and Tusting 2011; Copland and Creese 2015a; Snell et al. 2015), henceforth abbreviated to LE, to consider how fluid languaging practices (Jørgensen 2003) are employed by creative practitioners during the stages of production. My research involved a longitudinal ethnographic study of a United Kingdom-based grassroots community arts organization with short, intensive bursts of overseas fieldwork which focused on the making of a piece of street theatre. Throughout the process I collected and analyzed multimodal data (video, audio interactional data, field notes, photographs, interviews). In this way I also engaged in what Sara Childers refers to as 'multiple practices' within an 'interactive, rhizomatic process' (2012: 752). The aim of this chapter is to provide an insight into the research process and how this evolved in line with the participants and contexts under investigation.

In the first part of this chapter I summarize the focus and setting for my research and the theoretical frameworks I am working within. I give a short introduction to translanguaging as a descriptive and analytical concept and to linguistic ethnography as an approach to understanding language in society. I briefly highlight the challenges in 'flattening' research relationships in the field. In the second part, I set out **'liquidity'** as a framework and give empirical examples from my research. This draws on Zygmunt Bauman's 'Liquid Modernity' (2000) as a tool for understanding the fluidity of multilingual practice. Finally, I conclude by considering how a framework of liquidity and an ethical commitment to 'generous attentiveness' (Ingold 2014: 384) afford opportunities for rich ethnographic insights and more empathic and engaged research relationships within the field in research into language and social life.

Part 1: Texts and trajectories

My fieldwork centred around a group of aspiring multilingual street artists in Ljubljana, Slovenia, whom I studied from March to July 2015. The group was working on a co-produced piece of street theatre with the United Kingdom-based community arts organization with whom I had set up a research collaboration. The resulting multilingual production was performed across the country at street arts festivals in July 2015. During my fieldwork I followed the group from the inception of the collaboration through to the final performances. I use the trajectory of a text (Kell 2009) – a traditional Slovenian folk story which was developed into a street theatre piece using puppets, promenade and song – as a heuristic to frame and to structure my research. The resultant street theatre piece moved from street to street and from city to city. The story shifted mode throughout the development of the production. And my research moved with it. Likewise, my research methods shifted mode, and with them my analytical framework evolved.

My research project started life as a 2000-word research proposal, meticulously put together, clearly bounded and neatly annotated and referenced. The topic was concise, the setting was articulated and the timeline was fixed and structured. My research itself has emerged as something quite different to that which I set out to do. Yet, key building blocks remained almost unchanged. The settings changed, the location changed, the activity changed and the people changed. My own critical understanding of the three areas on which I was focusing – translation, translanguaging and superdiversity – developed. The methodology evolved throughout the research process, as did the methods employed. But my overarching research questions remained the same, almost unchanged. Likewise the ethnographic principles, including reflexivity and flexibility (cf. Hammersley and Atkinson 1983), which underpinned my research remained, although my understandings of these became deeper and my critiques became more sophisticated. I posit that these uncertainties and the fluidity that characterized my research, in terms of both focus and in terms of methodology, enhanced my understanding of the field and enriched my experience of working in this context. I argue that ethnographic principles in research require the acceptance of a certain degree of uncertainty and fluidity. In working with liquidity as both a research framework and focus, I was able to explore the interplay between 'strangeness' and 'familiarity' which, as Rampton et al. (2014: 2) suggest, ethnography should enable.

Liquid languaging

Liquidity also frames the languaging practices I investigate, for which I use translanguaging as a lens. As Li Wei puts it (2011: 1223), translanguaging is

> both going *between* different linguistic structures and systems, including different modalities (speaking, writing, signing, listening, reading, remembering) and going *beyond* them (my italics).

James Simpson (2016) describes translanguaging as a 'superdiverse practice' – a 'descriptive lens' (p. 2) for understanding multilingual interactions. Vallejo and Moore (2016, in press) argue that translanguaging is useful as an analytic lens when it explicitly seeks to challenge social structures reproducing language-based inequalities, therefore moving beyond documentation and description. A focus on translanguaging affords insights into what Ofelia García and Li Wei (2014: 43) explain as

> languaging actions that enact a political process of social and subjectivity transformation which resist the asymmetries of power that language and

other meaning-making codes, associated with one or another nationalist ideology, produce.

Therefore, in offering more than a descriptive lens, translanguaging can be considered in terms of social justice and transformation. As Otheguy et al. (2015: 281) put it, translanguaging is

> the deployment of a speaker's full linguistic repertoire without regard for watchful adherence to the socially and politically defined boundaries of names (and usually national and state) languages.

Translanguaging thus can act as a disruptor to 'the norm', as transformation which 'resists the asymmetries of power' (García and Li Wei 2014: 43). Likewise, the movement of the street arts production and the actors through the streets, from city to city (and country to country) could be seen to transform socially and politically defined boundaries into a performative space. In researching multilingual *street arts*, I am investigating the role of flexible languaging practices in a performative practice which also aims to resist and disrupt.

Linguistic ethnography: Engagement and collaboration

Blommaert (2007: 682) argues that ethnography allows for the comprehensive description and analysis of 'the complexity of social events'. He underlines the 'chaos' of behaviour and interaction in which, he summarizes, ethnographers wish to do justice to three elements: 'the perspectives of participants' (Boas and Malinowski); 'the micro-events' as 'combinations of variation and stability' (citing the 'tension between phenomenology and structuralism'); and reflexivity. Ethnography, Blommaert states, centres on the 'nature of social knowledge', and as part of this, he sees language as 'social and cultural knowledge' (p. 683). He also stresses the importance of seeing ethnography, not as method but as 'general theoretical outlook' (p.684), an idea taken up by Rock (2015), who, following Blommaert (2009: 260–261), considers LE to go beyond methods, providing a space for 'being in and knowing through research' (Rock 2015: 149). As Creese and colleagues put it, LE is not the 'welding together of two separate disciplines'; instead, they reinforce the **ontological** stance that studying language and social life is a unitary endeavour (Creese et al. 2015: 268). This builds on Dell Hymes's 'Ethnography of Communication' (for example 1972, 1974), resonating with what Snell and colleagues call the 'slow and intensive analysis of language and communication' (2015: 8).

My research with the street artists and visual artists has been intensive. I posit that Ingold's exhortations to commit 'generous attentiveness' (2014:

384) to those with whom we work invoke a collaboration between the researcher and the researched. Luke Eric Lassiter states that 'ethnography is, by definition, collaborative' (2005: 16), in that, as researchers, we engage with those with whom we work within the context. For Lassiter, collaboration and engagement represent two underpinning values of work within the social sphere. Lassiter takes this notion further in describing collaborative ethnography as one in which the researcher and the researched *cowrite* the ethnographic texts. He also differentiates between *collaborative* ethnography and *reciprocal* ethnography, which entails an exchange – denoting a finite enterprise – rather than an ongoing dialogue – denoting engagement.

As Heidegger explains, 'short distance is not in itself nearness. Nor is great distance remoteness' (1971: 193) and 'being there', in Geertz's terms (1988), does not necessarily translate to the 'generous attentiveness' that Ingold asks us to commit to our research relationships. It was important, therefore, for me to establish, to critique and to unpick how my work was ethnographic, and if indeed it was, reflexively throughout the process.

Liquid collaborations: Flattening the research relationship

In committing to enabling the voices of participants to be heard, researchers in LE are committed to 'flattening the relationship between researcher and researched' (Copland and Creese 2015b: 162). Copland and Creese also articulate the ethical commitment of many scholars to bringing back their research, and the knowledge that has been developed, to the people with whom they have worked – making it 'useful'. Giving back denotes that something has been taken away, and in that sense it creates a problem when it comes to reducing the power inequalities inherent in research. Yet, this can seem to represent an 'impossible place'. Hal Foster (1996: 303), in his essay on the artist as ethnographer, states:

> Just as the productivist sought to stand in the reality of the proletariat only in part to sit in the place of the patron, so the quasi-anthropological artist today may seek to work with sited communities with the best motives of political engagement and institutional transgression, only in part to have this work recoded by its sponsors as social outreach, economic development, public relations ... or art.

In this sense, the 'impossible place' is one which is occupied by researchers who, like the artists Foster writes about, can never not involve patronage of some degree in seeking to realign power imbalances. Childers draws from Derrida's 'deconstruction' to draw together theory and method in research which does not seek to simplify but instead to foreground messiness, complexity and intertextuality (2012: 752). From Childers' point of view, this 'impossibility' is 'what cannot be foreseen as a possibility', or, 'an affirmation of who or what is Other' (p. 754). The discomfort in reflecting on this as researchers is explained by Copland and Creese, who state that we often 'feel uneasy with our ethical decisions and remain unsure about our representations' (2015b: 1166), which serve to affirm the 'Other'. Yet these representations (and the decisions which lead to them) are entirely subjective. Their acceptance or rejection lies in the eye of the beholder (as with the artistic products which form the focus of this study).

Part 2: Liquidity as a framework

In my work, mobility and fluidity have particularly characterized the research process, the site, the creative practitioners and the communicative practices. I therefore developed an emergent framework which draws from Bauman's theories of liquid modernity. Bauman describes the world in 'liquid modern life' (2000, 2004), as 'sliced into poorly coordinated fragments while our individual lives are cut into a succession of ill-connected episodes' (2004: 12–13). This notion can help to explain the position of the ethnographer, who can quite easily feel 'wholly or in part "out of place" everywhere, not to be completely anywhere' (p.13). He describes 'floating' identities and this, as a metaphor, rings true for researchers. But how do we navigate these liquid sites and our own shifting, fluid identity? For Bauman there is a 'trick' to this – a trick developed through practice. Instead of seeking 'belonging' he exhorts that we should consider the benefits of being on the periphery, of 'continuous boundary-transgression' (p. 14). Bauman states:

> it is not true … that great art has no homeland – on the contrary, art, like the artists, may have many homelands, and most certainly has more than one'. (2000: 207)

In describing the exiled artist, Bauman explains that for an exile (he uses the example of Goytisolo), language can become less an everyday 'tool' for general **communication**, and instead become a talisman, an 'authentic homeland' (2000: 205). Bauman discusses Derrida and his obsession with 'being away' (p. 206). Derrida strongly endorsed the idea of to 'think travel'. To do so, in Derrida's mind, was

> to think that unique activity of departing, going away from chez soi, going far, towards the unknown, risking all the risks, pleasures and dangers that the 'unknown' has in store (even the risk of not returning).

This notion of 'travel' is not necessarily a literal one, and neither does exile have to mean a change of country. In my case, some of my fieldwork did take place overseas (following Pink and Morgan 2013) but the ethnographic research with the arts group was consolidated in the United Kingdom through prolonged engagement with their work. A framework of liquidity denotes that to conduct ethnographic research, the researcher must to some extent take on the role of an exile, 'departing' and going into the 'unknown', accepting the resulting unsettledness. I therefore use the concept of liquidity not solely to provide a useful analytical framework for the street artists and their work, but also to provide a methodological framework for ethnographic research into street arts.

Street arts performances occupy an ephemeral and transient space. The resultant 'product' – the performance itself – is a 'momentary outcome' (Ingold 2008: 80). It is iconically liquid, and packed up into a suitcase after the crowd has dispersed. Over the course of the production of the street performance, the group developed the traditional Slovenian folk story of the 'Zlatorog', or 'golden horned goat' for production. The following example is taken from the workshop in which the folk tale was introduced to the group.

Example 1: the telling of the tale

The story was first told within a workshop setting in a former church in the centre of Ljubljana.

Setting: Tabor, Ljubljana, Slovenia

We are sitting on chairs in a circle and about to break for lunch. One of the actors, Lyder, had chosen it as its provenance was his home region – the villages around Lake Bohinj which is surrounded by the Julian Alps. The mentor leading the workshop, Bea, is from the UK and she begins the session:

So this might be quite hard actually, I hadn't considered the fact that you would know these stories in your language and would have to TRANSLATE them for ME [.] I'm sorry, but yes (...)

In saying this, Bea is drawing attention to the fact that she is from the United Kingdom and does not speak Slovene. She is also recognizing that the stories will come from the actors' own country and background and that they would be known in Slovene rather than English. She apologizes for this. Lyder begins his story:

ok, so I'm originally from Bohinj (.) for several generations you probably know the place (...) (gestures to the group with his hand) and you probably don't (...) (looks at Bea)

Lyder places himself immediately as being from Bohinj, with generations of his family before him. He positions the majority of the group as 'insiders' to this place-related knowledge – to the story being told – and Bea as an outsider. One of the 'promises' of storytelling, according to Amy Shuman, is that stories are 'both ordinary and larger than life' which, in order to have meaning, must be 'tellable' and 'offer a shared experience' (2005: 27). In telling the story, Lyder is placing it as a possible starting point for the production. He is instigating a claim to ownership of the production. He was also telling something of his own story in selecting this particular tale. He was unable to perform in the final production as he was due to become a father for the first time during the same month. But he came to the performance, took photos and assisted the performers. He expressed his pleasure in the fact that his story had been chosen and that a story from his region of Slovenia should form the basis for the piece. The story moved seventy-six kilometres to the workshop space in Ljubljana, one cold morning in early March. But for Lyder it was talismanic. He was about to move back to his home town with his growing family, back into the family home after having been based in the city for a number of years. Travel – or homecoming – becomes a central consideration in the telling of the tale.

Multimodality: Liquid methods

Within the multilingual street arts activities I observed, the communicative practices not only coincide with but are also entangled with the diverse creative practices within the production process.

Example 2: photographs as analytical tools

The group engaged in making the puppets and the props for the performances themselves, and I was a participant-observer during this process. The making took place in the theatre studio on the outskirts of Ljubljana, and was seen by Bea as an integral part of the development of the piece. The room was a light and airy white space on the first floor of a municipal building. It was the end of May and the windows were wide open, the curtains blowing in the breeze. We had the radio on and we could hear the muffled sounds of live music coming from the arts venue below. There was a festival going on over the weekend and there was talk of us going to it later on. A blackboard was placed to the back of the room and Kaja and Sabina, two of the performers, wrote on it. The board became at times the place that the performers would congregate in to have a break from the making of the puppets. Kaja, an aspiring actress, was quoting Hamlet. Sabina was drawing chickens. There would be chickens in the production and chickens are also a symbol of Slovenia: the country itself is thought to look like a chicken. Veca, another performer, had said she was from the 'chicken's neck' when describing the location of her home town. I took photos of the board (Figures 8.1a–c):

FIGURE 8.1 *(a–c) Images on the blackboard in the theatre studio*

FIGURE 8.1 (*continued*)

FIGURE 8.1 (*continued*)

In my data analysis therefore, I started to move beyond linguistic communication and towards an analytical framework that encompasses the visual, the arts practices and the artistic products. For this I draw on and critique the conceptualization of translanguaging space (Li Wei 2011; García and Li Wei 2014), as being space that is coproduced by translanguaging, as well as produced 'for' translanguaging. García and Li Wei describe these spaces as enabling criticality and creativity (p. 74) and allowing 'linguistically diverse students to co-construct their language expertise, recognize each other as resources, and act on their knowing and doing' (p. 75). My investigation focuses on how these spaces are co-constructed by translanguaging, and how the arts practices intersect to enable 'critical and creative spaces' for production and performance in street arts. Visual ethnography therefore (for example, Pink 2014) became woven into my research design, as broadening the analytical framework to incorporate multimodality in translanguaging. The photographs become more than simply an aide-memoire for me when writing about the workshops and conducting linguistic analyzes of the interactions. They become a form of data in themselves, to be analyzed using a framework of translanguaging space.

For García (2016), translanguaging pedagogy requires a different type of teacher, a 'co-learner', and this aligns with the epistemological underpinnings of ethnographic research, which positions the researcher as engaged in 'educational correspondence' (Ingold 2014: 93). As Ingold puts it (p. 392):

> Knowledge is knowledge, wherever it is grown, and just as our purpose in acquiring it within the academy is (or should be) educational rather than ethnographic, so it should be beyond the academy as well.

Ingold is clear: less description and *more* education is needed when researching social life. As an approach, this leads organically to something more coproduced, more collaborative and a positioning of researcher as learner (or co-learner) rather than reporter, a shift in approach, which carries over to the analysis.

Liquid spaces: Unexpected fieldwork

Bourdieu challenges the scholar to make visible the messiness of the research process, and in presenting work to 'take risks' and to 'expose ourselves' (Bourdieu and Wacquant 1992: 219). There is an inherent risk when presenting methodological messiness. Bourdieu describes work at this stage as being 'in a state that one may call "becoming", that is muddled, cloudy, works that you usually see only in their *finished* state' (p. 219). The threads holding the work together are often invisible by the time a piece of work is published. Yet, it is these threads that demonstrate what Bourdieu calls *fermenting confusion*. Without making these processes visible, it could be said that we deny others the opportunity to learn from mistakes made throughout the research process, and we also sanitize the process, thus creating the impression that we leap seamlessly from data to polished scholarly publication.

Rebecca Coles and Pat Thomson (2016) call for more scholarship that reveals the behind the scenes, backstage writing that takes place in ethnographic research. They call this 'inbetween writing', and it happens between field notes and published work. The authors have started to categorize the different purposes that these kinds of *writings* have. Here my task is to make visible the inbetween and to attempt to describe and convey the liminality of linguistic ethnographic research, as well as the chaos of the lived experience of work in progress (Blommaert and Jie 2010).

This focus on the 'inbetween' and the messiness that lies in the space between what Geertz (1988) calls 'being there' and 'being here' is also inherent within the arts contexts I was investigating and in the area of coproduced research. My research focuses on the process of a production, on the 'inbetween', and in the same way that the elements within the conceptualization, making, devising and performance processes are crucial to the final production, so these elements of researching are also crucial to the final doctoral project. It is, in part, this focus on production processes in my research that has led me to focus on research processes in my writing.

Example 3: reporting as data

During my overseas fieldwork visits I would communicate via email and blog posts. These writings represented different kinds of 'inbetween writing' and became a form of data in themselves. In December, I went back to the theatre in Ljubljana to observe an education and training workshop that was being organized as part of a large European funding bid involving multiple countries, universities and practitioners. While I was there, I posted this on the TLANG project blog:

Thomson and Gunter (2011) write about the fluidity of researcher identity when conducting ethnographic fieldwork in schools. For me, although my work is in the street and in the theatre – not in a school – this seems to be particularly apposite. As I arrived at the studio, the group were waiting for me, and my role had been assigned: I was an observer. Officially. Of course, as a researcher drawing from ethnography, I'm used to this role. Observing. But generally I am an observer for my own research project. My observations are jotted down in notebooks, interactions are recorded onto my iPhone, my videos and photographs are stored into my own folders. But in this case, my 'outsider' status (I'm not a street artist, I have no practical experience in this area) was one that positioned me as someone who could document the workshops and produce a factual account of what was happening.

TLANG blog post, January 21, 2016

Here I am attempting to make visible the interwoven stories, or, following Bruno Latour, the 'delicate networks traced by Ariadne's little hand thread' (1993: 4). These interwoven stories also include decisions as to the paths not taken. In one sense these can be understood by what Tim Ingold refers to as 'the ethnographer's sideways glance' (2008: 84). My doctoral research project, or indeed any research project, is one that is limited both by time and funding. It falls upon the doctoral researcher, therefore, to make decisions throughout the process about the research focus, the research detail and final thesis. Sometimes, however, these decisions fall outside the researcher's hands, as was my experience. As a researcher working with, and 'attending to', community artists and street performers, key factors were austerity and funding regimes. One project I had anticipated using as a case study changed its form and focus. It disappeared from my research design. Another project that I had integrated into my research design received a number of funding rejections. However these factors also created opportunities, not solely in terms of my doctoral research, but also in terms of developing what Ingold refers to as 'educational correspondence' (2014: 390). Ingold describes the act of participant observation (as distinct from ethnography, which he sees as a 'practice of description') as being correspondence:

> to practice participant observation, then, is to join in correspondence with those with whom we learn or among whom we study, in a movement that goes forward rather than back in time.

Example 4: theorizing shifts in fieldwork focus

Entering into 'educational correspondence' required me to make a series of decisions about how I would 'follow' those with whom I was working and where I would go. In my research blog entry from December 2015, I wrote down a quotation from Zygmunt Bauman's 'The Art of Life' (2008: 53):

> *Between them, the stars might mitigate the darkness enough to allow the wanderers to trace a path in the wilderness – some sort of path; but which star should orient one's steps? And at what point should one decide whether selecting this star for a guide from among the multitude has been a felicitous or an unlucky decision? When should one conclude that the chosen path leads nowhere, and that the time has arrived to abandon it, turn back and make another, hopefully better choice? Notwithstanding the discomforts already brought by walking the previously selected road, such a resolution may be an unwise step: abandoning a hitherto followed star may prove to be an even graver and in the end more regrettable error, and you may find that the alternative path leads to even greater hardships; you don't know, nor are you likely to know all that for sure. Heads or tails, your chances of winning or losing look even.*

I was assessing whether the decisions to follow the arts group to Slovenia had been the right ones, and whether the final field trip I took in December during which I observed the beginnings of an education and training in street arts network had been a wise decision. I wrote in my research blog:

> *There's something that Zygmunt Bauman says in his book, 'The Art of Life'. Something about choices and decisions. A PhD seems to me to be a series of decisions. A series of decisions that you have to make as an 'apprentice independent researcher' who is on the path to becoming an 'independent researcher'. So does making these decisions, theorizing them, backing up your decisions and explaining why you didn't choose the different path – does all this mean that at the end of the three years you are suddenly 'independent'? When I've finished this process, will I have a new-found sense of clarity and faith in my decisions?*

Back to Bauman:
All that, however, only soon to find out that our choice of guiding star was in the last account our choice, pregnant with risks as all our choices have been and are bound to be – and our choice, made on our responsibility, it will remain to the end.

It's a weird dynamic with a PhD. I find myself questioning my every move. In contrast, I find myself with a new sense of confidence in what I used to do, coupled with a growing sense of confidence in what I am doing.
But I still make decisions that I don't feel completely sure about.
                          Research blog entry, 2 December 2015

Liquid roles: Researcher positioning

For the novice researcher, the unsteadiness caused by the fluid and shifting landscape I was catapulted into was not without its challenges. As Amy Shuman (2011: 149) writes:

Ethnographic work is unsettling. Doing ethnography places us on the verge, whether on the verge of knowing, on the verge of exploitation, on the verge of discovery, on the verge of desire, or on the verge of going native. For me, as for many others, ethnography is always a meeting place of the personal, the methodological, and the theoretical.

When we, as researchers, are placed on the 'verge', we are also positioned in a 'meeting place' – both in the ways that Shuman describes here and in terms of our status as insider or outsider. The binary division between these two 'positions' is problematic. Ethnographic research entangles and complicates the roles and responsibilities of the researcher and researched, making the divisions between insider and outsider unclear. Not simply unclear, these roles shift and mutate throughout the process. They are not, in Pat Thomson and Helen Gunter's words, 'singular, fixed and stable' (2011:17). Drawing from Bauman's theories of fluid identities, the authors argue that research which concentrates on the distinction between 'insider' and 'outsider' restricts understanding of the messiness of the lived experience of research in schools, creating an 'illusion of stability' (p. 27).

Conclusions

If we are placed on the verge, we have the opportunity to move inwards and outwards, and to gain a broader perspective. But it means that we relinquish some control of what we observe and the direction of our work. Likewise, Ingold, in his strong critique of ethnography, in which he argues that 'ethnographic methods' 'reproduce a pernicious distinction between those with whom we study and learn, respectively within and beyond the academy' (2014: 383), describes the 'existential risk' involved in 'attending to' those with whom researchers are working. This risk is foregrounded when researching in mobile and fluid contexts. It means we may not arrive at the destination we may have pictured when designing our research. It is this 'risk' which led me to shift the focus of my research to multilingual street artists, and undertaking my research overseas. Ingold states (2014: 389) (my italics):

> It is one that calls upon the novice anthropologist to attend: to attend to what others are doing or saying and to what is going on around and about; *to follow along where others go and to do their bidding*, whatever this might entail and wherever it might take you. This can be unnerving, and entail considerable existential risk.

Ingold warns against the overuse of 'ethnographic methods' or 'ethnography'. His argument is that in positioning our research as 'ethnographic', 'the priority shifts from engagement to reportage, from correspondence to description, from the co-imagining of possible futures to the characterization of what is already past'. Yet, Snell et al. (2015: 5), in summarizing the five characteristics of interdisciplinary scholarship in linguistic ethnography, underline the aspiration to 'improve social life' as one of the aims of LE research. Could research which simply 'reports', 'describes' and 'characterizes what is already past' also claim a commitment to creating a better world? It is not within the scope of this chapter to provide a comprehensive critique of either ethnography or of Ingold's critical call to arms. However, this chapter does take a critical stance on ethnographic approaches in research.

What does understanding more about the liquidity of research and generous attentiveness bring to the field? What does making visible the threads and the messiness mean for future research into translanguaging and community arts? For researchers to commit to what Lassiter describes as 'ethnography that is grounded in the ongoing ethical and moral co-commitment' (2005: 133), 'generous attentiveness' shifts towards a coproduced, collaborative framework. This framework allows for the liquidity and chaos of research into social and cultural knowledge. It also affords a space in which the messiness and liquidity of research can be accepted as fundamental and in which a commitment is made to keeping the threads visible.

I started this chapter with three lines from a poem by C.P. Cavafy, Ithaka. In the second verse of the poem, Cavafy writes:

Hope the voyage is a long one.
May there be many a summer morning when,
with what pleasure, what joy,
you come into harbors seen for the first time;

The poem itself was introduced to me by one of my PhD supervisors, and I remember thinking what an apt metaphor for the doctoral process it was – a voyage. I reproduce it here for three reasons: one, to provide a metaphor for research and as an exhortation to consider the process itself as important, as a site itself to be theorized and critiqued; two, to conceptualize this process as being one of *becoming* (in Bakhtinian terms); and three, to demonstrate the ways in which the community of scholars – also familiar with the fluidity, liquidity and chaos of research which takes an ethnographic approach – provides support and mentorship for the novice researcher. It is not a journey that is undertaken alone.

Transcription conventions
(adapted from Georgakopoulou 2007)
(0.03) time from beginning of extract
Overlapping utterances []
Intervals (.) less than 0.1 seconds; (..) between 0.1 and 0.5 seconds; (…) greater than 0.5 seconds
(italics) a gesture to the group or laugh from the group
CAPITALS speech louder than surrounding talk

References

Bauman, Z. (2000), *Liquid Modernity*, Cambridge: Polity.
Bauman, Z. (2004), *Community: Seeking Shelter in an Insecure World*, Cambridge: Polity.
Bauman, Z. (2008), *The Art of Life*, Cambridge: Polity.
Blackledge, A. and Creese, A. (2010), *Multilingualism: A Critical Perspective*, London: Continuum.
Blommaert, J. (2007), 'On Scope and Depth in Linguistic Ethnography', *Journal of Sociolinguistics*, 11(5): 686–688.
Blommaert, J. (2009), 'Ethnography and Democracy: Hymes' Political Theory of Language', *Text and Talk*, 29(3): 257–276.
Blommaert, J. and Jie, D. (2010), *Ethnographic Field work: A Beginner's Guide*, Bristol: Multilingual Matters.
Bourdieu, P. and Wacquant, L. (1992), *An Invitation to Reflexive Sociology*, Chicago, London: University of Chicago Press.
Childers, S.M. (2012), 'Against Simplicity, Against Ethics: Analytics of Disruption as Quasi-Methodology', *Qualitative Inquiry*, 18(9): 752–761.

Coles, R. and Thomson, P. (2016), 'Beyond Records and Representations: Inbetween Writing in Educational Ethnography', *Ethnography and Education*, 11(3): 253–266.

Copland, F. and Creese, A. (2015a), *Linguistic Ethnography*, London: Routledge.

Copland, F. and Creese, A. (2015b), 'Ethical Issues in Linguistic Ethnography: Balancing the Micro and the Macro', in P.I. De Costa (ed), *Ethics in Applied Linguistics Research: Language Researcher Narratives*, 1161–1178, New York: Routledge.

Creese, A., Blackledge, A., and Kaur Takhi, J. (2015), 'Metacommentary in Linguistic Ethnography', in J. Snell et al. (eds), *Linguistic Ethnography: Interdisciplinary Explorations*, 266–284, Basingstoke, New York: Palgrave MacMillan.

Foster, H. (1996), *The Return of the Real*, Cambridge, London: MIT Press.

García, O. (2016), 'What Is Translanguaging? An Interview with Ofelia García', (Interview conducted by Francois Grosjean). *Psychology Today blog*, 2 March 2016. Available at: https://www.psychologytoday.com/blog/life-bilingual/201603/what-is-translanguaging (accessed 4 January 2017).

García, O. and Li, Wei (2014), *Translanguaging: Language, Bilingualism and Education*, Basingstoke and New York: Palgrave Macmillan.

Geertz, C. (1988), *Works and Lives: The Anthropologist as Author*, Cambridge: Polity Press.

Georgakopoulou, A. (2007), *Small Stories, Interaction and Identities*, Amsterdam: Benjamins.

Hammersley, M. and Atkinson, P. (1983), *Ethnography: Principles in Practice*, London and New York: Tavistock Publications.

Heidegger, M. (1971), *Poetry, Language, Thought*, New York: Harper and Row.

Hymes, D. (1972), 'Models of the Iteration of Language and Social Life', in J. Gumperz and D. Hymes (eds), *Directions in Sociolinguistics: The Ethnography of Communication*, 35–71, Oxford: Blackwell.

Hymes, D. (1974), *Foundations in Sociolinguistics: An Ethnographic Approach*, Philadelphia, PA: University of Pennsylvania Press.

Ingold, T. (2008), 'Anthropology Is not Ethnography', *Radcliffe-Brown Lecture in Social Anthropology*, 69–92, Proceedings of the British Academy, volume 154.

Ingold, T. (2014), 'That's Enough about Ethnography!', *HAU: Journal of Ethnographic Theory*, 4(1): 383–395.

Jørgensen, J.N. (2003), 'Languaging among Fifth Graders: Code-switching in Conversation 501 of the Køge Project', *Journal of Multilingual and Multicultural Development*, 24(1–2): 126–148.

Kell, C. (2009), 'Literacy Practices, Text/s and Meaning Making across Space and Time', in M. Baynham and M. Prinsloo (eds), *The Future of Literacy Studies*, 75–99, Basingstoke/New York: Palgrave.

Lassiter, L.E. (2005), *The Chicago Guide to Collaborative Ethnography*. Chicago, London: The University of Chicago Press.

Latour, B. (1993), *We Have Never Been Modern*, Cambridge, MA: Harvard University Press.

Li, Wei (2011), 'Moment Analysis and Translanguaging Space: Discursive Construction of Identities by Multilingual Chinese Youth in Britain', *Journal of Pragmatics*, 43(5): 1222–1235.

Maybin, J. and Tusting, K. (2011), 'Linguistic Ethnography', in J. Simpson (ed), *Routledge Handbook of Applied Linguistics*, 515–528, London, New York: Routledge.

Otheguy, R. García, O. and Reid, W. (2015), 'Clarifying Translanguaging and Deconstructing Named Languages: A Perspective from Linguistics', *Applied Linguistics Review*, 6(3): 281–307.

Pink, S. (2014), 'Digital-visual-sensory-design Anthropology: Ethnography, Imagination and Intervention', *Arts and Humanities in Higher Education*, 13(4): 412–427.

Pink, S. and Morgan, J. (2013), 'Short-term Ethnography: Intense Routes to Knowing', *Symbolic Interaction*, 36(3): 351–361.

Rampton, B. (2007), 'Neo-Hymesian Linguistic Ethnography in the United Kingdom', *Journal of Sociolinguistics*, 11(5): 584–607.

Rampton, B., Maybin, J. and Roberts, C. (2014), 'Methodological Foundations in Linguistic Ethnography', *Working Papers in Urban Language and Literacies* (WP. 125). Available at: http://www.kcl.ac.uk/sspp/departments/education/research/Research-Centres/ldc/publications/workingpapers/the-papers/WP125-Rampton-Maybin-Roberts-2014-Methodological-foundations-in-linguistic-ethnography.pdf (accessed 2 December 2016).

Rock, F. (2015), 'Bursting the Bonds: Policing Linguistic Ethnography', in J. Snell et al. (eds), *Linguistic Ethnography: Interdisciplinary Explorations*, 147–165, Basingstoke, New York: Palgrave MacMillan.

Shuman, A. (2005), *Other People's Stories: Entitlement Claims and the Critique of Empathy*, Urbana, Chicago, and Springfield: University of Illinois Press.

Shuman, A. (2011), 'On the Verge: Phenomenology and Empathic Unsettlement', *The Journal of American Folklore*, 124(493): 147–174.

Simpson, J. (2016), 'Translanguaging in the Contact Zone: Language Use in Superdiverse Urban Areas, *Working Papers in Translanguaging and Translation* (WP.14). Available at: http://www.birmingham.ac.uk/generic/tlang/index.aspx (accessed 4 January 2017).

Snell, J., Copland, F., and Shaw, S. (2015), *Linguistic Ethnography: Interdisciplinary Explorations*, Basingstoke, New York: Palgrave MacMillan.

Thomson, P. and Gunter, H. (2011), 'Inside, Outside, Upside Down: The Fluidity of Academic Researcher "Identity" in Working with/in School', *International Journal of Research and Method in Education*, 34 (1): 17–30.

Vallejo, C. and Moore, E. (2016), 'Prácticas Plurilingües "transgresoras" en un Programa Extraescolar de Refuerzo de la Lectura', *Signo y Seño*, 29 (June): 33–61.

PART THREE

Looking Back – Reflections on Processes and Outcomes

The four chapters in Part 3 look back at completed projects to reflect on methodological issues, as well as findings. The authors reflect critically on what they learned about conducting ethnographic research through their engagement with its processes, and consider what their findings might mean for social justice in education in multilingual societies. In this framing section, I introduce the chapters, and then, in this final part of the book, consider methodological issues around research 'quality', and debates about the generic and contested themes of 'validity' and 'reliability'. Finally, I offer some thoughts about ethics in ethnographic research in education.

Introducing the chapters

The first two chapters in this part, by Samyia Ambreen and Valerie Nave, both originated in personal experience and the desire to enhance opportunities for success for multilingual pupils in mainstream school. Another common factor is that both researchers enjoyed – and were very aware of – their own positions of status and power in relation to their participants. Chapter 9 is a classroom-based study in which Samyia explores pupils' interactions in group activities in a Year 5 (9–10 year olds) class in a multilingual mainstream primary school in the north of England. Presenting excerpts from her observation and interview data, she reflects on the findings of her study, which reveal the ways that pupils' interactions in the classroom are influenced by social and cultural norms in their lives outside the school. Her discussion sheds light on the importance of developing an understanding of the reciprocal and bidirectional relationships between pupils' distinctive social and cultural backgrounds and their classrooms. Samyia argues that such understandings are vital in considering the factors that contribute to academic success.

This conclusion resonates with the motivation for the study featured in Chapter 10, where Valerie shows how she explored the experiences of three multilingual primary pupils attending schools in northern England, whose daily languages were English and French. As the mother of one of the children, she began her research with the personal aim of gaining a better understanding of how to help her daughter to maintain her multilingualism and to succeed in mainstream school. The process of researching from the inside-out allowed her to access information that she could not have obtained if she were not a parent and someone who shared the same linguistic repertoires as most of her participants. With great sensitivity to the ethical issues involved, she discusses the strategies she developed to avoid any disadvantages to her participants. She reflects on the role of the 'self' and how she maintained a position that allowed her to be both an insider and also to detach herself from the parent role and become a researcher, especially when analyzing her data.

The second two chapters in Part 3, by Janica Nordstrom and Katherine Fincham-Louis, both concern learners who may be considered privileged, compared to those whose lives feature in earlier chapters. But there are still issues of social justice to address, mainly to do with the recognition and representation of the learners' identities and of their voices. This way of thinking about social justice resonates with Nasir's theoretical constructions of recognition and misrecognition in Chapter 3. As Katherine points out, it sees social justice as temporal and context specific and helps to capture the ways in which justice in education is socially and historically contextualized.

Both Janica's and Katherine's chapters reveal the detail of the data collection processes used in the research projects they describe. In Chapter 11, Janica discusses her work in a Swedish complementary Saturday school in

Australia, and her use of participant observation with teenage students, whose motivations to attend the school she describes as 'rather complex'. She explores how her relationships with her student participants enabled her to gain insight over time and to generate otherwise difficult-to-obtain data. The challenges she faced included the need to monitor and analyze her own subjectivities and thus justify the reliability of the research as a whole to her own satisfaction. An important strand in this, which also had clear ethical implications, which she describes fully in the chapter, was her relationship with the teacher of the class in which she did her data collection.

Developing relationships and rapport with participants is also a major theme in Chapter 12, in which Katherine reports her participatory case study that explores language use and perceptions about identity among a select group of Greek/English bilingual/bicultural children in state elementary schools in Cyprus. Her main finding has implications for policy, as well as practice, in other places besides her research context. She found that this predominantly 'middle class' group of children was largely overlooked within the educational system in Cyprus. Katherine argues that this is due to a narrow and misinformed reading of the term 'bilingual'. In Cyprus, it is mainly seen as synonymous with 'immigrant and/or disadvantaged student'. This, of course, is also the case in many other contexts. This raises issues, as does every other chapter in the book, about what we do with 'difference' and how we address the needs of learners in our schools who do not fit the established moulds. In many ways, this is the central theme of the book, and the central concern of research that seeks to understand education for social justice in multilingual settings.

Research quality: 'Validity', 'reliability' ...

Debates about how to judge quality in research have gone on since people began doing research. The arguments about the unsuitability of using positivist models for assessing quality in educational research are well established (e.g. Carr 2007). Such models depend on externally derived criteria and externally imposed procedures to gauge a notion of absolute 'standards' of validity and reliability. We have for long had powerful alternatives, such as Mishler's model of validation and trustworthiness (1990). Instead of proposing alternative criteria, Mishler suggests a simple approach – to observe closely what researchers actually do, in other words their own 'cultural and linguistic practices' (p. 435). His definition of validation (p. 429) emphasizes the importance of the idea of a 'community of scholars':

[V]alidation is the social construction of a discourse through which the results of a study come to be viewed as sufficiently trustworthy for other investigators to rely upon in their own work.

This, he argues (1990: 420), allows us to see research as the socially constructed activity it is

> focusing on trustworthiness rather than truth displaces validation from its traditional location in a presumably objective, nonreactive and neutral reality, and moves it to the social world – a world constructed through our discourse and actions, through praxis.

In this way, the criteria for assessing research quality 'align[ing] the process more closely with what scientists actually do' (1990: 419).

Stressing that research, like any craft, 'is learned by apprenticeship to competent researchers, by hands-on experience and by continual practice' (p. 422), Mishler proposes a model of validation based on exemplars rather than abstract rules and absolute criteria. He suggests that 'exemplars contain within themselves the criteria and procedures for evaluating the "trustworthiness" of studies' and goes on to provide three detailed 'candidate exemplars' from his own and others' works. From these, he draws out practical principles to guide other researchers. These can perhaps be summed up in two key principles, both of which have strong implications for the writing of the thesis, which I will come on to in Chapter 13:

- the need for 'a continual dialectic between data, analysis and theory' (p. 427); in other words, the constant reiteration of reading, writing and working with data such as I have emphasized throughout the book;

- the need for 'the visibility of the work' (p. 429), which includes 'the direct linkages between data, findings and interpretation'; in other words, developing as much transparency as possible as you talk and write about what you actually did in the course of your fieldwork; the data you collected and what you did with the data.

Despite such powerful defences, findings from ethnographic research are still commonly seen as somehow less 'reliable' than the outcomes of quantitative studies. It is still a nagging concern among ethnographic researchers that their work will be judged as failing to meet some kind of absolute criteria. It is, sadly, a justifiable concern. A sense of unease can be discerned in some of the chapters in the book, and the authors have sometimes found their own ways to address it. In Janica's account of participant observation (Chapter 11), for example, she stresses the point that the researcher is the 'tool for collecting the data' (p. 22), and so the method is inevitably 'unpredictable'. As she suggests, 'two different researchers in the same setting can produce two very different descriptions of the field and the participants'. In naturalistic contexts, she argues, absolute notions of reliability and validity are not much use at all. In Valerie's case (Chapter 10), doing research with her own daughter in her own home was fraught with tensions about validation and trustworthiness, of which she was very well aware. In her chapter, she clearly delineates the different roles she needed to take in the course of her work. She found that, when it came to analyzing her observations and interview transcripts, physically moving her work site was a very helpful way of stepping into and out of these roles. So, most of her data analysis was done at her university workstation, rather than at her desk at home.

In assessing research quality, Mishler's models of validation and trustworthiness and the use of exemplars offer – I suggest – a much better way than the static, positivist concepts of validity and reliability that continue to hold such sway. As with so many contentious issues highlighted in this book, there is a need to recognize the established hierarchies and the uses and abuses of power in the relationships entailed in so-called 'communities of scholars'. Openness, trust and equality between novice researchers and those more senior is vital. A major matter in this regard is to do with teachers becoming researchers and the thorny issues that arise, such as their being made to feel disempowered by their apparent lack of the right kinds of knowledge in the new world they are entering. I mentioned this problem in Chapter 1 (p. 11) and will take it up again in Chapter 13 (p. 251). In Chapter 12, Katherine expresses such anxieties. Yet she had twenty-five years of experience as a practitioner, which no doubt gave her – among many other positive attributes – an intuitive expertise in building rapport with other teachers and in relating to her child-participants. It is a pity that, while completing her PhD, she did not seem to meet a senior researcher who was able to value what she brought to the enterprise and give her the time and space to recognize it in herself. Mishler ends his seminal paper (p. 438) with a call to researchers to work collaboratively, rather than in isolation or competition:

> Our collective task…is to engage with each other in vigorous debate about issues of validation as we move towards an alternative form of scientific life.

... and ethics

The boundaries between validity, reliability and ethics are hard to define and even harder, at times, to identify in practice. Valerie's care and sensitivity in negotiating her dual roles as mother and researcher are indicative of her own awareness of the ethical risks involved in doing research with your own children. They are also testament to the battles she had to fight to gain formal ethical approval for her project through the university's standard procedures. Similarly, when Samyia describes the issues she faced in maintaining trustworthy relationships with her participants, particularly the class teacher who seemed nervous about leaving the pupils to work together in groups when she was present in the classroom, she is revealing her awareness of the need to weave ethics through the processes of working with them. The strategy she introduced to overcome the problem, sharing her field notes with the teacher, shows the value of applying Mishler's principle of transparency in as many ways as possible. Finally, Janica's assertion that her friendly relationship with 'Britta', the teacher in whose classroom she spent so much time, was part of her data is a useful methodological, as well as ethical, point. And she goes on to show that she is fully aware of the ethical implications.

Ethics need to be considered in two ways, summed up by Kubanyiova (2008) as 'macroethical' and 'microethical' perspectives. The first, the formal ethical review procedures imposed by all universities, can be somewhat onerous. Indeed as Van der Aa and Blommaert (2011: 333) argue, sometimes their demands can create difficult tensions with the aims and design of ethnographic educational research as they can

> push educational research increasingly away from intensive case-based work toward abstraction and generalisation, toward the medians and averages that determine standards in education.

But, as Copland and Creese (2015: 184) remind us, formal ethical reviews can also be supportive in ensuring that students carefully consider all aspects of their project.

Much of the ways in which ethical reviews are constructed is based on medical models of research. It can seem a little odd for educational researchers to have to tick boxes in response to queries about working with human tissue samples! All of the studies in Part 3 deal with researching with children and young people under the age of sixteen, and so would require a tick in the box on the form denoting that the research involves working with 'vulnerable groups'. It is important to remember that a significant aspect of the form filling is necessary to meet obligations related to safeguarding the avoidance of risk and even litigation. The ethical responsibilities overlap, but go beyond this. The implications of 'informed consent', 'the right to withdraw' and 'ensuring anonymity' need to be fully activated, woven into the daily processes of the research and the ongoing conversations with the participants. Samyia (p. 168) talks about the need to solicit consent repeatedly from the young pupils in her study before she took photos in their classroom, even after parents and the head teacher had signed consent forms. In my own PhD research with nine- to ten-year-old pupils, I had to persuade them that it was necessary to give them pseudonyms, as without them, other participants in the study could be identified. For the children, using their real names was the honest and ethical thing to do, and they could not see why everybody did not see it in the same way as they did.

Kubanyiova (2008: 504) defines 'microethics' as the

everyday ethical dilemmas that arise from the specific roles and responsibilities that researchers and research participants adopt in specific research contexts.

This chimes with Copland and Creese (2015: 176), who contend that, in the end ethical issues 'must be resolved locally, drawing on contextual realities and mutual understandings'. Kubanyiova (2008: 507) provides suggestions for principles to underpin 'situated ethics' based on what she calls the 'cornerstones' of ethical practice; 'macroethical principles, ethics of care and virtue ethics'. Her examples show the tensions between the various demands of quality in research, such as 'pursuing technical excellence' which 'may be at odds with respect for persons' (p. 508). This is particularly the case where busy teachers may be asked to take part in interviews and diary-type data generation strategies, or even action research projects which make excessive demands on their time. Kubanyiova makes the important point that 'some data collection techniques may … emerge as unethical in the actual research practice' (p. 510), involving the need to make decisions about how to proceed and even change data collection strategies on the spot. In a discussion about her project, which aimed to promote change in teachers' classroom practices, she talks about 'ethically significant moments' (p. 511) – similar to the notion of 'rich points' in the data (p. 35) – which are often realizations about the distance between the researcher's perspectives and those of the participants. Addressing these can mean that the carefully planned and seemingly neat research design ends up much messier, but no less carefully considered. Some dearly held principles of good ethnographic research may seem less unquestionably 'good'; for example, she discusses the risks of developing close rapport with participants, arguing that it is 'no guarantee of ethical conduct', and can also 'violate the principle of respect for persons' (p. 515). In the end she concludes, as with so many issues in research as in life, it comes down to a matter of personal conscience.

Reflection and discussion points for Part 3

The chapters in Part 3 all focus on researching with children and young people, where issues related to status and power become very important. The authors are all concerned to form the right kinds of relationships which both empower and safeguard their young participants and also maintain ethical processes in their data generation and collection.

As you read Chapters 9, 10, 11 and 12, here are some questions to help you reflect on your own PhD project. You may also find them useful as discussion points with your peers:

- What ethical issues around researching with children and young people are raised in the chapters in this part?

- In accessing their child-participants, the authors all needed to consider carefully the ways they approached and negotiated with class teachers and other adult gatekeepers. As you read, take note of the issues that arose in this aspect of the research projects, and how the authors addressed them.

- In what practical ways do the authors show the trustworthiness of their research, in the sense that Mishler defines it?

References

Carr, W. (2007), 'Educational Research as a Practical Science', *International Journal of Research and Method in Education*, 30(3): 271–286.

Copland, F. and Creese, A. (2015), *Linguistic Ethnography: Collecting, Analyzing and Presenting Data*, London: Sage Publications.

Kubanyiova, M. (2008), 'Rethinking Research Ethics in Contemporary Applied Linguistics: The Tension between Macroethical and Microethical Perspectives in Situated Research', *Modern Language Journal*, 92(4): 503–518.

Mishler, E.G. (1990), 'Validation in Inquiry-guided Research: The Role of Exemplars in Narrative Studies', *Harvard Educational Review*, 60(4): 415–442.

Van der Aa, J. and Blommaert, J. (2011), 'Ethnographic Monitoring: Hymes's Unfinished Business in Educational Research', *Anthropology and Education Review*, 42(4): 319–334.

CHAPTER NINE

Exploring the Influences of Social Background and Parental Concern on Pupils' Participation in Ability-Based Groups

Samyia Ambreen

Guiding questions

1 In describing the processes of her field work, Samyia outlines some issues she faced in maintaining a 'trustworthy relationship' with the class teacher in the classroom where she spent quite a long time. Why do you think these issues arose and how did she mediate them? Do you think you might face similar issues in your own research?

2 In the discussion section of her chapter, Samyia provides an example of her data and data analysis, in which she claims that she used 'ethnographic principles'. What does this mean in practical terms for the nature of her analysis and her findings?

Introduction

This chapter shows the contribution that using an ethnographic research approach can make in understanding the influences of parental concerns on pupils' participation in ability-based groups in a multilingual primary classroom. In my research, I wanted to find out the ways that primary pupils engaged with different kinds of group work in their classroom, and the ways they perceived their roles in fixed and mixed ability groups. I conducted a small-scale study of children in one Year Five (nine- to ten-year-olds) multilingual classroom over one academic year. I observed and recorded the children working in different group settings, interviewed individual children, as well as their class teacher, and collected contextual information about the school, the curriculum and local and national policies. By the time I began my research, I had been working in the school as a volunteer for about a year.

In this chapter, I recount one aspect of my doctoral thesis to discuss the relationships between parental concerns and pupils' participation in ability groups. I begin with a brief account of group work, the ways it has been conceptualized in primary classrooms and their relevance for my research. I reflect on my experiences of developing an interest in studying primary pupils' interactions in their classrooms and narrate my experiences of becoming an ethnographic participant observer of the routinely organized classroom activities in a primary school. Through this, I illustrate the role of ethnographic principles in identifying relationships between pupils' classroom experiences and their households. In conclusion, the chapter highlights the importance of adopting inductive and open-ended approaches to explore classroom practices linked with the distinctive social and educational needs of the pupils in multilingual educational settings.

Group work

Group work is a renowned instructional pedagogy which can enable pupils to interact and communicate with others to achieve common goals (Galton and Hargreaves 2009). Pupils are expected to cooperate and collaborate with their peers (Lazarowitz 2008) to work, think and make sense of the given activities together in groups (Mercer 2002: 1). The emphasis on group work as an educational strategy emerged in the 1970s. Research on group work (Johnson and Johnson 2002) identified that peer interaction and collaboration can be an effective means to enhance pupils' achievements and to maximize their learning opportunities.

The relationship between pupils' interactions and their cognitive and social development is highlighted in the constructivist theories of Vygotsky and Piaget (Howe and Mercer 2010). The theories assert that pupils interact and learn from one another through participating in group-based activities (Baines et al. 2009). Pupils communicate, share ideas, confront and elaborate their knowledge based on one another's views and contributions (Webb et al. 2009). According to the Piagetian perspective, language facilitates change in pupils' thinking and cognitive abilities. Piaget claims that learners assimilate new information with their existing knowledge while interacting with others (Meggitt 2012). In the Vygotskyan perspective, thought is the internalized form of language. Vygotsky claims that language plays a major role in constructing people's thinking when they interact with the outside world. People use language to communicate with others and later on, the language is internalized to control their inner thinking (Bruner 1978). Therefore, thought and speech are related processes in both Piagetian and Vygotskyan views (Vygotsky 1986: 119), and interaction is vital for learning. In educational settings, the claims of such constructivist theories, which link peer interaction with pupils' cognitive and social development, are put into practice in the form of group work. There is an extensive body of research (Wegerif et al. 1999; Mercer and Littleton 2007; Baines et al. 2008; Gillies 2014) based on either Piagetian or Vygotskyan views, which advocates group work as a means to enhance pupils' cognitive, social and moral development. In the current educational system, group work is mostly organized in forms of performance and ability-based groups. In English primary classrooms, pupils are usually grouped in high, average and low ability groups, mostly based on their end of year's academic attainment.

The concept of assessing pupils' abilities to group them according to their innate intelligence emerged in the early 1930s in the British primary educational system. From then, the debates among policy makers, either to assess pupils' innate abilities/intelligences to teach them accordingly in different schools or to introduce comprehensive education for pupils according to their interests and learning needs have continued for many decades (Cox 2011). From the 1990s, the emergence of the National Curriculum and the introduction of statutory programmes of study required all school teachers to differentiate learning to teach core subjects. The statutory programmes (DFE 2014) considered ability groups as the best way to foster differentiated teaching, matched to the distinctive learning demands of pupils to maximize their achievements. Ability-based differentiation was presented as a suitable pedagogy to raise pupils' learning standards (Hallam and Ireson 2007). From the 1990s onwards, in most primary classes, pupils are grouped in two main (fixed and mixed) ability groups.

As a primary teacher and teacher educator in Pakistan, I always recommended pedagogical practices from the Western educational system because of their interactive nature. Interactive and child-centred educational activities including group work (Gillies 2008) claim to encourage pupils' participation in teaching and learning processes. My idealization of group work as a means to enhance social interactions among pupils was shaken when I found pupils discussing with each other their placements in various ability groups. Once, during a stay in the United Kingdom, I overheard pupils talking about their placements in high ability groups and stereotyping their peers due to their being placed in low ability groups. I heard them saying things like, 'I don't want to play with her as she is in the low group.' This made me begin to think about the role of ability-based groups in developing and effecting social interactions among pupils. Research has shown that interaction with others pupils can participate in socio-cognitive discussion to elaborate their thinking (Tolmie et al. 2010), and can generate discussions among more and less competent peers to create existing and potential zones for their development (Daniels et al. 2007). At the same time, pupils' dialogues about their placements in particular ability groups appeared to me discriminatory and perhaps very different from the theoretical expectations of group work with which I was familiar. Pupils' remarks about their placements in high ability groups made me wonder; why is it important for them to befriend or play with their peers from high ability groups only? I started questioning the role of ability-based groups in influencing pupils' attitudes to participation during their group work.

There is an extensive body of research on group work (e.g. Baines et al. 2008, Gillies 2014, Franke et al. 2015), which has attempted to identify the ways in which it promotes social interactions (Blatchford and Baines 2007), task-related discussions (Howe and Mercer 2010) and productive social behaviours (Gillies 2008) among pupils. However, most of this research is conducted through experimental research design. In it, teachers, as well as pupils, seem to have a limited role, only to respond to the tightly structured questionnaires. It seemed to me there was a gap for an in-depth, longitudinal and ethnographic-based research study to explore pupils' own perspectives on group work. In my own research into pupils' group work in a mainstream multicultural classroom, I came to know that there can be various factors in pupils' educational, as well as their social, contexts which can influence their participation inside the classroom. These factors may include pupils' classroom context, the classroom itself, parental teaching and their distinctive sociocultural backgrounds. In this chapter, I recount one aspect of my doctoral thesis to discuss the influences of parental concerns on pupils' participation in ability groups. I demonstrate how the application of ethnographic research principles enabled me to identify these factors and to advocate the application of ethnographic-based research methods and methodologies to research pupils' participations in multicultural classrooms.

The study

I was interested in exploring pupils' interactions and the influences of pupils' educational and social contexts on their participations in ability groups following the principles of open-ended ethnographic research.

The processes of generating and collecting data in ethnographic research are very different from collecting data from other research paradigms (Sapsford and Jupp 2006). Ethnographic fieldwork in itself is a learning process that can bring chaos, frustrations and confusions (Blommaert and Aa 2011). During my fieldwork, I went through all these emotional states. I did my fieldwork in a state primary school situated in a highly diverse and multicultural area in Leeds. University students enrolled in the nearby campuses were among the families living around the school. I was familiar with the school context due to volunteering there for a year. I contacted the head teacher as a gatekeeper to negotiate access and recruit pupils and their class teacher to my research. After overcoming various pitfalls, I managed to begin my fieldwork in one Year Five class. My fieldwork lasted for almost a year due to the unpredictable processes that emerged during the data collection.

Developing the researcher role

In the beginning, the ethnographer is seen as an outsider (Hymes 1996). Because I had worked as a volunteer and helper in the school, I began my fieldwork with a little understanding about the particular classroom, teaching activities, the class teacher and pupils. I began my project in the Year Five classroom by familiarizing myself with the classroom context and also negotiating through information sheets and conversations with the class teacher, pupils and their parents about their participation. Gaining their consent to begin my observations took nearly a month. Afterwards, I began to formally observe pupils' group work in fixed and mixed ability groups. I took notes of pupils' interactions, their conversations, and verbal and non-verbal expression while working with others in group or pair work. My process of writing field notes began with the general and moved to the specific. Initially, I took notes of the school infrastructure, building, staff, parents and community in order to develop an understanding about the classroom context. Later on, I limited my observational lens to record details of the pupils' interactions only. I recounted pupils' actions, their conversations and behaviour towards their peers to analyze the nature of their interactions in ability-based groups. I also noticed the social environment including the physical setting, group structure, the group's members, learning tasks and other relevant details to understand the context of pupils' interactions. I took snapshots of the classroom, pupils' work and samples of teaching plans, which helped me to remember details about place, participants and all other significant moments after the fieldwork (Fabian 2008). Prior permission was gained from the head teacher, class teacher, pupils and their parents before taking snapshots of the classroom, pupils and their work. However, as Renold et al. (2008) assert, informed consent in ethnographic participative research inquiries is not limited to getting nonambiguous permission and the signing of agreement forms. Therefore, on each occasion when I intended to take photos, I asked my participants including the class teacher and pupils whether they want to be photographed or not in order to respect their rights of ownership (Prosser and Schwartz 1998). The photos were taken by me and were solely used in the reporting of my dissertation. These were not shared publicly during my formal and informal academic discussions with others to make my participants less recognizable in the public spheres.

In addition to taking notes, with consent from the class teacher and the parents, I used a digital audio recorder to record pupils' conversations electronically. These recordings helped me to recall teaching plans, learning tasks and the pupils who were involved in the particular conversations. In the beginning, pupils were conscious of being recorded and got involved in irrelevant conversations, which disrupted my observations. However, after negotiating with the class teacher, I placed the audio recorder in corners of the classroom, which helped to make pupils calm and respond naturally, and allowed me to record pupils in their normal lessons. Permission had been taken from pupils' parents beforehand to record their children in this way during their group work. At the same time, I also took further notes of pupils' conversations, which I used as a backup to amplify the recordings with additional details. This meant that I could not avoid capturing some of the less relevant voices and conversations that were happening in the classroom at the time. I felt content that I had attempted to capture detailed descriptions of the event that was my focus, but I ended up having very long recordings with low quality sound, which were difficult to transcribe later on.

Some issues in roles and relationships

Ethnographic fieldwork requires face-to-face direct interaction between researchers and participants in a real, situated environment. This brings unpredictability and complexity during the processes of data generation and collection (Blommaert 2009). While I was transforming my role from a participant to an observer, I found some of the things that I had become accustomed to in the field had changed. I was familiar with the classroom's physical structure and teaching and learning practices organized in it. The pupils were also familiar with me and with my presence in their classroom. They were aware that I would observe their group work, as we had discussed this during the process of gaining informed consent. But I found that it was difficult to maintain trustworthy relations with the class teacher. Initially, she treated me well, explaining her teaching plans which helped me to understand the classroom practices. However, this cooperation fluctuated once I started observing pupils in her classroom. The relationship between me as an observer and her as an informant was transformed, perhaps because of the observer's effect (Blommaert and Jie 2010). For instance, whenever I sat with a group of pupils to observe them, she would also join that group and start explaining the lesson to the pupils. It was normal practice that the pupils needed the teacher's instructions to complete their tasks appropriately, but I felt it a bit unusual when she remained there almost throughout the lesson. To some extent, my observations were spoiled because I was focusing on peer interaction among pupils and the extended presence of the class teacher seemed to limit opportunities for them to interact with one another. I wondered if the class teacher perhaps misunderstood me, and doubted my presence in her classroom, despite the fact that I had clearly communicated the purposes of my research to her before starting the project.

Similarly, I was keen to discuss my experiences of working with the pupils during the break time with her. This had been the usual practice during my volunteer work and at the beginning of the fieldwork. Later, when I attempted to discuss anything related to pupils' group work or about their interactions after observing them, she appeared to respond to me reluctantly. She seemed to doubt my inquiries as an observer and outsider. The hesitation of the class teacher seemed to confirm the idea that, though ethnographic researchers take part in their participants' lives as a member of their communities, they are not perceived as normal members (Blommaert and Aa 2011). There may have been several personal, emotional, ideological and cultural aspects of my personality which influenced my relationship (Al-Natour 2011) with her. For instance, I was a university student observing her classroom for my research, so I might have been perceived as an expert due to my pursuing a higher level degree. Also, my sociocultural background was different from hers. Moreover, I was already familiar with the school before, whereas she was a newly appointed teacher. Despite all these differences, removing such confusions and contradictions to maintain trustworthy relations with the class teacher was essential for me. Hence to overcome these confusions, I decided to share my field notes and other details relevant to pupils' group work with her. After reading those a couple of times, she seemed to be less bothered by my presence in her classroom. Sharing field notes with the class teacher helped me to gain her trust. It also aided me to ensure the accuracy of my observations. I was able to correct invalid descriptions of my field notes, according to the teacher's feedback. For instance, once I found a participant from a low ability group was a slow writer: however, on sharing my notes with the class teacher, I came to know that she had weak eyesight; therefore, she took time to copy things from the board. Similar kinds of discussion were helpful to identify the influences of 'outsiderness' on my field notes and improve my data recording (Barbara 2005).

Coping with unpredictability

In ethnographic fieldwork researchers focus on human beings so, they cannot follow a pre-set plan or outline to gather data from the field. Researchers' plans are constantly adjusted and readjusted to accommodate the unforeseen circumstances that emerge in the field. Several times I could not follow my preplanned observational schedule. Sometimes, I planned to observe my participants and made all arrangements for recording and observing, but had to postpone my observations due to unpredictable events in the classroom. For instance, once I could not complete my observation of a participant in the low ability group because of the arrival of a guest, which changed the lesson format. Another time, I intended to observe pair work in the mixed ability group, but the planned pair work was changed into group work due to the nature of the experiment. In their groups, the pupils became very noisy and it became difficult to concentrate on their actions. Every so often, I had to switch my role from researcher to support teacher, and this restricted me from observing or interviewing pupils. After going through these unpredictable processes, I concluded that data generation in ethnographic work needs to be flexible. Researchers need an open heart and mind to accept that, while we may get huge amounts of data one day, it is more likely that we spend days without having any data (Blommaert 2009). Therefore, we need to possess and demonstrate flexibility, adaptability and open-mindedness to go through the challenges and obstacles to successfully complete the intense fieldwork.

Making sense of the data

Ethnographic research is inductive in its nature. It studies empirical data and generates theories from the data (Fabian 1983). Ethnographers enter in the field with some theoretical knowledge and use their data to challenge or extend the theories (Charmaz 2006). In following ethnographic principles, I did not set a tentative hypothesis (Emerson et al. 2011) about the nature of pupils' interactions in group work as either cooperative and helpful or noncooperative and unhelpful. I treated my data as emergent without hypothesizing any theory to draw specific conclusions. I collected data in the form of lengthy observational recordings, which I transcribed, and field notes. I used qualitative data analysis computer software (NVivo) to arrange, sort and classify the gathered data. In ethnographic inquiry, participants' language is perceived as situated in their social lives (Hymes 1996). I analyzed the pupils' language as a social performance which creates, as well as represents, a social phenomenon (Morgan 2010). This seemed to serve as a functional tool to understand the social world around the pupils and their links with various social and cultural groups (Gee 2011: 176). I analyzed the pupils' words as a representation of their social, institutional and cultural backgrounds to explore the situated meanings that they constructed in their specific contexts (Gee 2011). In the following section, I explain how the application of ethnographic principles helped me to explain the complexity of the observed events (Hymes 1983), their 'truth' from the pupils' perspectives and to explain the influences of pupils' contexts on their interaction while working in ability groups.

Discussion

My analysis of both observational and interview data suggested that pupils exhibited both cooperative and noncooperative interactions towards their peers while working under different group structures. Prominent features of their interactions included competition and gender segregation, which influenced them to behave noncooperatively towards their peers. By ignoring or not listening to their peers, they showed that they did not seem to want to help or to be helped by their peers. They appeared to segregate their peers on the basis of their gender. I began to wonder about the factors which affected pupils to exhibit such kinds of noncooperative interaction. In this section, I explain the role of the ethnographic research approach in helping me to identify the relationships between pupils' participation and their sociocultural backgrounds, which seemed to be influential in generating noncooperation among the pupils in the immediate classroom setting.

The ethnographic approach enables researchers to understand their participants holistically by considering both microscopic and macroscopic (Blommaert and Jie 2010: 12) contexts. I focused on the pupils' micro classroom context to elicit its role in influencing them to exhibit competition towards their peers. My data about the composition of group structures and the learning tasks helped me to identify the relationships between the micro classroom context and pupils' interactions. It revealed how pupils made sense of the learning environments in which their teacher placed them to work in groups. For instance, I show below an extract from pupils' group work in which they interpreted the allocation of individual work sheets as evidence that they needed to do individual work, and did not need to interact with their peers to take help from them. I also exemplify the processes I adopted to analyze my data ethnographically.

Babar: why have you written 26?
Ahsan: it's partitioning
Babar: it's not partitioning. We are doing division man.
Ahsan: no I'm right.
Babar: I am telling you how to do it
Ahsan: no I'm doing my own I can do it....miss gave me my own sheet.
Babar: you can ask me for help...you can ask miss as well
(Extract from fixed ability group work, 21/10/13 between 10:05-10:40)

Contextualization: Pupils in an average ability group were given individual task sheets to solve in a numeracy lesson. The given task sheets comprised the same mathematical questions in different sequences. Each pupil tried to finish their own questions. They were sitting close so they could see one another's notebook.

Analytical commentary: Ahsan refused to accept his peer's feedback to correct his work. He denied his fault and refused to change his answer. He emphasized that the class teacher gave him his own (individual) work. Therefore, he did not need to interact with someone or to get help from them. The individualistic group structure of the particular classroom seems to encourage competition among pupils. It seems to serve as a hurdle which prevents pupils from discussing their work or listening to one another's suggestions to improve their work. The pupils considered that they were not expected to interact with others and failed to develop positive interdependency to work together as a group. Consequently, they reacted negatively towards their peers by rejecting their feedback to correct their mistakes.

Discussion: The level of cooperation among the pupils was not entirely dependent on pupils themselves. The teaching strategies to group pupils in an individualistic group structure played an important role in influencing and constructing pupils' interactions as noncooperative. The pupils were not interlinked with shared or common goals (Johnson et al. 2008) to work cooperatively as a group. The allocation of individual work was interpreted as evidence that they were expected to do things individually. Pupils' inferences that they were not expected to interact or work together generated competition and mistrust among them.

As shown in the given example, ethnographic principles allowed me to capture the social, educational and organizational factors that shaped and constrained the social actions of the pupils in a classroom setting (Blommaert 2009). I was able to analyze the influences of the micro classroom structures, as well as the macro organizational structures, which influenced the pupils to be competitive. Teaching strategies in English state primary classrooms are planned and designed according to the specifications of the National Curriculum (Tomlinson 2004) which, as identified in the above extract, seem to hinder the cooperation among pupils through implementing ability groups with individually designed teaching content (Cazden 2001).

I was able to analyze the influences of the micro classroom structures, as well as the macro organizational structures, which are interlinked to influence pupils to be competitive. For instance, observational data also revealed that pupils' sociocultural backgrounds also seemed to play an important role in encouraging competition and gender-based noncooperation among pupils. The sociocultural backgrounds and pupils' ethnicities are positioned as macro structures in the organizational ecology of the classroom (Johnson 2008). I interviewed pupils informally to explore their perspectives on the nature of competition that they showed during their group work. Pupils referenced their parents who inculcated the importance of getting good grades in them. Here I quote one of the pupils from high ability group (I = interviewer; P = participant):

I: So do your parents know your level?
P: Yeah. They ask me every day after school when I go home what did you learn at school how was it and they are happy with my levels? *(... pause of informal discussion)*
I: How do you think can good levels help you in your life?
P: hhhhh... just so I will get good job and it will be easier for me like to have a good job
(Extract from interview with a pupil from the high ability group on 6/12/13 at 2:45)

The participant mentioned that he is encouraged by his parents to consider good academic records as means of gaining a better position in society (Thapar and Sanghera 2010). The particular pupil was of British Asian ethnicity. In such cultures, academic success is not linked with individuals' quests for knowledge only, but it is also considered as a means of bringing success, fame, pride and wealth to the family (Tao and Hong 2014: 112). Pupils in Asian communities often strive hard to do better in education to fulfil parents' and significant others' expectations. They consider superiority in academic achievement as an obligatory endeavour (Tao and Hong 2014), which motivates them to focus on their individual performances. In the above extract, the participant's parents appear to have inculcated the importance of getting good results in their child. They construct the job sector as competitive in which good academic grades are vital. Parental concerns about pupils' academic grades appear to motivate the pupils to concentrate on their individual work and success. Consequently, they disregard the importance of interacting and learning from others during their group work.

Similarly, parental influence also remained prominent in influencing pupils to show gender-biased noncooperative interactions towards their peers. Pupils appeared to create gender-based identities for themselves and for their peers. Gender segregation seemed to serve as a prominent influence to inspire pupils to be noncooperative with other-sex peers. Pupils preferred to be grouped and worked with same-sex peers only (Mehta and Strough 2009). The pupils and the class teacher clearly saw pupils' sociocultural backgrounds as a main factor behind their gender-biased interactions. The class teacher did not organize mixed gender group work due to respecting pupils' social, cultural and religious backgrounds and adopting a culturally sensitive approach (Gonzalez 2005). However, my analysis from my perspective of sharing the same sociocultural background as the pupils enables me to identify that the pupils' decisions for working with same-sex peers are not linked with their religion, as the teacher seemed to think. Pupils also appeared to mistakenly link it with religion, whereas it is more part of their cultural norms as practised in various social settings, including their homes and schools. Their religion (Islam) in itself does not create sex segregation. However, the problems of gender division in Muslim communities arise when many followers, despite following the fundamental tenets of the same religion (Basit 2012), adopt various religious affiliations influenced by their distinctive ethnic origins, local cultures and day-to-day interactions (Basit 2012: 408). So, pupils confused religion with culture and appeared to exhibit sex segregation, portraying it as a fixed pattern of behaviour (Gonzalez 2005) which cannot be addressed by their class teacher.

The deep analysis of the data showed that the individualist and competitive structures present in the social and cultural lives of the pupils influenced their educational lives (Rogoff 2003; Bakker et al. 2007). This encouraged pupils to concentrate on their individual work and ignore the affordances for collaborative learning offered by working in groups.

Conclusions

The application of open-ended and flexible research principles of ethnography made it possible for me to participate in pupils' educational lives for an extended period of time. They enabled me to explore and identify the relationships between pupils' micro and macro contexts including the classroom and broader sociocultural backgrounds, which can influence pupils' performances in the classroom setting. The close exploration of pupils' interactions in this way enabled me to conclude that their sociocultural interpretations of success, competition and gender affected the nature of their interactions during their group work. Pupils' relationships with classroom, home and community contexts influenced them to interpret the assigned learning tasks, group placement, gender identities and academic success in specific ways to concentrate on individual performance, and thus undermine the importance of collaborative group work. The identification of such relationships and their influences requires recognition and attention from policy makers, educational researchers and class teachers to better understand pupils' interactions as part of successful group work.

Some methodological conclusions

As an ethnographic researcher, I attempted in my study to balance both etic and emic lenses (Hammersley and Atkinson 2007) to gain a holistic understanding of my participants and their context (Young 2005). My understanding of the theoretical underpinnings of group work facilitated an etic approach to identify the relationships between pupils' classroom contexts and their interactions. Along with this, my emic perspective because of sharing cultural backgrounds with the pupils enabled me to critically interpret the relationships between pupils' interactions and their social and cultural backgrounds. One outcome of this for me is the realization that class teachers need to work closely with educational researchers to adopt sociocultural and critical perspectives to understand their pupils' performances and interactions from diverse cultural perspectives. Teachers can collaborate with researchers to investigate and understand the personal, social, cultural and national norms that exist in pupils' social lives and influence their educational lives. Class teachers need opportunities to participate in open-ended and qualitative modes of exploration to understand the social contexts of pupils' households, which can reveal factors such as the competitive and gender-divided structures revealed in my study. Educational researchers can illuminate the communicative barriers between schools and pupils' households to assist teachers to conceptualize the norms of interactions that exist in pupils' social worlds. Teachers can integrate the learned knowledge about pupils' households into classroom pedagogies to encourage cooperation and mixed gender group work in multicultural classrooms. Their research-informed efforts to integrate pupils' social and cultural values into classroom practices need to be recognized by educational policy makers, who – in turn – need to support initiatives to make learning processes consistent with pupils' educational, social and cultural needs.

Chapter 9

Al-Natour, R.J. (2011), 'The Impact of the Researcher on the Researched', *A Journal of Media and Culture*, 14 (6). Available at: http://www.journal .media-culture.org.au/index.php/mcjournal/article/viewArticle/428 (accessed 4 January 2017).

Baines, E., Blatchford, P. and Kutnick, P. (2008), 'Pupil Grouping for Learning: Developing a Social Pedagogy of the Classroom', in R. Gillies, A. Ashman and J. Terwell (eds), *The Teacher's Role in Implementing Cooperative Learning in the Classroom*, 56–72, New York: Springer-Verlag.

Baines, E., Davies, C.R. and Blatchford, P. (2009), 'Improving Pupil Group Work Interaction and Dialogue in Primary Classrooms: Results from a Year-long Intervention Study', *Cambridge Journal of Education*, 39(1): 95–117.

Bakker, J., Denessen, E. and Brus-Laeven, M. (2007), 'Socio-economic Background, Parental Involvement and Teacher Perceptions of these in Relation to Pupil Achievement', *Educational Studies in Mathematics*, 33(2): 177–192.

Barbara, B.K. (2005), 'Participant Observation as a Data Collection Method', *Forum Qualitative Sozialforschung /Forum: Qualitative Social Research*, 6(2): Art. 43.

Basit, T.N. (2012), '... But That's Just the Stereotype': Gender and Ethnicity in Transition to Adulthood', *Race, Ethnicity and Education*, 15 (3): 405–423.

Blatchford, P. and Baines, E. (2007), *Pupil Grouping Strategies and Practices at Key Stages 2 and 3*, Research Report 796. Nottingham.

Blommaert, J. (2009), 'On Hymes: Introduction', *Text and Talk*, 29(3): 241–243.

Blommaert, J. and Aa, J.V.D. (2011), 'Ethnographic Monitoring: Hymes' Unfinished Business in Educational Research', *Anthropology and Education Quarterly*, 42(4): 319–334.

Blommaert, J. and Jie, D. (2010), *Ethnographic Field Work: A Beginner's Guide*, Bristol: Multilingual Matters.

Bruner, J.S. (1978), 'The Role of Dialogue in Language Acquisition', in A.J. Sinclair, R. Jarvella and W.J.M. Levelt (eds), *The Child's Conception of Language*, 241–256, Germany: Springer-Verlag.

Cazden, C.B. (2001), *Classroom Discourse: The Language of Teaching and Learning*, Portsmouth: Heinemann.

Charmaz, K. (2006), *Constructing Grounded Theory: A Practical Guide through Qualitative Analysis*, London: Sage Publications.

Cox, S. (2011), *New Perspectives in Primary Education: Meaning and Purpose in Learning and Teaching*, New York: Open University Press.

Daniels, H., Cole, M. and Wertsch, V.J. (2007), 'Inside and Outside the Zone of Proximal Development: An Eco-functional Reading of Vygotsky', *The Cambridge Companion to Vygotsky*, 276–331, Cambridge: Cambridge University Press.

Department for Education (2014), *The National Curriculum Framework*. Available at: https://www.gov.uk/government/collections/national-curriculum (accessed 4 January 2017).

Emerson, R.M., Fretz, R.I. Shaw, L.L. (2011), *Writing Ethnographic Field Notes*, Chicago: University of Chicago Press.

Fabian, J. (1983), *Time and the Other: How Anthropology Makes Its Object*, New York: Columbia University Press.

Fabian, J. (2008), *Ethnography as Commentary: Writing from the Virtual Archive*, Durham: Duke University Press.

Franke, M.L., Turrou, A.C., Webb, N.M., Ing, M., Wong, J., Shin, N. and Fernandez, C. (2015), 'Student Engagement with Others' Mathematical Ideas: The Role of Teacher Invitation and Support Moves', *The Elementary School Journal*, 116(1): 26–148.

Galton, M. and Hargreaves, L. (2009), 'Group Work: Still a Neglected Art?', *Cambridge Journal of Education*, 39(1): 1–6.

Gee, J.P. (2011), *An Introduction to Discourse Analysis: Theory and Method*, New York: Routledge.

Gillies, R. (2014), 'Cooperative Learning: Developments in Research', *International Journal of Educational Psychology*, 3(2): 125–140.

Gillies, R.M. (2008), 'Teachers' and Students' Verbal Behaviours during Cooperative Learning', in R. Gillies, A. Ashman and J. Terwal (eds), *The Teacher's Role in Implementing Cooperative Learning in the Classroom*, 238–257, New York: Springer.

Gonzalez, N. (2005), 'Beyond Culture: The Hybridity of Funds of Knowledge', in N. Gonzalez, L. Moll and C. Amanti (eds), *Funds of Knowledge: Theorizing*

Practices in Households, Communities and Classrooms, 24–46, New York: Routledge.

Hallam, S. and Ireson, J. (2007), 'Secondary School Pupils' Satisfaction with Their Ability Grouping Placements', *British Educational Research Journal*, 33(1): 27–45.

Hammersley, M. and Atkinson, P. (2007), *Ethnography: Principles in Practice*, London: Routledge.

Howe, C. and Mercer, N. (2010), 'Children's Social Development, Peer Interaction and Classroom Learning', in R. Alexander, C. Doddington, J. Gray, L. Hargreaves and R. Kershner (eds), *The Cambridge Primary Review Research Surveys*, 170–194, London: Routledge, Taylor and Francis.

Hymes, D. (1983), *Essays in the History of Linguistic Anthropology*, Amsterdam: John Benjamins.

Hymes, D. (1996), *Ethnography, Linguistics, Narrative Inequality: Toward an Understanding of Voice*, London: Taylor and Francis.

Johnson, D.W. and Johnson, R.T. (2002), 'Learning Together and Alone: Overview and Meta-analysis', *Asia Pacific Journal of Education*, 22(1): 95–105.

Johnson, D.W., Johnson, R.T. and Roseth, C.J. (2008), 'Promoting Early Adolescents' Achievement and Peer Relationships: The Effects of Cooperative, Competitive, and Individualistic Goal Structures', *American Psychological Association*, 134(2): 223–246.

Johnson, E.S. (2008), 'Ecological Systems and Complexity Theory: Towards an Alternative Model of Accountability in Education', *Complicity: An International Journal of Complexity and Education*, 5(1): 1–10.

Lazarowitz, R.H. (2008), 'Beyond the Classroom and into the Community: The Role of Teacher in Expanding the Pedagogy of Cooperation', in R.M. Gillies, A.F. Ashman and J. Terwal (eds), *The Teachers' Role in Implementing Cooperative Learning in the Classroom*, 38–55, New York: Springer.

Meggitt, C. (2012), *Child Development: An Illustrated Guide*, Harlow: Pearson Education.

Mehta, C.M. and Strough, J. (2009), 'Sex Segregation in Friendships and Normative Contexts Across the Life Span', *Developmental Review*, 29(3): 201–220.

Mercer, N. (2002), 'Developing Dialogues', in G. Wells and G. Claxton (eds), *Learning for Life in the 21ˢᵗ Century: Sociocultural Perspectives on the Future of Education*, 141–153, Oxford: Blackwell.

Mercer, N. and Littleton, K. (2007), *Dialogue and the Development of Children's Thinking: A Sociocultural Approach*, London: Routledge, Taylor and Francis.

Morgan, A. (2010), 'Discourse Analysis: An Overview for the Neophyte Researcher', *Journal of Health and Social Care Improvement*, 5(1): 1–7.

Prosser, J. and Schwartz, D. (1998), 'Photographs within the Sociological Research Process', in J. Prosser (ed), *Image-based Research: A Sourcebook for Qualitative Researchers*, 115–130, London: Falmer Press.

Renold, E., Holland, S., Ross, N.J., and Hillman, A. (2008), 'Becoming Participant Problematising "Informed Consent" in Participatory Research with Children and Young People in Care', *Qualitative Social Work*, 7(4): 431–451.

Rogoff, B. (2003), *The Cultural Nature of Human Development*, Oxford: Oxford University Press.

Sapsford, R. and Jupp, V. (2006), *Data Collection and Analysis*, London: Sage Publications.

Tao, V.Y.K. and Hong, Y.-Y. (2014), 'When Academic Achievement Is an Obligation: Perspectives from Social-oriented Achievement Motivation', *Journal of Cross-Cultural Psychology*, 6(1): 1–27.

Thapar, S. and Sanghera, G.S. (2010), 'Building Social Capital and Education: The Experiences of Pakistani Muslims in the UK', *International Journal of Social Inquiry*, 3(2): 3–24.

Tolmie, A.K., Topping, K.J., Christie, D., Donaldson, C., Howe, C., Jessiman, E., Livingston, K. and Thurston, A. (2010), 'Social Effects of Collaborative Learning in Primary Schools,'*Learning and Instruction*, 20(3): 177–191.

Tomlinson, C.A. (2004), 'The M'Obi'us Effect: Addressing Learner Variance in Schools', *Journal of Learning Disabilities*, 37(6): 516–524.

Vygotsky, L.S. (1986, 2012), *Thought and Language*, Cambridge: The Massachusetts Institute of Technology Press.

Webb, N.M., Franke, M.L., De, T., Chan, A.G., Freund, D., Shein, P. and Melkonian, D.K. (2009), '"Explain to Your Partner": Teachers' Instructional Practices and Students' Dialogue in Small Groups', *Cambridge Journal of Education*, 39(1): 49–70.

Wegerif, R., Mercer, N. and Dawes, S.L. (1999), 'From Social Interaction to Individual Reasoning: An Empirical Investigation of a Possible Sociocultural Model of Cognitive Development', *Learning and Instruction*, 9(6): 493–516.

Young, J. (2005), 'On Insiders (Emic) and Outsiders (Etic): Views of Self, and Othering', *Systemic Practice and Action Research*, 18(2): 151–162.

CHAPTER TEN

The Importance of Self: Insider and Outsider Perspectives on the Researcher's Role

Valerie Nave

Guiding questions

1 Valerie writes, 'I needed to take various roles in the processes of designing my project and collecting and analyzing my data.' What roles does she outline in her chapter and how does she mediate them through the course of her research? How do they relate to your own researcher roles in your project?

2 What ethical issues did Valerie face in mediating her roles as both mother and researcher? What strategies did she develop to overcome them?

Introduction

My longitudinal ethnography study explores the experiences of three multilingual primary school pupils in the north of England, whose daily languages are English and French. It highlights the tensions and contradictions families face in maintaining their home language(s) in monolingual educational systems and in the wider community. Before I began my research, in my daily life, I encountered parents who had similar experiences as me: parenting multilingual children in the United Kingdom. I decided to carry out this research after years of questioning the fact that children of mixed backgrounds gradually lose their mother tongues after a couple of generations (Fishman 1966).

In order to produce trustworthy qualitative research, social researchers must be aware of their position (insider/outsider) all through their study as it has a huge impact on the research process and outcomes. An insider approach (emic) corresponds to the point of view of a researcher who is part of the culture under study. On the other hand, the outsider insight (etic) represents the position of an investigator who has no familiarity with the researched community (Breen 2007). Assuming both roles is challenging (Gerrish 1997; DeLyser 2001), as researchers of this type often struggle to balance their diverse positions. In this chapter, I trace the ways I developed my roles to show my readers how insider/outsider perspectives can be tackled. The fact that the researcher carries heavy responsibility in describing and analyzing a culture to achieve a maximum of authenticity makes my topic noteworthy.

The starting context for my project was a French complementary school (*la petite école*) that met on Saturdays in the multilingual city where I live. My daughter was a pupil in the school and I volunteered as an assistant in her class. In order to understand how children and their families experienced and mediated their multilingualism, I tracked the experiences of five children in the class, including my daughter, in the complementary and their mainstream schools and in their homes. It took me a year of observation in addition to shared discussions with teachers, parents, friends and colleagues before I was sure of what needed to be investigated in order to highlight the complex home language experiences of the young multilingual children. One main outcome of my study was to illustrate the lack of cooperation and negotiation between the main institutions that played key roles in the children's lives: home, complementary and mainstream schools.

As can be seen from this brief description of my research, I needed to take various roles in the processes of designing my project and collecting and analyzing my data. During the data collection period, I was a member of the complementary school as an assistant inside the classroom (insider) and also a member of the university, a researcher (outsider) who, after gathering enough data, handled and analyzed them via the important perspective of the mother of one of the participants. In this chapter, I share my journey as a mother-researcher who experienced a variety of roles during the research process and reflected on them in order to validate my results. The process of researching from the inside out allowed me to access information I could not obtain if I had not been a mother. Smyth and Holian (2008) acknowledge the insider's valuable knowledge that can be collected, compared to the outsider who would spend much more time to gather similar pieces of information if only they are accessible.

The purpose of my chapter is to offer readers a self-reflexive account of my experience as a researcher with multiple roles: a researcher, a mother and also a classroom assistant in the field of multilingualism in the United Kingdom. I present my research procedure and discuss the strategies I developed during data collection and analysis to minimize the disadvantages of having a researcher's insider role. I reflect on the roles I needed to construct, and how I maintained a position that allowed me both to be an insider and also to detach myself from the mother role and become an outsider researcher when I analyzed my data.

Researcher roles

When I first started my research, I was constantly reminded by my supervisor that I had to reflect on my roles during fieldwork, especially because I was both a qualitative researcher and a mother. It was crucial to clarify my position because of its multifaceted aspects, which had advantages in validating my data, but possible disadvantages that needed to be considered and overcome. Moreover, although research regarding one's own children is increasing these days, especially in the field of language development and learning, pondering on the importance of the self is scarcely found in literature (Greene 2014).

Like Adler and Adler (1996: 35) who discussed the multiple roles a researcher may undertake and their implications because of the nature of his or her research, I will elaborate on

- role identification (e.g. who am I in each part of the research process?);

- role change (e.g. how is my role evolving from one status to another?/how does one impact on another?);

- roles in the relationships (e.g. what role do I take in a relationship with my interviewees?/relational self).

In some circumstances, I was an insider and at other times, I was an outsider, but the move from insider to outsider was not always obvious; it was at times rather a process that needed to be reflected upon in order to highlight the mother-researcher's multi- and complex identities during the transformative process. Ergun and Erdemir (2010: 16) state:

the insider-outsider relationship can be conceived as a dialectical one that is continuously informed by the differentiating perceptions that researchers and informants have of themselves and others.

Each researcher has his or her personal style and particular way to relate to their participants: I present here my own view of the insider/outsider relationship.

The journey of the self: Identifying roles and relationships

At first, when I was asked how I was going to overcome the challenge of undertaking the dual role of a mother and a researcher, I simplistically explained that in some places, I would be an insider (e.g. in the French complementary school) and in other places, I would partly be an outsider and play the role of a researcher (e.g. in the office while doing my data analysis). This kind of binary division between the two positions seemed a priori a good way to construct my multi-identities (mother, researcher, teaching assistant). I soon realized when I conducted my first interviews that it was more complicated than this: my relationship with my interviewees would necessarily be different from one individual to another, and sometimes, particularly with my daughter, in relation to the same person. Instead of thinking about the places in which I was carrying out my research, it was rather by reflecting on my own attitudes that I could develop or act roles, in sites under investigation, in relation to children, parents and teachers. My presumed roles were facilitated thanks to my multiple identities; the roles of an assistant, a teacher (on one occasion), a mother and a researcher did not have to be constructed, they were present de facto. Adler and Adler (1996: 40) state:

> [My] presence and role in the settings [...] [was] understood and expected by participants; children and the adults who surrounded them interacted with [...] [me] naturally during the course of conducting everyday business.

Being a mother-researcher is often overlooked in research (Adler and Adler 1996), but it gave me the opportunity to understand the children's worlds via my own child in a variety of contexts that were naturally occurring. My parental role has opened doors for me in places where entrée may have been difficult. Long negotiations between parents and teachers could only be managed when frequent contacts and interaction took place. As a parent interacting with a range of people (other children and their parents, Special Needs and English as an Additional Language (SEN-EAL) teachers, class teachers, complementary school teachers, headmasters and secretaries) who could impact on my daughter's home language maintenance, I benefited from deep knowledge of diverse perspectives highlighting the complex multilingual situation. My position allowed me to be readily familiar with the British educational system through my daughter and her school. Indeed, before the formal data collection stages, while preparing for my research project, I volunteered as a 'helping mum' in the different classrooms of my daughter's school in order to gather data on the school approach towards home languages.

I was part of a variety of interactions with my daughter-participant's friends, classmates, secretaries, teachers (mainstream and complementary), headmasters, headmistresses and neighbours. I also happened to be part of activities that took place in the complementary school such as coffee mornings, school festivals and pedagogical meetings as a parent or teacher assistant. I attended all of these events naturally because of my various roles, and they also enriched my research process offering a range of opportunities for observing and discussing cultural, social and linguistic matters with French mothers as an insider. This led to my finding that parents found it hard to contribute to home language maintenance. As an outsider interested in EAL, I remember sitting informally among mainstream school teachers and mentors who chatted over issues they encountered when multilingual children with little English registered in their school. I noticed then that EAL pupils were often seen as a problem. Thus, as I moved forward, I was able to pinpoint what was causing tensions among monolingual teachers, as well as multilingual families. Experiences such as these were key in my developing research design. Issues I knew about in the field of home language maintenance, which were occurring in my personal life, and also in many other multilingual families, led me to investigate on the policy of three multilingual families, as well as of other educational institutions.

Most of the time, my various roles (researcher, mother, assistant) merged into one another, but there were times when I deliberately split my roles in order to clarify my task in hand. For example, when I had finished a set of interviews and after transcribing them, I needed to distance myself from my data to consider issues of bias. Instead of working at home which was my normal practice, I went and sat at my university workstation where the fact that I was in a formal institution surrounded by other PhD students helped me to move into a researcher's state of mind. This enabled me to develop criticality and to question my initial position if the new cases showed this was appropriate. In fact, months of training and writing descriptions of what I had noticed before the data collection period were very helpful in moving away from my parental role and reminding myself that my emotions involved in this piece of research needed to be reined in. To avoid bias, other researchers such as Unluer (2012: 8) try hard to consider:

> [her] research within the current social circumstance and by clarifying the research process and the researcher role while writing the research report.

Actually, an ethnographic study requires a transparent explanation of the research process, which optimizes the objectivity of the project. Rooney (2005) suggests that the impact of bias could be addressed by enlisting the help of another researcher who is not engaged in the same type of research. Consulting my PhD colleagues was also part of my practice. This surely supported me to observe my data with a more objective eye.

Parent/researcher tensions

Issues about parental roles as researchers have only recently begun to be addressed because of the fact that there are not many studies whose participants are children and particularly the researcher's child. There are many ethical issues, which can lead to ethics committees in some universities rejecting proposals which involve research on one's own child, such as the concentration of the research on one individual, the age of participant, relationships between the participant and the researcher, and so on. Other institutional ethics committees have accepted such proposals, 'as long as [...] [parents] restricted [...][themselves] to interacting naturalistically within the confines of the "parental" role' (Adler and Adler 1996: 54). In order to minimize the ethical problems, I added other participants to my research design. Thus, the focus of the study was not entirely directed onto my daughter. At the same time, keeping my daughter as one of the participants benefited my research, thanks to easy access to my own child's world and for many other reasons, as I discuss below. Obviously, any researcher who crosses the boundaries of the parental role and other roles needs to work by the formal ethical procedures of gaining consent while maintaining confidentiality and anonymity, avoiding sensitive matters in questioning, and maintaining the full right for participants and actors to opt out of various forms of data collection.

Researching with my daughter

A doctorate implies years of investigation, which can heavily affect the child-parent relationship. Adler and Adler recognize this, and discuss how studying their own children and community may impinge upon researchers' relationships with their children or other community members (1996: 45). This said, the fact that one of my participants was constantly available for me to observe, discuss, question in formal and informal circumstances, in public and private places and during term time and holidays was undoubtedly an advantage of great value. My immersion in the life of my daughter was very valuable in highlighting the complexity of interactions between multilingual children and monolingual individuals in the light of maintaining their home languages. This reinforced the validity of the research through capturing and portraying a more comprehensive picture of multilingual children's experiences in preserving their home language(s) that could then triangulate the data I was able to gather from the other children in the study. As mentioned below in my account of the research procedure, my position as a mother-researcher was an advantage that offered me plenty of opportunities to triangulate data and thus validate my outcome. I benefited from several sources of information with which I could grasp a sense of participants' and actors' perspectives on home language maintenance.

In effect, my daughter really became a co-researcher; her consistent willingness to answer my questions and her thorough understanding of what my research was about contributed significantly to the richness of the naturally occurring data, although there were times when I had to make sensitive judgements about when it was most appropriate to approach her. I did not want to intrude into her personal life at all times. I was also aware of the feeling of boredom that could be caused for her by my investigation or with my topics I wanted to know about that could have been overwhelming and could have jeopardized my research outcome. For example, she did not want me to talk to her mainstream teacher about particular issues taking place in the school. On several occasions, because my child was very concerned about her teachers' and peers opinions of herself in her mainstream school, I had to negotiate tactfully with her class teacher through emails and once through face-to-face discussion, requesting her to be discreet. She wanted to keep a low profile, as she did not want to be different from the rest of the class. Comments such as 'you are the teacher's pet' did not please her or at other times, a pupil mentioned to the language teacher that 'Emilie speaks French to her mother every day and so she must know well the gender of a noun in French.' Emilie was ridiculed by the teacher who retorted that 'if she was French, she would not have made any mistake', pointing out her homework. Obviously this particular teacher had not grasped the concept of being multilingual. A series of small events such as the ones exemplified above led to Emilie's withdrawal into herself, attempting to become invisible in the French class. For example, she could spend several lessons without being addressed. She dedicated her time doing extra exercises at her mother's request. No comment or correction was suggested to value her effort.

Research procedure

At the beginning of my project, I intended to explore mainly the government's policies on multilingualism, but as the research progressed, I quickly realized that the driving force in this study was the families and their relationships with other institutions. Thus, the project focused on multilingual English/French children, and became an investigation of the home language experiences of three multilingual families in home, mainstream and complementary schools. My aim was to capture a better insight into the factors that could lead to language shift and possible language loss.

Selecting participants and collecting data

The final design of my project was an ethnographic study involving five ten-year-old multilingual French/English-speaking children whose mothers were French (except one who was Belgian), and fathers were British (except one who was Iraqi). They were all from upper working-class to middle-class families (this was decided according to level of educational qualifications, job/ home and car ownership/occasional family holidays). They were all in the same class in their French complementary school. I contacted all the pupils' parents just before the summer holidays. This was done through the headmistress, who emailed all the parents inviting them to a meeting in the complementary school, where I offered them coffee, tea and brioche and presented them with my research project. Two parents out of seven attended. They showed much interest in my topic as they genuinely wanted to understand more about multilingualism in our context, Yorkshire, in the United Kingdom. Following this, two other parents responded positively through emails and informal conversations to my request. At last, I had five participants including my daughter. I asked them to fill a consent form which contained a description of my research topic, a list of data collection tools and a timeline showing the approximate dates of interviews and observations. The data collection was planned to last over an academic year, with one observation in each child's mainstream school. In addition, I asked parents to write a diary on their family's language experiences at home three times during the year of data collection in order to help me grasp a more comprehensive view about the home linguistic and sociocultural situation.

I also collected data from the five child-participants through conducting fifteen semi-structured interviews with them and ten interviews with their parents (in most cases with the mothers). By organizing my interviews with the participants in three different phases, I could trace both the consistencies and the contradictions in the participants' beliefs about their home language and triangulate the data resulting from the perspectives of my participants and those close to them (Denzin 1989). Furthermore, as the data collection progressed, I could question certain beliefs and attitudes in the second or third phase of interviews and deepen my general understanding of the processes of retaining home language in the United Kingdom.

The data collection started in the complementary French school in CM2 (*Cours Moyen 2*) where the five participants gathered every week for two-and-half hours on Saturday mornings. In their English mainstream schools, four participants were in Year Five and one in Year Six. I first interviewed the five participants, as well as their teacher, after an observation session in unoccupied rooms or corridors in the complementary school. Following that, I met parents in their homes where I also interviewed them on their background and language practices. I conducted the same procedure three times with the children in the complementary school and twice with the parents, one at the beginning of the study and one towards the end. I eventually managed to visit three mainstream schools, undertook three observations and interviewed teachers including two SEN-EAL teachers at the end of the data collection period in order to highlight other forces and other settings impacting on home language maintenance. Apart from the participants' homes and two of the mainstream schools I visited, I was familiar with all other settings. In one of the cases, when I asked him if I could contact one of the participants' mainstream schools, the child's father objected, fearing that it would lead to his child's French identity (and so his 'difference') being reinforced. At first, I was concerned that my dataset would not be complete. However, I soon understood that the refusal actually reflected the family's challenges while raising their multilingual children in a specific setting. The father's reason for refusing was thus significant and worth analyzing. This shows that undertaking social research demands permanent consideration and reflection on the participants and actors' reactions and responses. All data are important and meaningful in this particular type of ethnographic research. In the other case study where I could not gain access to the school, the headmaster apologized as he could not accommodate me due to the teachers' busy schedules.

I believe that the participants' age helped to gain naturally occurring information because ten-year-olds are often spontaneous compared to other age groups such as adolescents, who are more self-conscious. Even when I progressed through the study, neither child-participants nor the complementary class teacher behaved differently. The interview schedules developed gradually through my numerous informal discussions with participants and others in the different settings and a year observation in my daughter's mainstream school. I also consulted official documents mainly related to National Curriculum and other policies, and Year Five textbooks in order to capture an insight into a variety of perspectives regarding multilingualism in the United Kingdom and other similar countries (such as the United States, Canada, Australia, France and so on). I could gather copious information with my daughter as a participant, and through this draw a more comprehensive picture of the tensions the other four multilingual children and families encountered in the 'monolingualising' (Heller 1995) society in which we live. After completing five datasets on my participants, I realized I had a vast amount of data, but that two sets did not add any new concepts to the research. I then decided to focus on three participants' home language experiences for further analysis and presentation in my thesis.

Positioning myself in the research setting – Some advantages and some dilemmas

On different occasions, the place in which I was situated was the key factor in my positioning and researcher role. For example, in the complementary school, my role as an assistant superseded my position as a mother. However, if someone in the class had insulted or mocked my daughter, I would have probably reacted as a mother. That is what Adler and Adler mean when they discuss their researcher roles:

> As in any complete-member-research, our attachment was stronger to our parental membership role. We had a greater investment in this dimension because it was primary, deeper, longer lasting, and more central to our core identities and goals. (1996: 42)

As I found out in the course of my research, the parent-researcher stance affords great advantages. It was a significant element that could have influenced my research outcome either positively or negatively. I was cognizant of this possibility; thus, for any minor incident in the Saturday school classroom, I treated everybody the same way when they transgressed the teacher's set of good conduct rules or when they needed help with their exercises. However, my dual position involved the enforcement of certain obligations. I was surely more concerned about my daughter's performance than her classmates' but attempted to hide the fact that I was related to her even though my relationship with her was constantly apparent, since she called me 'Maman' in the playground and in the classroom.

I often managed to combine both roles of parent/researcher in most settings without encountering objections. However, the demands of my role could sometimes prevent me from gaining useful information. I overcame this issue through negotiation. For example, my daughter-participant faced a time when she was bored in her French class in the mainstream school because nothing appropriate for her level was offered. My duty as a mother was to investigate and see what could be done to improve her situation. But my daughter refused to allow me to contact her teacher. On this occasion, I was torn between my role as a mother and my position as a researcher. As a matter of principle, I never intervened in my other participants' affairs because I had the strict responsibility to adopt a nonjudgemental approach while researching, whereas in my daughter's case, I simply could not remain quiet. My parental role obliged me to deal with the issue. Even though in general, teachers listened to my comments and attempted, successfully or unsuccessfully, to provide my daughter with better strategies to help her, I often found myself misunderstood when I dealt with her mainstream language teacher. I must admit that, while my parental role and intervention implied a risk that could affect my data, it surely presented fewer risks than other types of research within which the researcher is not an insider. Indeed, my membership role facilitated the exchange I needed to maintain with my participants and their parents. I am sure that the fact that I offered the parents hope to bring more light into the complexity of multilingualism in their contexts nourished reciprocal exchange. One family took opportunities to reflect on their past history of multilingual experiences. My interviews were another way that they could clarify their issues. Moreover, the fact that I supported their children in the complementary school was another factor that motivated them to pursue the research adventure.

In the public arena, the research was conducted smoothly: no one ever mentioned that they wanted to withdraw from my study. Following ethical principles, I asked my participants their permission to proceed to more investigation and every time a date was set for data collection, they always accepted my request. I assume that the parents' constant enthusiasm was certainly determined by an urge to understand the reasons why our multilingual children might struggle to preserve their home languages. In addition, the child-participants were always keen on being interviewed and videotaped. For them, it was gratifying; it was a way to have their point of view valued. In my private sphere, however, I was aware of the negative perspectives and attitudes children and sometimes parents had towards the French complementary school. I had moments of doubt about registering my daughter in this institution. However, my role as a parent was to encourage my child and make sure she received quality teaching, contributing to home language maintenance in line with the family beliefs. I was in contact with mainstream teachers who, consciously or unconsciously, could have impacted negatively on my child with regard to her home language due to the fact that they had no concept about the ways to treat a multilingual child in a class where French was taught as a second language. In fact, the teachers I interviewed had hardly received any training in EAL. I attempted to negotiate the situations in order to gain a full sense of their views on multilingual children, raising key questions that could challenge the teachers' points of view. I also contacted other parents and gained a sense of their views in order to grasp what could be done. I communicated face to face or through emails with French teachers, bearing in mind that I should never use any vocabulary of blame but rather explain to them as transparently as I could what I was trying to do.

Relationships with participants

My role as a parent-researcher reinforced my ties with certain actors in the settings under study. My close relationships with other teachers, assistants, headmistresses, parents and the pedagogical team from the complementary school opened spaces for them to assert freely their perspectives over the place of the home language in education. But I had some concern about the settings in which I would be an outsider. For example, in mainstream schools, I was a foreigner who may have been perceived as an intruder, demanding to know about teachers' attitudes towards multilingual children. Even if the meeting happened only once at the end of the data collection period, I had to reflect a great deal on the way I approached the school from the head teacher to the class teacher or even the SEN-EAL teachers. Through them, I could highlight two mainstream schools' beliefs, attitudes and practices and their impact on two multilingual children. Thus, they were a significant part of my study as they could influence heavily multilingual children's home attitudes to their languages. The fact that my daughter was a member of one of the mainstream schools afforded me various contextual data. My parental role provided me with much evidence of teachers' perspectives/ attitudes on home language and cultural matters from this point of view. My communication with other parents who were themselves multilingual with a home language different from English was also an essential source of information, extracted from naturally occurring settings. Whenever I needed to triangulate my data to confirm issues, I had easy access to data through weekly conversations with multilingual families on Saturdays or during school festivals, morning coffees or pedagogical meetings, all within the complementary school.

In the second mainstream school I visited, I was an outsider. The only element that connected me to the class teacher was my participant and his parents. To facilitate my meeting with the mainstream teacher, I first asked permission of the mother and her son if they would agree that I could consult the mainstream school in order to do an hour-long observation and one interview with the grade five teacher. They both agreed. The mother mentioned it to the school and from there, I could call the school. I talked to the secretary and explained my project. She asked me to call back after she was able to mention the scenario to the headmaster and the class teacher concerned. When I did, I was nicely welcomed and was told that I could send an email to the class teacher with a consent form attached addressed to all the classroom parents. It was a condition from the ethical committee that all the parents were informed and accepted my presence in their child's classroom. Following this procedure, the teacher agreed on a date with me. I observed the class in July while she was teaching fifty-five minutes of mathematics. After the observation, when all the children were having lunch, she sat with me in the quiet classroom where I interviewed her for forty-five minutes. At that time, to her, I was only a French female researcher with no other attribute that she was aware of. I was pleased to see that she had nineteen years of experience in a school where 50 per cent of the pupils were multilingual and multicultural children. She was British but with a culture different from her husband's. I immediately began to look for the similar characteristics I shared with her: female, European, a positive attitude to the concept of multiculturalism, to start with. The atmosphere was friendly and the meeting informative. I made sure that I was neutral in the face-to-face conversation but I am sure that the teacher might have started answering me with the preconceived idea that I was in favour of multilingualism due to my nationality and position in the French complementary school.

Whether her respect for her pupils' culture was genuine or created for the occasion, my observation revealed that she was a professional educator and showed interest to all types of pupils. In the corridor near the entrance, the school had a big photo frame which included a picture of all the pupils. This showed their pride in diversity. However, I was cautious about such information that could be said to please me as a researcher, although my longitudinal study offered me numerous details at different times and in a variety of settings with participants and actors whose perspectives on the teacher and school were valuable in my research and strengthened my outcomes. In fact, my data from the school could only be validated when I related them to the data I had from the family. I could not just rely on the teacher's words and actions to draw conclusions about the school policy regarding the value the teacher gave to her pupils' home languages or cultures because the data of one interview and one observation were not sufficient to validate my outcome.

Conclusions

I would say that, in my case, my journey as a researcher has taught me to observe without judging. It also directed me towards the concept of negotiation. I have learned that investigating on social, educational and cultural issues demands patience, time, communication skills and trustworthiness. In addition, my theoretical approach to my research guided me in putting any emerging issues in context attempting to understand a variety of layers encompassing individuals, communities, bodies and agencies interacting and influencing one another. By following this layered framework, I could highlight complex cases and bring forward the contradictions and tensions that impeded home language maintenance. My research role along with my parental role was a positive advantage. The information exchange I have experienced with my daughter seems to have enhanced our bond. This journey has empowered my child, who has often been given the space to think and decide for herself with family guidance when needed. I received much feedback from my own child asserting that my study has transformed me and the guidance she obtained through years of exchanges over French lessons and French teachers' and other monolingual teachers' attitudes has helped her to balance and reinforce her language abilities. It was not a matter of prioritizing the French language over the English language; it was about valuing both in order to facilitate communication in both languages. Furthermore, this intimacy between mother and daughter, developed during the study years, has reinforced the mother's involvement in the child's academic and her social life: a parental characteristic not negligible in the child's school life. This research took place at an age (nine to ten years old) when my child still welcomed her mother's closeness, and I had the constant insight that my participant was transparent in our discussion and that the data I accumulated from her was trustworthy.

This study has permitted me to expand on the way I accessed key settings and negotiated with participants and actors in order to gain insight into their multilingual experiences. I perceive my experience of a mother-teacher-assistant-researcher as a spectrum within which I constantly moved from a familiar setting (complementary school, home, my daughter's mainstream school to unfamiliar places such as other parents' homes and one of the participants' mainstream school). As a native speaker of French, I could easily position myself as one of the members of the French complementary school and thus facilitate the concept of trust among my participants. However, in other settings, I had to establish this idea by negotiating with schools in order to be perceived as a person who is not there for judging but rather to understand classroom or home experiences. Even within such a delicate area of research, I have been rewarded by acquiring the knowledge necessary to make a difference among multilingual individuals who often struggle to maintain their home language(s) in 'monolingualising' settings (Heller 1995: 374).

In this chapter, I have presented the way I conducted my research and introduced my readers to the multifaceted aspect of my 'self' during my investigation. I have reflected on my different roles in the research process in relation to cooperating parents, children, teachers and my personal actions and reactions in this study. I conclude that the 'self' is a concept that needs to be constantly observed and analyzed in relation to events, time, contexts and types of participants. It is a matter of awareness of one's own biases in any setting relevant to the topic under study. Rogers (2003: 18) signals a gap in the literature by affirming that 'there is still relatively little on the actual practicalities of the problem of managing the self when close to the research material'. In other articles, different writers present their experiences with the 'self'. For example, Dwyer and Buckle (2009) defend the twofold roles of the researcher within which they sometimes face the double position of an insider and outsider at the same time. They reject the dichotomous view that consists of separating the insider's position from the outsider's one. They conclude that a dialectical approach is more appropriate for a qualitative researcher whose 'self' is a key element in his or her study.

References

Adler, P.A. and Adler, P. (1996), 'Parent-as-Researcher: The Politics of Researching in the Personal Life', *Qualitative Sociology*, 19: 35–58.
Breen, L.J. (2007), 'The Researcher "in the middle": Negotiating the Insider/Outsider Dichotomy', *The Australian Community Psychologist*, 19(1): 163–174.

DeLyser, D. (2001), '"Do you really live here?" Thoughts on Insider Research', *Geographical Review*, 91(1): 441–453.

Denzin, N.K. (1989), *The Research Act*, 3rd edn, Englewood Cliffs, NJ: Prentice-Hall.

Dwyer, S.C. and Buckle, J.L (2009), 'The Space Between: On Being an Insider-Outsider in Qualitative', *Research International Journal of Qualitative Methods*, 8(1): 54–63.

Ergun, A. and Erdemir, A. (2010), 'Negotiating Insider and Outsider Identities in the Field: "Insider" in a Foreign Land; "Outsider" in One's Own Land', *Field Methods*, 22(1): 16–38.

Fishman, J.A., ed (1966), *Language Loyalty in the United States*. The Hague: Mouton.

Gerrish, K. (1997), 'Being a "Marginal Native": Dilemmas of the Participant Observer', *Nurse Researcher*, 5(1): 25–34.

Greene, M.J. (2014), 'On the Inside Looking In: Methodological Insights and Challenges in Conducting Qualitative Insider Research', *The Qualitative Report*, 19 (29): 1–13. Available at: http://nsuworks.nova.edu/tqr/vol19/iss29/3 (accessed 12 March 2017).

Heller, M. (1995), 'Language Choice, Social Institutions, and Symbolic Domination', *Language in Society*, 24: 373–405.

Rogers, C.A. (2003), 'The Mother/Researcher in Blurred Boundaries of a Reflexive Research Process', *Auto/Biography* XI (1 and 2): 47–54.

Rooney, P. (2005), *Researching from the Inside – Does It Compromise Validity?* Dublin Institute of Technology. Available at: http://level3.dit.ie/html/issue3 /rooney/rooney.pdf (accessed 12 March 2017).

Smyth, A., and Holian, R. (2008), 'Credibility Issues in Research from Within Organizations', in P. Sikes and A. Potts (eds), *Researching Education from the Inside*, 33–47, New York, NY: Taylor & Francis.

Unluer, S. (2012), 'Being an Insider Researcher While Conducting Case Study Research', *The Qualitative Report*, 17 (29): 1–14. Available at: http://nsuworks .nova.edu/tqr/vol17/iss29/2 (accessed 12 March 2017).

CHAPTER ELEVEN

Participant Observations in Community Language Schools in Australia

Janica Nordstrom

Guiding questions

1 In what ways did Janica construct her 'participation' in participant observation in her research? Are any of the ways she describes relevant to your own research?

2 What ethical issues arose in Janica's research as a result of her participant observer role? How did she mediate them?

Introduction

Fieldwork is central to ethnographic inquiry, striving towards understanding and interpreting people, behaviour and the meaning ascribed to local practices and phenomena in naturalistic settings. As such, participant observations have become one of the foundations for ethnographic data collection, involving the researcher not only observing, but taking part in the common (and uncommon) activities in the field and over time. In this chapter, I explore how participant observations can be applied to gain insight to multilingual educational settings by drawing on my research into a Swedish community language school in Australia. A key element of participant observation in this study was in the development of appropriate field relationships with the participants, particularly the community language teacher in whose classroom I observed. This chapter will focus on these relationships, how they were negotiated and how they affected the outcome of the study.

Community language schools have been established all over the world by minority immigrant communities to support the maintenance of their heritage languages. They are also known as ethnic, heritage, supplementary and complementary schools, and are held out of normal school hours, often in premises borrowed or rented from mainstream schools. In Australia, classes are held for about two hours per week to the descendants of migrants and are attended by more than 100,000 students in approximately seventy different languages across the country (Community Languages Australia 2014). While parents often value that these schools encourage a stronger sense of heritage identity and belonging, one of the key findings from previous research into these schools has indicated that students', parents' and teachers' reasons for attending community language schools are both complex and sometimes contradictory (e.g. Blackledge and Creese 2010; Francis et al. 2009, 2010; Li Wei and Wu 2010).

In the late 1990s, some community language schools in Australia began offering courses taught online or in blended mode (alternating face-to-face and online teaching) in attempts to increase student enrolment and motivation. Research in the field of computer-assisted language learning (CALL) has shown several benefits of computer-mediated communication in teaching, including more equal student participation, better attitudes towards learning, the reduction of target language use anxiety, as well as an increase in authenticity and vocabulary development (e.g. Fitze 2006; Fitzgerald and Debski 2006; Warschauer 1996). In the light of these previous findings from research into community language schools and the emergence of online teaching within these schools, I wanted to gain an inside understanding of how a community language class taught in blended mode met the needs of students and their families, which was how I came to conduct fieldwork in one Swedish community language school in Australia for my doctoral research.

Aiming for a rich, in-depth understanding of why and what people do in community language schools, I adopted an ethnographic perspective and chose to focus in-depth on one class, a group of sixteen students aged twelve to fifteen. Generalizability was never a desired outcome, but I sought to understand and describe how this group of people constructed meaning and purpose within their social, political and historical context. The participating class was taught in blended mode, alternating between face-to-face and distant, online, synchronous text-based lessons. The teacher had introduced this approach in an attempt to increase student motivation and attendance. At the participating school, this was the only class that was taught in blended mode.

Data were gathered during a five months' participant observation field period where I engaged with people formally and informally, formed relationships, collected artefacts (teaching material, curriculum documents, notes from teachers meetings, etc.). I also video-recorded students during their online lessons. In this chapter, I will look back at my experience as a participant observer, reflecting on the data and the knowledge I gained through this method and some of the issues I faced.

Participant observation

While the development of participant observation as a systematic method of data collection is often credited to the anthropologist Malinowski for his work in the Trobriand Islands of the east coast of Papua New Guinea (DeWalt and DeWalt 2011), the principles of participant observation are nevertheless transferable to school contexts where the method can afford in-depth and insightful understanding of people and their behaviours (Erickson 1984). When adopting an ethnographic perspective, we strive towards **idiographic** rather than **nomothetic knowledge**. That is, rather than aiming to generalize, we seek to understand people and their behaviours as context-embedded; to interpret and understand reality from the perspectives and actions of the participants; and to reconstruct this knowledge in thick descriptions (Geertz 1973). Researchers participate in and observe the events of the people they seek to describe; they form relationships with and engage in conversations with participants about their lives, all the while striving to gain an inside understanding of the meanings and values people and groups place on (sometimes seemingly mundane) routines and events (Barton and Hamilton 1998; Cohen et al. 2007; DeWalt and DeWalt 2011). We thus *observe*, listen to and react to our surroundings, as well as *participate* 'within the current of activity' (Ingold 2014: 387) in the field. By observing and participating, and asking questions as we do so, researchers strive to develop a tacit understanding of a 'culture', which is not always easily put into words by those we seek to understand (Blommaert and Jie 2010). Participant observation thus becomes both a method of data collection and a process of learning, where the researcher is committed, attentive and sensitive to the contexts they seek to describe (Atkinson and Hammersley 1994; Schensul and LeCompte 2013; Ingold 2014).

However, participant observation is an unpredictable method; we rarely know prior to fieldwork what data we will leave with in the end (Atkinson and Hammersley 2007; Brockmann 2011; DeWalt and DeWalt 2011). When, where and how we can (or even should) participate and observe is determined by our role in the field and the relationships we form with participants, the culture of the group we seek to describe and the characteristics of the researcher. For example, the researcher's own trajectory (age, ethnic background, languages, interests, gender, life history, personality and so forth) becomes relevant in the research, influencing what, how and with whom relationships are formed, the nature of those relationships, what knowledge and information will be shared with him/her and subsequently also the outcome of the study (Atkinson and Hammersley 2007; Cohen et al. 2007; Brockmann 2011; Schensul and LeCompte 2013). Conducting participant observations, we (as researchers) thus inescapably become part of the research and the analysis (Adler 1990; DeWalt and DeWalt 2011).

Ethnographic endeavours are therefore inevitably of an interpretive and subjective nature, where the researcher is both within and of the world being researched (Blommaert and Jie 2010; Cohen et al. 2007: 171). In traditional positivist research, such subjectivity causes unease and concern, particularly because it can become uncomfortably clear that two different researchers in the same setting can produce two very different descriptions of the field and the participants, and thus threaten the idea of validity and reliability. However, because naturalistic inquiry works on the assumption that human knowledge is bound to context and reality is multiple (Guba 1981), trustworthiness of naturalistic research is not met in objectivity, validity and reliability but achieved through clear, in-depth delineation of methods, critical reflexivity of the researcher's presence (Stake 1978; LeCompte and Goetz 1982; Lincoln and Guba 1985) and thoughtful reflections on how these influenced the outcomes of the research. Rather than working on the assumption that a single and stable 'truth' is to be found that becomes timeless and context free, naturalistic inquiry works on the assumption that generalizations are not possible, but that results may allow for 'naturalistic generalizations' (Lincoln and Guba 1985) where the readers can recognize themselves in the research so that certain audiences can benefit through their own experience. A vital aspect of this is 'trackable variance – variance that can be ascribed to sources' (Guba 1981: 81), requiring thick descriptions not just of the findings, but also of how these findings came to be.

Field relations

In my research, I conducted participant observations for five months (May–September), participating and observing in the routines and events of one Swedish community language class in Australia. As such, I took part in the weekly lessons, interacted and formed relationships with students and teachers 'as one of the means of learning the explicit and tacit aspects of their life routines and their culture' (DeWalt and DeWalt 2011: 1). I participated in face-to-face and online lessons where I assisted the teacher and helped the students; I hung around the school speaking to parents and staff members before and after lessons; I asked four students to video-record themselves during their online lessons; and I attended any meetings that occurred during my time in the field.

Throughout this period, the field relations I formed and the roles I took on came to affect what data were available to me. Some of these roles were nonnegotiable. For example, I am a woman, born in Sweden, speak Swedish and have taught Swedish as a community language both face to face and online. I was thus familiar with the customs and language, and I had fairly extensive experience of community language schools which clearly afforded me with some 'insider perspective' that likely gave me great advantage when negotiating field entry and ensuring initial trust with the participants (Haniff 1985; Labaree 2002; Ryberg and Christiansen 2008). However, the boundaries of 'insiderness' need also to be understood as situated in the context (Tedlock 1991; Labaree 2002). Insiderness is a degree of measurement on a continuum rather than one aspect of a binary of inside or outside. It does not imply that the researcher has 'somehow achieved an inside understanding of the community's culture' (Labaree 2002: 104), just as 'being born an ethnic minority does not automatically result in "native" consciousness' (Tedlock 1991: 80).

Despite having some insiderness, my level of participation still needed to be negotiated with the participants through the course of the field period. It unfolded as 'active' participation (DeWalt and DeWalt 2011), a level of participation that was not particularly chosen by me, but was influenced by the way I was treated by the participants. For example, upon entering the field, the teacher (Britta) explained to me that she had difficulties in teaching this particular group because of their diversity in proficiency. She therefore welcomed my presence and asked me to assist as much as possible, which I did. Rather than position myself at the back of the room as a 'passive' or 'moderate' participant (DeWalt and DeWalt 2011: 23), observing but with no or limited interaction, I walked around helping students when they needed help, paired with them when there were uneven numbers working together, distributed papers, chatted and so forth, while writing up my field notes as quickly as possible after the lesson had finished.

While students initially were reluctant to speak to me, or only did so briefly, I persevered and chatted with them about all sorts of things: their interests, hobbies, what they did on the weekend, things we saw and heard around us that had nothing at all to do with learning Swedish. While I certainly did not become 'friends' with the students, the suspicion I sensed from them glaring at me in the beginning (both as a university researcher, but more so as a 'teacher') soon seemed to change as they perceived a new role for me – not a friend, but not a teacher either. Rather, I became someone they could chit-chat with and ask for help if needed, but not someone who told them what to do (or not to do). They soon learnt that I would not take on the teacher's role and tell them to keep focused if they were off-task and they became more relaxed around me. Creating these relationships with the students through active participation, I thus came to gain their trust

(Atkinson and Hammersley 2007). Gaining this trust, I was also able to observe things not otherwise easily observed. For example, one day Britta left the classroom and took the authority (and discipline), with her as she went. I was no threat to the students by this stage, and some of them took the opportunity to stop the work they had been instructed to do in favour of what seemed to be more appealing activities such as talking about things unrelated to the task. The spoken language of the classroom instantly changed from Swedish to English, and I noted that some of the boys down at the back were laughing. As I walked over to them, I saw that these boys were having the time of their life writing a short story in Swedish. The story, focusing around the clumsy character Sven Johnson, went on for several pages in one of the boys' book, accompanied with creative illustrations. It was, and still is, unknown to me whether Sven was the result of an earlier teacher-initiated project or not. Nevertheless, two noteworthy observations were made: first that the students enthusiastically engaged in an activity that involved written Swedish language (which was a very rare observation), and secondly that while they did so, they were translanguaging (García and Li Wei 2014), drawing on both Swedish and English to construct meaning with each other in a way that included even the least proficient student in the activity. As Britta reentered the classroom, the students reverted to their instructed activity, and kept the use of English language to a minimum.

My relationship with Britta, the teacher of my study

The relationships I formed with students and staff at the school were particularly valuable in gaining insight and depth in my observations. However, the relationships I formed with the adult participants were different to those with the students. As it unfolded, these relationships were often grounded in characteristics beyond my nationality, background, language proficiency and teaching experience. In particular, being a woman in my thirties and a mother in a relationship with an Anglo-Australian partner were aspects of my own trajectory that assisted in forming relationships and trust with participants, and allowed me access to data that might otherwise have been difficult to gain. The similarities in age and gender in many ways allowed me greater acceptance among the adult participants than that afforded by my nationality and profession, as we engaged in discussions around how and why we wished to teach our children Swedish.

During my second visit to the school, I was surprised to hear that Britta had handed in her resignation after six years of community language teaching. As the field period unfolded, Britta and I developed a close relationship that led to inside understanding of the issues she faced in her teacher role, and I left the field with a wealth of insight to her work that I had far from anticipated in my preparations for fieldwork. While Britta and I had no personal relationship before the field period, we did know of each other prior to the research. Britta had previously lived in Sydney, where both of us taught at a local Swedish community language school. The school operated over geographically dispersed locations, and thus while Britta and I had been colleagues, we only saw each other at any of the four annual teachers' meetings. Britta soon moved interstate and started teaching at a different Swedish community language school, the one where I came to conduct my research. I commuted by flight every second weekend (Friday–Sunday) to attend the face-to-face lessons.

When I came for my first visit, Britta invited me to come and stay the Friday night at her house and meet her husband and twins. Meeting with Britta outside of school hours was probably the first unanticipated aspect of my fieldwork. However, making choices is a part of engaging in participant observations (Tedlock 1991), and these choices affect our experience in the field and the relationships we form. We make choices to whom we should speak and what we talk about and when, choices that in turn affect what data is collected, when, why and from whom (Atkinson and Hammersley 2007). After considering the ethical issues involved in the decision, I accepted the offer and spent that night at Britta's house together with her family. Had she been a complete stranger to me, I probably would not have agreed (and she probably would never have asked).

As time unfolded, both that night and throughout the field period, we spoke about many things not related to teaching Swedish, but engaged in conversations any two women about the same age could engage in: about our experiences of raising children, our families and anything else that would come to mind. I often came to see Britta outside of school hours and she several times told me that she was looking forward to my visits: we would have coffee together, go out for dinner and twice we also shared a hotel room in the city together. *Getting to know her* I also came to *understand her*. She was smart and witty, and had a tendency for sarcasm. Our informal conversation about children, chickens (Britta convinced me to get some), politics, languages, husbands and wine thus did not only facilitate the collection of future data more aligned with the topic of my study, but more importantly, 'they were data in their own right' (Atkinson and Hammersley 1994: 72), a pathway and a process towards gaining a deep insight to her teaching at the Swedish school.

To illustrate this point about data, I provide an example. Britta explained in one of our formal interviews that she '*avskyr*' (loathes) speaking English with her students and observing her lessons, I came to see that all formal classroom interaction was in Swedish only. This, as I observed in the classroom, resulted in less proficient students becoming peripheral in the learning environment, at times restricted from participating in classroom discourses due to their lack of proficiency in Swedish. Such monoglossic ideologies and policies are common in community language schools where the minority language is often favoured and valued, while the approach to students' dominant language ranges from ignoring it (Choudhury 2013; Chung 2013) to explicitly discouraging it (Wu 2006; Blackledge and Creese 2010). Often, this is done in the attempt to strengthen the identity of the students, increase language exposure and to prevent language attrition. Such beliefs in keeping languages separate are also not unique to community language teachers. Cook (2001: 403) describes how 'assumptions' have affected many generations of students and teachers' belief that students first language (L1) should be discouraged in the language learning classroom, ranging from explicit policies that L1 is banned from the classroom to more positive framing of maximizing the target language.

Through our informal conversations around families and children however, I came to gain an in-depth understanding of Britta's perceptions around languages, and the theme of English language use in the classroom soon became intertwined with the narratives of her own children. Britta had twins, a boy and a girl aged six at the time of the field period. At home, she tried to speak as much Swedish as possible with her children. However, at times Swedish was difficult to sustain. When her twins came home from school they were tired, and '*frågar jag på svenska [hur deras dag har varit] så får jag inga svar*' (if I ask in Swedish [how their day has been] then I get no answer). To ease communication with her children, she used English, as well as Swedish, explaining that because the children '*har upplevt det på engelska, de tänker på engelska, och då frågar jag på engelska för att jag vill veta*' (have experienced it in English, they think in English, and then I ask in English because I want to know). Recognizing this translanguaging as a natural aspect of everyday conversations, Britta felt that the two weekly hours at Swedish school was the only opportunity for many children to speak the language. Upholding monoglossic practices in the classroom was then embedded in her experiences of raising her own children, where she found that her twins were not exposed to enough Swedish throughout the week. Reluctance towards the use of English in the classroom was a pragmatic response to her everyday translanguaging practices (García and Li Wei 2014). She wished to maximize the students' exposure to Swedish in the community school to 'make up' for the rest of the week.

Recording the data

The recording of my data was a recurring issue and source of reflection, even long after I left the field. Observations are never data until they are recorded (DeWalt and DeWalt 2011) and while formal interviews were audio-recorded, much of my data was produced through the writing of field notes. Following suggestions by DeWalt and DeWalt (2011), I sought to make the field notes of my observations highly descriptive; they included a high level of detail, even the most trivial observations of behaviours and surroundings and as much verbatim quotes as possible. I had a note book with me at all times during my visits, as well as during online lessons, where I jotted down quick phrases, quotes and thoughts whenever I had the chance and transformed these to lengthy field notes on my small laptop as soon as I left the field to ensure that the experiences were still fresh in my memory. This was a lengthy process, and I spent as long writing the field notes as I did observing, and sometimes more. I began with writing highly descriptive notes, and always finished with reflective remarks where I recorded any thoughts, feelings and ideas that ran through my head. These reflective thoughts and ideas were invaluable at the later stages of analysis and thesis writing, as they assisted in reconstructing my process of learning and my relationship with the participants (DeWalt and DeWalt 2011), noting when (and under what circumstances) a particular insight had emerged (or had been discarded as seemingly inaccurate).

There were many times I wished that I had audio-recorded some of the face-to-face lessons, particularly because many of my field descriptions and analyzes came to be focused around people's use of language. I wrote field notes for both face-to-face and online lessons, but online lessons were also supplemented by excellent transcripts of participants' interactions, which were automatically generated through the chat provider. Some of the (unanticipated) findings from the online lessons in my study included more equal student participation where less proficient participants were able to partake actively in lessons (see Nordstrom 2015), while the same students were often peripheral in the face-to-face classroom. This was a strength of the online learning environment, and while I had the raw data to describe this for online learning environment, I could only describe the interaction in the face-to-face lessons based on what I had noted in my field notes.

However, while video- and audio-recordings can generate detailed information about participants' talk, gestures and behaviours, permanent recording such as audio and video 'can shape the process of ethnographic work in ways that are undesirable' (Atkinson and Hammersley 2007: 147). Fine-grained linguistic analysis lay beyond the scope of my study, both in focus and in time. Furthermore, audio-recordings would have been pragmatically challenging, as students were spread out and often on the move, with plenty of chatting going on simultaneously during lessons. Rather, field notes provided a different set of data that included daily events and behaviours, overheard conversations and informal interviews, and assisted in achieving the holistic aim of the study, which was to understand and appreciate community language schooling from the perspectives of the participants (Emerson et al. 2011). Having worked on other projects since my PhD, I have come to learn that while audio-recordings can be very efficient, it is unfortunately all too easy (for me at least) to put audio-recordings aside when leaving the field in favour of other, seemingly more urgent matters, and so waiting to transcribe them at a later time (see also DeWalt and DeWalt 2011 for a similar experience). This makes it more difficult to capture the immediacy of what has taken place. Being reliant on field notes, I was forced to 're-live' the experiences I had been through while they were still fresh in mind and to think deeply about them, affording that first level of analysis required for the ethnographic perspective (Kozinets 2010).

It is important to remember that data generated from field notes are products constructed by the researcher who chooses what is recorded and what is not, and so have been through an initial stage of analysis. Choices are made *in situ* of what seems relevant and what is not, in comparison to a recorder that is allowed to run throughout a lesson. Thus field notes are always selective (Atkinson and Hammersley 2007) and if something is not recorded in the field notes, then it did not happen as far as analysis is concerned, as analysis can only be concerned with what has been recorded in field notes (DeWalt and DeWalt 2011). Field notes, regardless of how detailed they are, then become a process of simultaneous data collection and data analysis, which can never be unbiased (DeWalt and DeWalt 2011). The choice of not bringing a recorder to the classroom thus limited the comparative insight between online and face-to-face learning environments in terms of language use, but on the other hand provided me with a richer perspective of the context in which event occurred and the participants' perspectives.

Conclusion

Participant observation is not a static or straightforward method of data collection; it is continuously constructed in the field; it is fluid, messy and influenced by the researcher's identities, roles, choices and relationships formed in the field. The researcher is the tool collecting the data, and he or she evolves, adapts and changes through the field process. It is an unpredictable method of data collection and difficult to plan for or anticipate in preparation for fieldwork: who we are, our level of participation, and the choices we make will affect the direction of the study, the data available to us and the outcomes of the research. Our roles and relationships in the field affect which participants we will gain insight from and what we will learn. This makes the characteristics, personality and identity of the researcher inseparable from the research we are conducting. Approached with reflexivity and criticism, however, these roles and relationships can be transformed into strengths in ethnographic research. Furthermore, to ensure the trustworthiness of the research, there needs to be clear delineation in any accounts of the research of how participant observations were conducted and how this may have affected the outcomes of the research.

Although space in this chapter prohibits a detailed thick description of how the tacit and explicit understanding of a Swedish community language school emerged, some examples from my participant observations have highlighted how the ethnographic principles of my research affected the outcomes of my study, afforded in-depth understanding of this particular class and in particular an insightful understanding of Britta's position as a community language teacher. Applying ethnographic principles with critical reflection of data collection methods and of my own presence and relationships with participants to my data, I was able to strengthen the trustworthiness of the research and the holistic understanding of this particular group of participants, including myself, at this particular time and place.

References

Adler, P. (1990), 'Ethnographic Research on Hidden Populations: Penetrating the Drug World', in E.Y. Lambert (ed), *The Collection and Interpretation of Data from Hidden Populations*, 96–112, Rockville, MD: U.S Department of Health and Human Services.

Atkinson, P. and Hammersley, M. (1994), 'Ethnography and Participant Observations', in N.K. Denzin and Y.S. Lincoln (eds), *Handbook of Qualitative Research*, 248–261, Thousand Oaks, CA: Sage Publications.

Atkinson, P. and Hammersley, M. (2007), *Ethnography: Principles in Practice*, Milton Park, Abingdon, Oxon: Routledge.

Barton, D. and Hamilton, M. (1998), *Local Literacies: Reading and Writing in One Community*, London and New York: Routledge.

Blackledge, A. and Creese, A. (2010), *Multilingualism a Critical Perspective*, London: Continuum.

Blommaert, J. and Jie, D. (2010), *Ethnographic Field Work: A Beginner's Guide*, Bristol: Multilingual Matters.

Brockmann, M. (2011), 'Problematising Short-Term Participant Observation and Multi-Method Ethnographic Studies', *Ethnography and Education*, 6(2): 229–243.

Choudhury, R. (2013), 'Raising Bilingual and Bicultural Bangladeshi-American Children in New York City: Perspectives from Educators and Parents in a Bengali Community Program', in O. García, Z. Zakharia and B. Otcu (eds), *Bilingual Community Education and Multilingualism: Beyond Heritage Languages in a Global City*, 60–73, Bristol: Multilingual Matters.

Chung, J. (2013), 'Hidden Efforts, Visible Challenges: Promoting Bilingualism in Korean-America', in O. García, Z. Zakharia and B. Otcu (eds), *Bilingual Community Education and Multilingualism: Beyond Heritage Languages in a Global City*, 87–98, Bristol: Multilingual Matters.

Cohen, L., Manion, L. and Morrison, K. (2007), *Research Methods in Education*, 6th edn, Abingdon, Oxon: Routledge.

Community Languages Australia (2014), Available at: http://www
.communitylanguagesaustralia.org.au (accessed 2 December 2016).

Cook, V. (2001), 'Using the First Language in the Classroom', *The Canadian
Modern Language Review*, 57(3): 402–423.

DeWalt, K.M. and DeWalt, B.R. (2011), *Participant Observations: A Guide for
Field Workers*, Lanham: AltraMira Press.

Emerson, R.M., Fretz, R.I. and Shaw, L.L. (2011), *Writing Ethnographic Field
Notes*, Chicago: The University of Chicago Press.

Erickson, F. (1984), 'What Makes School Ethnography "Ethnographic"?',
Anthropology and Education Quarterly, 15(1): 51–66.

Fitze, M. (2006), 'Discourse and Participation in ESL Face-to-Face and Written
Electronic Conferences', *Language Learning and Technology*, 10(1): 67–86.

Fitzgerald, M. and Debski, R. (2006), 'Internet Use of Polish by Polish
Melburnians: Implications for Maintenance and Teaching', *Language Learning
and Technology*, 10(1): 87–109.

Francis, B., Archer, L. and Mau, A. (2009), 'Language as Capital, or Language as
Identity? Chinese Complementary School Pupils' Perspectives on the Purposes
and Benefits of Complementary Schools', *British Educational Research Journal*,
35(4): 519–538.

Francis, B., Archer, L. and Mau, A. (2010), 'Parents' and Teachers' Constructions
of the Purpose of Chinese Complementary Schooling: "Culture", Identity and
Power', *Race Ethnicity and Education*, 13(1): 101–117.

García, O. and Li, Wei (2014), *Translanguaging: Language, Bilingualism and
Education*, New York: Palgrave Macmillan.

Geertz, C. (1973), *The Interpretation of Cultures*, New York: Basic Books.

Guba, E.G. (1981), 'Criteria for Assessing the Trustworthiness of Naturalistic
Inquiries', *Educational Communication and Technology*, 29(2): 75–91.

Haniff, N.Z. (1985), 'Toward a Native Anthropology: Methodological Notes on
a Study of Successful Caribbean Women by an Insider', *Anthropology and
Humanism Quarterly*, 10(4): 107–113.

Ingold, T. (2014), 'That's Enough about Ethnography!', *HAU: Journal of
Ethnographic Theory*, 4(1): 383–395.

Kozinets, R.V. (2010), *Netnography: Doing Ethnographic Research Online*, Los
Angeles, CA: Sage Publications.

Labaree, R.V. (2002), 'The Risk of "Going Observationalist": Negotiating the
Hidden Dilemmas of Being an Insider Participant Observer', *Qualitative
Research*, 2(1): 97–122.

LeCompte, M.D. and Goetz, J.P. (1982), 'Problems of Reliability and Validity in
Ethnographic Research', *Review of Educational Research*, 52(1): 31–60.

Li, Wei and Wu, C.-J. (2010), 'Literacy and Socialisational Teaching in
Chinese Complementary Schools', in V. Lytra and P. Martin (eds), *Sites of
Multilingualism: Complementary Schools in Britain Today*, 33–44, Stoke on
Trent: Trentham Books.

Lincoln, Y. and E. Guba (1985), *Naturalistic Inquiry*, Newbury Park: Sage
Publications.

Nordstrom, J. (2015), 'Flexible Bilingualism through Multimodal Practices:
Studying K-12 Community Languages Online', *International Journal of
Bilingual Education and Bilingualism*, 18(4): 395–408.

Ryberg, T. and Christiansen, E. (2008), 'Community and Social Network Sites as Technology Enhanced Learning Environments', *Technology, Pedagogy and Education*, 17(3): 207–219.

Schensul, J.J. and LeCompte, M.D. (2013), *Essential Ethnographic Methods: A Mixed Method Approach*, Lanham, MD: AltaMira Press.

Stake, R.E. (1978), 'The Case Study Method in Social Inquiry', *Educational Researcher*, 7(2): 5–8.

Tedlock, B. (1991), 'From Participant Observations to Observation of Participation: The Emergence of Narrative Ethnography', *Journal of Anthropological Research*, 47(1): 69–94.

Warschauer, M. (1996), 'Comparing Face-to-Face and Electronic Discussion in the Second Language Classroom', *CALICO Journal*, 13(2–3): 7–26.

Wu, C.-J. (2006), 'Look Who's Talking: Language Choice and Culture of Learning in UK Chinese Classrooms', *Language and Education*, 20(1): 62–75.

CHAPTER TWELVE

Striving for Participation in a Case Study of Bilingual Children's Experiences of Language and Identity in State Primary Schools in Cyprus

Katherine Fincham-Louis

Guiding questions

1   In her chapter, Katherine is very concerned to justify the need for social justice for the group of pupils in Cyprus who were her participants. Why do you think she had these concerns and how did she justify her claim for social justice? Are there any implications here for your own research?

2   What issues did Katherine face in engaging children in her data collection? How did she attempt to overcome them and was she entirely successful?

Introduction

This chapter reflects on a small-scale case study of a select group of Greek/English-speaking children of mixed heritage in the Republic of Cyprus. The research examined how these children reported on their experiences of language and identity at monolingual state schools on the island. The goal was to examine the experiences of the children from their perspectives by focusing on the children's voices rather than those of teachers or administrators. The chapter illuminates issues arising from the research. It begins by examining the context of the study and the issues of positionality for the researcher and then explores the difficulties which arise when making claims of social justice for a group which is not part of an identified or clearly recognized minority group. It moves on to explore the role of the novice researcher and concerns over researcher identity and their influence on the research process. Next, the chapter examines some of the methodological issues faced when conducting research with children, particularly concerns over ownership, tokenism and participation, which can emerge when research that makes claims to participation is driven by the researcher. The chapter concludes by examining some of the claims regarding dual heritage bilingual students in state elementary school in Cyprus which emerged from the study.

The Cypriot educational system

A small Mediterranean island, Cyprus has had a turbulent and tempestuous history of occupation and conflict (Mallinson 2009). The result is a country with a vibrant and varied populace which, though primarily Greek and Turkish Cypriot, includes Maronite, Armenian, Roma, Lebanese and English communities among others. In 2004, European accession caused significant shifts to the populace, which have filtered down to the children entering schools. Cyprus Ministry of Education and Culture (Cyprus MoEC) statistics reveal that the number of non-Cypriot children entering schools has steadily increased from approximately 4 per cent in 2007/2008 to 10 per cent in 2009/2010 to over 15 per cent for 2014/2015 (Cyprus MoEC 2007, 2009, 2014). The Cypriot educational system, due in part to the conflicted history of the island and the de facto division since 1974, has been characterized as heavily politicized and monocultural and one which marginalizes non-Cypriot students (Trimikliniotis and Demetriou 2009). The MoEC's approach to non-Cypriot students has been characterized as focused on assimilation rather than integration (Angelides et al. 2003; Panayiotopoulos and Nicolaidou 2007). The statistics may not present a complete picture of Cypriot education. Indeed it is likely that the school system is even more diverse than they indicate. This is due to two main reasons: first the MoEC statistics categorize students based only on their nationalities, and 'official' minority groups such as Armenians, Roma or Latins. Local dual heritage students with 'non-official minority' backgrounds are recorded solely as Cypriot. Secondly, the MoEC statistics reflect the numbers of 'foreigners' without clearly recording the linguistic backgrounds of all children entering schools. This perpetuates the general assumption that 'foreigners' are not fluent in Greek while Cypriots are. Consequently, although Greek language Support Programmes are provided through the MoEC's multicultural education efforts, these are focused on Greek as an Additional Language learners, ergo 'foreigners'.

As a third culture English woman raising two Greek Cypriot/English children in Cyprus, I was interested in the disconnect between what I noted anecdotally regarding the experiences of bilingual dual heritage children in state schools and the official position of the MoEC. As part of my doctoral research, I chose to explore the language and identity experiences of a select group of dual heritage Greek/English bilinguals enrolled in state primary education. I was interested in how the children experienced their bilingualism and identity at school and particularly whether they needed any additional linguistic support (Cummins 2000; Meisel 2004). My objective was to try to understand the linguistic needs of this group while uncovering their school experiences through their voices.

I began by exploring the literature around children's primary school experiences in Cyprus. This was of particular importance as I was embarking on a project outside of my direct professional context and knowledge base. I discovered that although there was a developing literature on the experiences of Greek-Cypriot children within the primary school setting, it had an emphasis on the experiences of these students in relation to 'others'; mainly Turks, Turkish-Cypriots or new immigrant children (Spyrou 2000, 2001, 2006; Angelides et al. 2003; Trimikliniotis 2004; Theodorou 2010; Zembylas 2010; Zembylas and Lestas 2011). There was little recognition in the literature of the distinct group of bilingual mixed heritage students. As the children in my study were bilingual or multilingual, I sought out local literature exploring the linguistic experiences of such learners. Again, I could identify a developing literature on the needs of Greek language learners and issues related to the teaching and learning of Greek by new immigrant children to Cyprus (Papamichael 2008), but not on the growing group of Cypriot children being raised as bilinguals or multilinguals. It was clear that, at least in the current literature, there was no applicable recognition of this group of students or acknowledgement of their school experiences. This, along with the statistics of the MoEC, afforded me some validation in establishing that this was a distinctly underrepresented, unidentified and unaccounted group of children.

Claims of social justice

The lack of recognition for this group was fundamental to my decision to move forward with the study as it reinforced what I saw as critical educational research and an issue of social justice. My understanding of this was influenced by Griffiths (2003) and Clark (2006) and, as such, concerned with inequality and distribution but not an absolute equality (Clark 2006: 276). My concern was rather the need to work towards an understanding of when, why and how justice and injustice take place (Walker 2003). What I struggled with was that my chosen group did not fit the traditional idea of one for which claims of social justice could be made.

However, as I explored ways of thinking about social justice, I came to understand that it can be viewed as more than distributional. It is temporal, context specific (Cribb and Gewirtz 2003) and particularly concerned with issues of respect and recognition (Taylor 1997, Griffiths 2009). Within this understanding, I appreciated that cultural justice as a component within social justice must place the absence of cultural domination, nonrecognition and disrespect as paramount in the fight for social justice for all groups (Fraser 1997: 13) – a situation which I believe applied to this case. Beyond this, I was influenced by Apple's (1988) understanding of the student and hoped, as he suggests, to be able to 'see the classed, raced and gender subjects' of the school, recognizing the experiences and lives of these children and how they are linked 'to the economic political and ideological trajectories of their families and communities, to the political economies of their neighbourhoods' (Apple 1988: 5) and as such all need a voice.

Concerns over claims of social justice were further complicated, once I began to identify my participants for the study. This was due to the families' socioeconomic statuses and demographic profiles. It quickly became evident that the children I had identified were from predominantly middle-class homes, with professional, university educated parents. As such, they enjoyed the related status and advantages of education and social economic class afforded to members of this 'advantaged' group. However, if we understand, as Apple (2008) advocates, that people do not belong to class categories in uncomplicated, straightforward ways and that social justice is temporal, context specific and concerned with issues of recognition and respect, then those who in one context might be perceived as advantaged may need the justice of recognition in another.

Researcher positionality – Insider/outsider status

Even before I began the study, I recognized that my interests in the language and identity experiences of this group stemmed directly from my own experiences with my dual heritage bilingual children. This had fed my desire and commitment to understanding what I believed was an unacknowledged group, and brought about additional issues of concern related to my positionality. To begin with, I was a mature student returning to studies after twenty years of practice: I had not engaged in any sustained research before this project. Thus, I brought with me all the insecurities connected to redefining myself as a researcher. I worried that I was too far removed from the research experience to make the needed adjustments to create and sustain a successful project. I worried about my capabilities in managing the research while raising a family and working full time in a different environment. Both of these factors impacted my self-confidence, and often left me feeling as though everyone else 'knew more' and was 'doing better'. A further complication was that I had no experience or knowledge of working directly with children in primary school, beyond that with my own children. Thus, I was legitimately fearful of my abilities and competencies to conduct the study, particularly as so much of the literature on researching with children highlighted the importance of duty of care and the connection a researcher needed to develop when working with this vulnerable group.

While recognizing the fluidity and complexity of researcher positionality in research (Merriam et al. 2001), my position was complicated by the fact that I was bridging both insider and outsider status in relation to this group (Kusow 2003; Young 2004). I claimed insider status as a foreign woman raising two mixed heritage bilingual children in Cyprus. This was reinforced by the fact that I was easily able to directly identify my sample of participants rather than go through the MoEC. Indeed, for several of the children involved in the study, I was a 'known quantity' thereby easing not only issues of access but also of trust building; for example, several participants identified with me as 'so and so's mother' or as an 'aunty'. On the other hand, I occupied outsider status in several ways. I was an adult researcher striving to gain access to the experiences of children and as such I was part of the inherent power dynamic which results when an adult researcher seeks to work with children (Mayall 2000). Punch (2002a) argues that to conduct research with children, one of the fundamental issues an adult must address is that of superiority and the belief that as adults we somehow have an advantaged understanding. He contends that we must put these assumptions aside as they present methodological issues for the researcher. This is especially because although we have all 'been' children, it is only those who 'are' children who truly understand and can represent contemporary childhood. Adults can be caught up in a sense of nostalgia for their own vanished childhoods and unless we dispel these feelings they will lead to problematic issues within our research as we will fail to acknowledge our inherent outsider status. The recognition of this outsider status and attempts to address the fundamental concern of adult superiority is necessary in achieving children's participation in the research process.

Researching with children

I entered the study guided by the contention that the primary contemporary challenge of research concerning children has been the shift from seeing children as objects to be studied to seeing them as social actors involved in constructing their own social worlds and adept at making direct contributions to research which concerns them. Thus it was important to me that I adopted a child-centred participatory approach to the research, accessing the children's experiences from their own perspectives. I hoped, as Hill (2006) argues, to respond to the need for more studies which capture children's views through methods involving joint researcher-respondent interaction. As such, I began the study committed to exploring child-friendly research methods and applying them within my research context (Alderson 2008). Though I was inexperienced in the mechanics of how to achieve it, I hoped to achieve an 'ethical symmetry' (Christensen and Prout 2002: 482), taking as the starting point that the relationships I developed with my participants would not be influenced by generationalism (Mayall 2000). This did not mean that I would not acknowledge the differences involved in researching with children, but rather that I would work to ensure that these relationships were guided by the same ethical principles I would have used if I was researching with adults, irrespective of age, social maturity or power. I hoped that any differences which might arise would stem from differences in the values, interests, experiences and everyday routines of children, not from my own preconceived ideas of what these differences might be.

Accordingly, I worked to shift my own understanding of childhood to a perspective which actively recognized children's ownership of the knowledge of childhood (Mayall 2000). This allowed me to approach the study with the intention of learning from children's own experiences, acknowledging children's ownership of knowledge. Critical to this acknowledgement was the recognition that the processes of researching children's experiences from their own perspectives are unlikely to be equal (Alderson 2001), because the impetus for the research usually stems from the needs of an adult researcher, as was the case in this study. Additionally, there can be intrinsic practical difficulties associated with researching with children, for example, issues with gatekeepers, access, scheduling and so on (Cree et al. 2002). What is important is that researchers committed to the involvement and participation of children do not use these difficulties as barriers or excuses to avoid directly involving children in studies connected to their own lives.

Another developing concern about the children's participation in the study was that, though I knew I wanted to access and honour the children's voices (Fielding 2001) I was unclear on the best methods to do this. Most of the research I had come across consisted of studies situated within a school setting, often conducted by a teacher, head teacher, principal or researcher/practitioner in collaboration with one or more of these people. The complications of gaining permission and access to primary schools presented by the MoEC meant it was unlikely that I would have gained permission to work with individual students at school. Beyond this, the dispersed nature of the group meant that working within one school would not have afforded me access to a large enough group. Additionally, I had seen that there was a lack of studies that explored children's school experiences from the child's perspective. Indeed, a critique of the area was that the prevalence of studies was from an adult perspective (Thiessen and Cook-Sather 2007). As a consequence, I decided to focus on accessing the voices of the children so that they could illuminate their own experiences from their own perspectives. I hoped they would express what they thought, what their experiences were and what they saw as the issues they experienced.

Subsequently, I approached the study with an understanding of my own status, the complications of the social justice claims being made, the subjectivity of the research process and how this was influenced through my own political and social background. I was aware of the role and influence of the researcher and how this influenced decisions, from the questions to be asked and the areas to be explored to who the participants were and how they would be involved. I embraced the idea that research interpretations and meanings are subjective to both the researcher and the researched. I wanted, as Robinson and Fielding (2007) state, to focus more fully on student experience within educational research. I wanted to provide for the recognition of these voices and this influenced my interest in participatory research (Hill 2006). What I did not yet know was how best to achieve this.

The pilot

Given my limited experience with research and even less with children, I decided to conduct a preliminary focus group to try out some of the data gathering methods I had read about. Thus, I arranged a small focus group with six children, four girls and two boys, in friendship pairs, to discuss common methodological choices used in participatory research. The use of friendship pairs, where each child-participant is asked to bring a friend, allows for them to feel comfortable and willing to contribute. Mauthner (1997) advocates the use of focus groups with children in helping to redress the inherent issues of power that are at work in adult researcher and child-participant relationships. Furthermore, the pilot study would improve my confidence and identity as a researcher. Ultimately, only four children attended as one child and a friend opted out on the day, foreshadowing an issue of participation which would become all too familiar in the main study.

Though I had set out to conduct a focus group, upon reflection I characterized it as more of a group interview as, I felt, it failed to meet the criteria of a focus group as outlined by Morgan et al. (2002), who view a lack of sustained group interaction as a common weakness, but as fundamental to the success of focus groups. The results of the group interview informed several of my decisions in moving forward into the main study. The first was to hold the interviews beyond the school setting as the children had characterized school as an 'unsafe space' where conversations could be 'listened to' and 'judged'. Thus, I offered participants a choice of location for the interviews, and they were held in a variety of spaces such

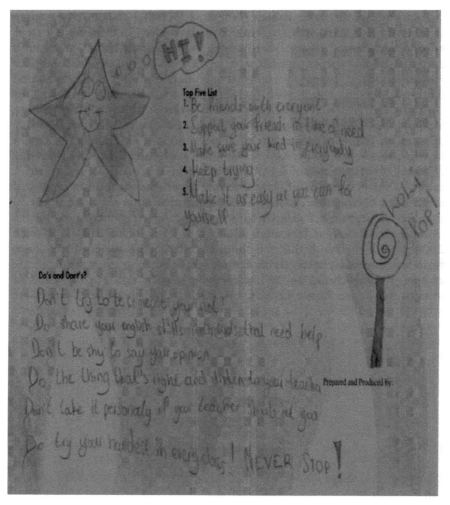

FIGURE 12.1 *(continued)*

collaboration, consent and involvement with each child, while at the same time emphasizing nonparticipation as a choice.

My goal was to achieve an ethical participatory research project with the children. Alderson (2001) refers to children's involvement in research as like the rungs of a ladder, whereas Christensen and Prout (2002) view the process as a continuum where there are several levels of possible involvement. Ladder or continuum, my goal was to avoid 'tokenism' (Alderson 2001: 145), a term used to describe studies where claims of children's involvement are made, but where in practicality there is not true involvement. I hoped to achieve a reflective research process (Davis 1998; Punch 2002a) so the children's voices could permeate the research at all its levels from designing and collecting data to interpreting.

Complications

Once I began the interviews, I soon experienced a series of problems. The first was related to participation, collaboration and responsiveness, despite my efforts to provide child-friendly research methods throughout the study. Many of these were practical, such as the cancelling and rescheduling of interviews. Indeed, I was struck by how full and busy the lives of the children and the families were. I had one family who rescheduled so much that I ended up conducting the second and third interviews almost back to back rather than allowing for the reflective break I had between interviews with other children. These issues frustrated the research process and the collaborative and interactivity of the research and upon reflection influenced my ability to establish greater rapport and a flow for the study, as there were occasions when more time passed between interviews than I would have wanted.

The second issue was related to the interviews themselves. Though I worked hard to establish a connection with the children through implementing child-friendly methods and responsive semi-structured interviews, I experienced incidents of children losing interest within the interview process. On two separate occasions a child decided to call the interview to a close and basically told me 'I'm done', 'I'm bored', 'I don't want to talk anymore', at which point I ended the interview. One child decided, upon my arrival, that he did not want to do the interview that day, although I had called ahead of my visit to reconfirm. These incidents were frustrating as they impeded the progress of the research, but I felt there was not much I could do to foresee or respond to them.

My final challenge was perhaps the most significant and related to the active participation of the children in the research. I had employed child-friendly methods in the pilot study like the use of 'Mosaic Approach' (Clark and Moss 2001), which provided free choice of any method to produce artefacts on the topic '*My life as a bilingual child*'. But, when I checked on the progress of the artefact production only two children had produced anything at all, both in the form of pictures – one from the computer and the other from the family pictures. Ultimately, I found I had to be more prescriptive by providing a sentence completion task and a brochure template for the children to complete. Here again there were issues with participation as, although all the children completed the sentence charts, when it came to the brochure a couple of children were uninterested in completing it. Again, I was frustrated as it had been my hope that the children would engage more fully within the research process and I certainly had not intended to prescribe the artefact production by offering templates. However, once

I evaluated the lack of response I was left struggling with issues of data production for the study. On reflection, I feel this lack of commitment to producing artefacts reflected larger issues of ownership of the study. This was *my* study and the children knew it. Though I considered that I had tried to engage with the children, I had not been able to surpass *my* ownership and need for the study. Ultimately, I ended up hoping I had at least avoided tokenism.

I felt many of these issues were complicated by the fact that I conducted the project in different settings with the children. This meant they were not necessarily known to each other and there was no group interaction, momentum or sense of group ownership of the project – an issue which, upon reflection, I could have accounted for by organizing some group activities with all the children together, even though scheduling would have been an issue in achieving this. Additionally, I was asking the children to participate in a project which infringed on their own private time and lives. This was not a study where children were corralled into a common space away from the routine of lessons during the school day, to be observed or to produce pictures for the teacher. The children here were often within their own homes, and though this had the advantage of allowing for a more 'comfortable' and accessible approach to our discussions it was clear that my visit meant time away from videogames, TV, friends or other activities.

In the end, I felt, many of these issues were ones I could have better anticipated, had I had greater research experience. There is a strong chance that they could have been mitigated if I had established some other methodological approach which would have increased the children's ownership of the research project. However, though there were concerns throughout the process, I worked at being responsive to these and adjusted and redesigned as I went along. While there were certainly things I would change, or do differently were I to conduct a similar project, ultimately, I believe I was able to accomplish the goal of accessing the voices and experiences of the children.

Making claims

Despite these methodological issues, the study did uncover thought-provoking issues in terms of language use and social justice. Primarily, it revealed that the linguistic and educational needs of this group were often overlooked by the current educational system. This was mainly because the families were characterized as professional middle class and thus did not present as 'bilingual' in the manner in which teachers and school officials had come to understand the term – 'immigrant', predominantly third country nationals from a lower income bracket and synonymous with 'disadvantage'. At the same time, the results showed that the children inadvertently reported struggling with 'managing' an unacknowledged bilingualism within a school setting, where they sometimes needed help that was not available. The children recounted that overall, they 'kept their languages separate' at school as, in their experience, there was no space for English within the classroom. They recounted incidents of translanguaging (García 2009) to gain understanding, which were unacknowledged by their teachers. Indeed, in most cases the teachers were characterized as being wholly unaware of how the children worked with their languages during class. The children recounted incidents such as asking friends for translations of how to say something in Greek or of 'using my brain' to figure out understandings. They reported that, as a rule, they did not seek the help of the classroom teacher with their linguistic needs for fear of being reprimanded and because – as they understood it – the classroom was an 'English free zone'. In the excerpt below Maria, aged ten, describes what she does in class when she is working to express herself in Greek:

> I try to use help from the kids that know English too and sometimes it's kind of I don't really get it right, but my teacher understands it, but mostly I think I know the words but some of them cause they are kind of hard and I can't pronounce them right, I just use my mind.

Maria's characterization of her language use at school was typical of the responses of the children, with the notable exception that Maria felt that her teacher understood her regardless of her mistakes. This was not the case for most of the other children who expressed feeling more pressure for correctness in their Greek language production at school.

Although the MoEC offers a programme of Greek language intervention for students, none of the children were enrolled in it. Additionally, no family reported having had any teacher or school administrator address their child's linguistic issues by suggesting involvement in these additional classes. This lack of acknowledgement of their linguistic needs conflicted with the reports from the children and their parents who, to varying degrees, acknowledged that they had 'linguistic gaps' and often needed support with Greek. Indeed, many families had engaged help with Greek beyond school by employing private teachers, or relatives, often grandparents, to help their child manage schoolwork. The result was that families had taken the educational needs into their own hands, a decision afforded them largely through their relative social and economic advantage. This raises serious questions about the ability of less advantaged dual heritage bilingual students within the school system.

The one exception to school being an English-free zone reported by the children was during their school English as second language classes. Here they described that they might be called upon by the teacher to demonstrate a language feature or participate in a dialogue in English. Additionally at school festivals and assemblies, particularly when they involved visiting dignitaries or parents, the children were often called upon to 'perform' in English. What resulted was a characterization of their experiences as performative and subject to the will of the individual classroom teacher or school.

What emerged from the data was a situation analogous to that outlined by Theodorou (2010), who characterized the use of 'difference blindness' within the Cypriot educational system with regard to the position of others – particularly migrant children. In the case of these mixed heritage multilingual children there appeared to be a blending of their *otherness* so that issues of difference in terms of language and identity were melded and overwhelmed by the dominant Greek Cypriot rhetoric of the school. The result was a lack of recognition of their varying and shifting identities and language needs, and therefore children who may have required linguistic support were not identified as their differences were essentialized to that of being solely Greek Cypriot. Ultimately, the study shed light on a growing group of children, not only in Cyprus but in other contexts. It uncovered a need for us to broaden our understandings of what it means to be a bilingual child and to remove the 'stigma' associated with the label, which is so often essentialized to the negative connotation of 'migrant'.

Conclusions

This chapter has recounted my experiences on my research journey and the struggles I experienced as the research unfolded. These were several fold and involved methodological, representational and social justice issues. Initially I struggled to come to terms with my own identity as researcher. Beyond this, I dealt with issues of positionality and participation, particularly in terms of how ownership, inclusion and voice are reflected in research with children. Finally the chapter concludes by making a case for expanding our understandings of bilingual children on the basis of a social justice platform which involves working for inclusive, participatory research addressing the context-specific needs of our local populations while continually reflecting and striving to improve our research practices.

References

Alderson, P. (2001), 'Research by Children', *International Journal of Social Research Methodology*, 4(2): 139–153.

Alderson, P. (2008), 'Children as Researchers: Participation Rights and Research Methods', in P. Monrad, P. Christensen and A. James (eds), *Research with Children: Perspectives and Practices*, 2nd edn, 276–290, London: Falmer Press.

Alderson, P. and Marrow, V. (2004), *Ethics, Social Research and Consulting with Children and Young People*, Essex: Barnardo's.

Angelides, P., Stylianou, T. and Leigh, J. (2003), 'Multicultural Education in Cyprus: A Pot of Multicultural Assimilation?', *Intercultural Education*, 15(3): 307–315.

Apple, M. (1988), *Teachers and Texts: A Political Economy of Class and Gender Relations in Education*, New York: Routledge.

Apple, M. (2008), 'Can Schooling Contribute to a More Just Society?', *Education, Citizenship and Social Justice*, 3(3): 239–261.

Baker, C. (2006), *Foundations of Bilingual Education and Bilingualism*, 4th edn, Clevedon: Multilingual Matters.

Christensen, P. and Prout, A. (2002), 'Working with Ethical Symmetry in Social Research with Children', *Childhood*, 9(4): 477–497.

Clark, A. and Moss, P. (2001), *Listening to Young Children: The Mosaic Approach*, London: National Children's Bureau/Joseph Rowntree Foundation.

Clark, J. (2006), 'Social Justice, Education and Schooling: Some Philosophical Issues', *British Journal of Educational Studies*, 54(3): 272–287.

Cree, V., Kay, H., and Tisdall, K. (2002), 'Research with Children: Sharing the Dilemma', *Child and Family Social Work*, 7: 47–56.

Cribb, A. and Gewirtz, S (2003), 'Towards a Sociology of Just Practices: An Analysis of Plural Conceptions of Justice', in C. Vincent (ed), *Social Justice, Education and Identity*, 15–29, London: RoutledgeFalmer.

Cummins, J. (2000), *Language, Power and Pedagogy: Bilingual Children in the Crossfire*, Cleveland, OH: Multilingual Matters.

Cyprus Ministry of Education and Culture (MoEC) (2007), *Ministry of Education and Culture Annual Report in English*. Available at: http://www.moec.gov.cy/etisia-ekthesi/index.html (accessed 4 January 2017).

Cyprus Ministry of Education and Culture (MoEC) (2009), *Ministry of Education and Culture Annual Report in English*. Available at: http://www.moec.gov.cy/etisia-ekthesi/pdf/Annual_report_2010_EN.pdf (accessed 4 January 2017).

Cyprus Ministry of Education and Culture (MoEC) (2014), *Ministry of Education and Culture Annual Report in English*. Available at: http://www.moec.gov.cy/en/annual_reports/annual_report_2014_en.pdf (accessed 4 January 2017).

David, M., Edwards, R. and Alldred, P. (2001), 'Children and School Based Research "Informed Consent" or "Educated Consent"?', *British Education Research Journal*, 27(3): 347–365.

Davis, J. (1998), 'Understanding the Meaning of Children: A Reflexive Approach', *Children and Society*, 12: 325–335.

Fielding, M. (2001), 'Students as Radical Agents of Change', *Journal of Educational Change*2: 123–141.

Fraser, N. (1997), *Justice Interruptus: Critical Reflections on the "Postsocialist" Condition*, London: Routledge.

García, O. (2009), *Bilingual Education in the 21st Century: A Global Perspective*, Oxford: Wiley-Blackwell.

Greene, S. and Hogan, D. (2005), 'Researching Children's Experience: Methods and Methodological Issues', in S. Greene and D. Hogan (eds), *Researching Children's Experiences: Approaches and Methods*, 1–22, London: Sage Publications.

Griffiths, M. (2003), *Action for Social Justice: Fairly Different*, Buckingham: Open University Press.

Griffiths, M. (2009), 'Action Research For/as/mindful of Social Justice,' in S.E. Noffkle, B. Somekh (eds), *The Sage Handbook of Educational Action Research*, 85–99, London: Sage Publications.

Hill, M. (2006), Children's Voices on Ways of Having a Voice', *Childhood*, 13(1): 69–89.

Kay, H., Cree, V., Tisdall, K. and Wallace, J. (2003), 'At the Edge: Negotiating Boundaries in Research with Children and Young People', *Forum: Qualitative Social Research*, 4(2) Art 33.

Kusow, A.M. (2003), 'Beyond Indigenous Authenticity: Reflections on the Insider /Outsider Debate in Immigration Research', *Symbolic Interaction*, 26(4): 591–599.

Mallinson, W. (2009), *A Modern History of Cyprus*, London: I.B. Tauris and Co Ltd.

Mauthner, M. (1997), 'Methodological Aspects of Collecting Data from Children: Lessons from Three Research Projects', *Children and Society*, 11: 110–116.

Mayall, B. (2000), 'Conversations with Children: Working with Generational Issues', in P. Christensen and A. James (eds), *Research with Children: Perspectives and Practices*, 120–135, London: RoutledgeFalmer.

Meisel, J. (2004), 'The Bilingual Child', in T. Bhatia and W. Ritchie (eds), *The Handbook of Bilingualism*, 91–113, Malden, MA: Blackwell Publishing.

Merriam, S.B., Johnson-Bailey, J., Lee, M.Y., Kee, Y., Ntseane, G., and Muhamad. M. (2001), Power and Positionality: Negotiating Insider/outsider Status Within and Across Cultures', *International Journal of Lifelong Education*, 20(5): 405–416.

Miles, M.B. and Huberman, A.M. (1994), *Qualitative Data Analysis*, 2nd edn, Thousand Oaks, CA: Sage.

Morgan, M., Gibbs, S., Maxwell, K., and Britten, N. (2002), Hearing Children's Voices: Methodological Issues in Conducting Focus Groups with Children Aged 7–11 Years', *Qualitative Research*, 2(5): 5–20.

Panayiotopoulos, C. and Nicolaidou, M. (2007), 'At Crossroads of Civilizations: Multicultural Educational Provision in Cyprus Through the Lens of a Case Study', *Intercultural Education*, 18(1): 65–79.

Papamichael, E. (2008), 'Greek Cypriot Teachers' Understandings of Intercultural Education in an Increasingly Diverse Society', *The Cyprus Review*, 20(2): 51–78.

Punch, S. (2002a), 'Research with Children: The Same or Different from Research with Adults?'*Childhood*, 9(3): 321–341.

Punch, S. (2002b), 'Interviewing Strategies with Young People: the 'Secret Box', Stimulus Material and Task-based Activities', *Children and Society*, 16: 45–56.

Robinson, C., and Fielding, M. (2007), *Children and Their Primary Schools: Pupils' Voices (Primary Review Research Survey 5/3)*, Cambridge: University of Cambridge Faculty of Education.

Spyrou, S. (2000), 'Education, Ideology and the National Self: The Social Practice of Identity Construction in the Classroom', *The Cyprus Review*, 12(1): 61–81.

Spyrou, S. (2001), '"Those on the Other Side" Ethnic Identity and Imagination in Greek-Cypriot Children's Lives', in H.B. Schwartzman (ed), *Children and Anthropology: Perspectives for the 21st Century*, 167–185, Westport, CT: Bergin and Garvey.

Spyrou, S. (2006), 'Children Constructing Ethnic Identities in Cyprus', in Y. Papadakis, N. Peristianis and G. Welz (eds), *Divided Cyprus: Modernity, History and an Island in Conflict*, 121–139, Bloomington: Indiana University Press.

Taylor, C. (1997), The Politics of Recognition', in A. Heble, D. Palmateer Peenee and J.R. (Tim) Struthers (eds), *New Contexts of Canadian Criticism*, 98–131, Ontario: Broadview Press.

Theodorou, E. (2010), '"Children at Our School Are Integrated. No One Sticks Out": Greek-Cypriot Teachers' Perceptions of Integration of Immigrant Children in Cyprus', *International Journal of Qualitative Studies in Education*, 24 (4): 501–520.

Thiessen, D. and Cook-Sather, A. (eds) (2007), *International Handbook of Student Experience in Elementary and Secondary School*, Dordrecht: Springer.

Trimikliniotis, N. (2004), 'Mapping Discriminatory Landscapes in Cyprus: Ethnic Discrimination in a Divided Education System', *Cyprus Review*, 15(2): 53–86.

Trimikliniotis, N. and Demetrou, C. (2009), 'The Cypriot Roma and the Failure of Education: Anti-discrimination and Multiculturalism as a Post-accession Challenge', in A. Varnava, N. Coureasm and M. Elia (eds), *The Minorities of Cyprus: Development Patterns and the Identity of the Internal-exclusion*, 241–264, Newcastle upon Tyne: Cambridge Scholars Publishing.

Walker, M. (2003), 'Framing Social Justice in Education: What Does the "Capabilities" Approach Offer?', *British Journal of Educational Studies*, 55(2): 168–187.

Young, A.A. Jr. (2004), 'Experiences in Ethnographic Interviewing About Race: The Inside and Outside of It', in M. Bulmer and J. Solomos (eds), *Researching Race and Racism*, 187–202, London: Routledge.

Zembylas, M. (2010), 'Children's Construction and Experience of Racism and Nationalism in Greek-Cypriot Primary Schools', *Childhood*, 17(3): 312–328.

Zembylas, M. and Lestas, S. (2011), 'Greek-Cypriot Students' Stances and Repertoires towards Migrants and Migrant Students in the Republic of Cyprus', *Journal of International Migration and Integration*, 12(4): 475–495.

CHAPTER THIRTEEN

Drawing the Threads Together and Telling the Stories

Jean Conteh

In this concluding chapter, I offer some guiding principles for developing good ethnographic research in education in multilingual contexts. These are developed from the two criteria for ethnographic research that I introduced in Chapter 1 (p. 17) and the five key themes that I wove through the framing sections to the three parts of the book. Following this, I share some ideas about the importance of writing in ethnographic research; both writing the PhD thesis and writing to disseminate the outcomes of the research in order to promote change in society – in other words, to make an impact. Finally, I offer some thoughts about dissemination and impact, and what – at least, from my perspective – it really means to be a teacher-researcher. My hope in doing this is that, in the future of ethnographic research in education, the interests of 'teachers' and 'researchers' can be more equitably and productively brought together than they currently are in the shared endeavour of developing research that will contribute to social justice and really make a difference to people's lives in multilingual societies.

Guiding principles for ethnographic research in education

In Chapter 1, I argued that research needed to meet two main criteria in order to be good ethnographic research in education. These were about of your chapters (including those which you have not yet written), and keep adding, removing, changing and moving things about as you develop your arguments. Include all the chapter sections and subsections and number them systematically as you go along. This will help you to make sure the thesis is coherent, well structured and that the steps in the development of your arguments are clear. It will also save a great deal of time in the final stages as you work, probably against the clock, to get everything together and ready to submit.

Perhaps the most common question that doctoral students ask is 'How should I organize my thesis and what should it look like?' The answer I usually give: 'there's no right or wrong way', is probably quite frustrating and not totally accurate. All doctoral theses have to contain the same elements:

- a theoretical framework for the research questions and the methodology;

- a contextualization of the issues surrounding the 'problem' and the practical contexts of the research;

- a clear account and justification of the methodology and the data collection strategies (the methods);

- a full and transparent display of the data, the analytic frameworks and the findings;

- a discussion of the findings in relation to the theoretical frameworks and the research questions;

- a strong conclusion that clearly shows the contribution to knowledge of the research, with implications for future research, policy and practice (where relevant).

Generally, institutions do not lay down prescriptions about how theses should be structured and organized. But it is wise to bear in mind Sikes's cautionary note about the need for early career researchers to 'gain entry into the community' (2006: 108) and so avoid the risks of adopting nontraditional writing styles. This can come later. There are some particular stylistic features of doctoral theses that are important to comply with, and which make them a writing genre distinctive from other academic texts such as research articles, presentations, research reports and so on. The main one is the need to 'signpost' what you are writing, making it clear why you are writing it, how it links with other parts of the thesis, where the reader can find linking material and so on. This is because the main task of the examiners is to test out the strength of your arguments on their own terms, not to agree or disagree with them. And the best way to make their job easier and thus encourage them to be more sympathetic to your work is to keep reminding them how you have done it. This is one of the few times in writing when it is better to 'tell' rather than 'show'. Make the signposting effective by cross-referencing as much as possible, reminding your reader where you previously said something relevant to the point you are making now; where they will find the data that will help them understand the issues they are reading about; how you justify a particular assertion elsewhere in the thesis and so on. You cannot do this kind of writing until you are at a fairly late stage in the process. It is a painstaking, iterative process, which involves reading and rereading your own work, inserting and removing content, going back and forth across the chapters to ensure consistency and coherence. It is one of the signs that the examiners will be looking for, to reassure them that your work is of the required academic standard.

A second key feature of thesis writing, suggested by Mishler's criteria quoted above, is the need to reveal as fully as possible the data you collected and the ways you have interpreted and analyzed them. This is also part of the author's responsibilities to their participants in the writing, and thus part of the ethical processes of the research. Among the case study chapters, it is perhaps Robert's (Chapter 7) which provides us with the clearest articulation of the tensions entailed in this aspect of the writing, including the need to be aware of the risks of 'othering' your participants (Sikes 2006: 114) by not paying enough attention to the distinctive qualities of their voices.

Ethnographic research inevitably generates a huge amount of data, far more than can be analyzed in the thesis, or even shown in its entirety. I always ask my students to provide a 'mapping' of their data. By this I mean some kind of chart, list, table, timeline or other way of showing the 'what, when, where and how' about all the data they collected (the 'why' comes in the written discussion). Figure 13.1 is an example of what I mean. It is a chart which shows all the school observation visits I made in the course of my PhD research, over two years or so (I did it part-time, so the fieldwork was stretched out). It is very simple, and I did other charts to show other components of the data, such as home visits, interviews with teachers and so on. I used them as part of my signposting and cross-referencing to show where the data I actually analyzed and presented in the thesis came from in the whole dataset, because they were only a very small proportion of the whole data. I justified my selections explicitly with reference to the theoretical frameworks, the questions and the methodology. I also 'told the story' of what happened when I collected the particular piece of data. These contextualizing sections ended up as some of the most effective writing in the thesis. All of this appeared in the main body of the thesis, alongside the actual piece of data (e.g. an interview transcript, notes from an observation, an analyzed document and so on). I tried to ensure that the selections showcased the range of the data. In addition, in my appendices, I included examples of field notes (photocopied from my notebook), floor plans of the classrooms I worked in, further interview transcripts and other examples of 'raw' data. The examiners commented that the thesis was too long, but they did also say that the transparency of the data was well done! This way of doing it did not emerge fully formed from a textbook or from my own mind,

DATE	SCHOOL	NATURE OF VISIT(S)
Jan. 1996–June 1998	First school 1	Weekly or fortnightly visits of one morning or afternoon duration to observe, assist in working with groups of children and collect audiotaped data in one classroom (50 visits altogether)
May 1997	Middle school 1	Initial liaison visit with 3 children before transfer
Dec. 1997	Middle school 1	Whole day visit to observe and audiotape in classrooms (4 different teachers observed)
Dec. 1997	Middle school 2	Half day visit to observe and audiotape in classrooms (3 different teachers observed)
March 1998	Middle school 1	Whole day visit to observe and audiotape in classrooms (3 different teachers observed)
April 1998	Middle school 2	Half day visit to observe and audiotape in classrooms (2 different teachers observed)
Dec. 1998	Middle school 1	Whole day visit to observe and audiotape in classrooms (5 different teachers observed)
June 1999	Private primary school	Half day visit to observe in classrooms (1 teacher observed)

FIGURE 13.1 *An example of a data 'map'*

nor it is the only way it could have been done. It was developed piece by piece, as the data collection, analysis and writing were going on. It fitted the needs of my thesis. I would not recommend replicating it in its entirety, but it illustrates what is needed for this essential element of doctoral writing. This 'laying your cards on the table' will also work to your advantage with the examiners, as it allows them to test the quality of your research. As an external examiner of PhD and EdD theses, I know how important this is, and have contributed to many viva reports which ask, as part of the revisions, for further transparency on the data. And as a supervisor, I also know how difficult it can be to pull off this vital part of the thesis.

Once your thesis is submitted and the viva is safely over, you can then think about other kinds of writing, to satisfy the needs of other audiences. Copland and Creese (2015: 178) argue that this is part of the ethical commitment of many scholars, reflecting the need to bring back their research, and the knowledge that has been developed, to the people with whom they have worked – in other words, making it 'useful'. But it is not a straightforward process. Kubanyiova (2008: 514) talks about the dangers of conflicting responsibilities in writing for different audiences; there is the need to 'honestly report' research results in order to contribute to knowledge and the equally important need to maintain a nonjudgemental relationship with participants.

This strongly resonates with my own dilemmas in writing about the views, which I had found quite disturbing, of some of the teachers I interviewed as part of my PhD, and that I mentioned in Chapter 1 (p. 39). I felt it was very important to include them in some way in the book I published soon after completing my thesis, as they revealed some of the intractable pressures that teachers had to work under. Before I did so, I asked colleagues I trusted to read drafts and let me know if they thought anything was likely to cause offence. I made revisions, following their advice carefully and the final outcome appeared in Conteh (2003: 110–115). To my knowledge, there has been no negative feedback whatsoever about this piece of writing, but I still feel slightly uneasy when I see the words on the page and hear the teachers' voices in my head. It can be very daunting when participants show that they are eager to read things you have written, and you fear that you may disappoint them. The most positive feedback, in my view, is when people you have written about tell you that they can recognize themselves in your words. One useful rule-of-thumb is not to write anything that you would find difficult to say to your participants, though this may not always be possible. As I demonstrate above, peers and trusted colleagues can be valuable sounding boards for your work.

Dissemination, impact and teacher-researchers

Dissemination and impact are all about making research make a difference, contributing to change for the better and thus promoting social justice. All researchers seeking funding know about the importance of being able to argue that their research will have a powerful impact in the 'real world', as they write successive 'impact plans', 'pathways to impact' statements and so on to support their research bids. Writing about research in academic journals, reports and conference presentations is clearly a key contribution to impact, and publications addressed to practitioners are just as important. But perhaps the most effective route to impact is through working with practitioners themselves, who can take the ideas straight back into their classrooms and other workplaces. More and more teachers are applying to do EdDs and PhDs, so the possibilities are there.

At several points in this book, I have argued for the importance of teachers and researchers working together, but some of the models offered in the academic literature are perhaps not altogether helpful. In my view, researchers need to work to understand better the perspectives of teachers, and to find out what it is really like to work in schools these days. Many academics have written about 'researching with teachers', and it bothers me that the prevailing message seems to be the need to induct teachers into the ways of researchers, rather than for researchers to understand better the ways teachers work within the education system and cope with the pressures involved. In their account of doing linguistic ethnography (LE) in 'educational settings', for example, Rampton et al. (2015: 38–40) talk about the 'educational focus', which 'has to incorporate national targets, pre-determined curriculum goals and the measurement of individual competencies'. They contrast this with 'the researcher's gaze', which

> needs to open to a more holistic understanding of what is going on within the local constructions of meaning on the one hand, and the configuring of the school environment by broader linguistic and sociopolitical processes on the other.

But is it really the case, as they go on to suggest, that the linguistic ethnographer has to 'set aside the institutional lenses'? Surely, the key issue here is that researchers need to understand better the ways in which institutional factors play into the work of teachers and the experiences of learners. Rampton et al. go on to illustrate their argument by discussing the very opposed models of literacy that prevail in school on the one hand and in most ethnographic research on the other. They suggest that teacher-researchers have to 'move' from one to the other and conclude by talking about 'the route from education into LE' as if it is a one-way street. As a teacher educator, I love working with skilled teachers who – certainly in my experience – do not see it in this way at all. They are hungry for access to the complex theoretical perspectives on literacy and other pedagogic themes that help them to understand what actually happens in their classrooms and support them in considering the practices that will improve their pupils' opportunities for success. One of the joys of working with the teachers on my practice-based MA course was in the way they took theoretical ideas back to their classrooms with enthusiasm and dedication, then came back to university sessions and discussed what they had done and finally wrote about it all in their assignments and critical studies.

In their chapter on researchers and teachers working together on a Master's course in LE, Lefstein and Israeli (2015: 196) say that part of their focus is 'contrasting pedagogical and LE perspectives', not in drawing them together. They make some interesting comments about how we understand learning, which reveal the differing perspectives of teachers and researchers. In response to the views expressed by a teacher on their course discussing an example of interaction from his own classroom, they indicate the differing assumptions of teachers and themselves about how to understand learning:

Rather than assuming that students are by definition engaged in learning, we assume that much of what happens in classrooms is related to managing one's identity and social relations, and performing school-appropriate roles.

They go on to propose that LE is 'not very good at investigating learning', because of its 'tendency to focus more on social interaction than on cognitive processes'. This seems to beg the question about what we understand 'learning' to be. There are plenty of theoretical approaches that helpfully consider 'managing identity and social relations', 'performing roles' and so on as aspects of learning. My argument is that, instead of seeing teachers' and researchers' views as being in opposition, the two need to be brought together into one, complex vision of what happens in classrooms, so that models of learning are widened and enriched, moving beyond a narrow model of 'cognitive processes'. Surely, the way forward is to construct dialogues to play to the strengths of both communities.

I think that a key element in developing better relationships between teachers and researchers and creating more equal spaces for collaboration is the sharing of theoretical perspectives, leading to the shared construction of new ways of thinking about language, learning and pedagogy. I have written about this elsewhere (see, for example, the introduction to Conteh and Meier 2014: 4–8). Instead of trying to help teachers to move away from their practice-oriented understandings to the more overtly theory-supported ones offered by researchers, the ways forward, surely, are in constructing dialogues to develop a shared, complex perspective that offers much more productive ways forward to promote social justice and meaningful change. This has clear implications for the kinds of research we need, and which needs to be supported by funding bodies, Master's courses and EdD and PhD projects.

Some closing comments

As I was reading and rereading the case study chapters, thinking about what to include in my own framing sections and in the generic chapters that begin and end this book, I was struck by the ways the contributors bring their participants to life, and also the feeling that many of them give of their own sense of belonging, and yet not quite belonging, to the communities they were researching. Knowing some of the contributors face to face, I am aware that this feeling sometimes applies to their everyday lives as well, and this resonates strongly with my own identity. I often find myself on the margins of things, not quite fitting in and yet not quite a stranger either, often arriving in the middle of things and leaving before they are finished. This has certainly been the case in my professional life. For many years, working in universities on initial teacher education programmes while meeting my commitments for research and writing, I felt deeply the gap between 'teacher' and 'researcher'. As time went on, I began to find this an exciting – if not altogether comfortable – place to be. In her chapter (Chapter 8), Jessica reminds us how, for Bauman (2004: 14), there is a 'trick' to benefiting from this sense of not quite belonging, this liquidity of identity. It is 'a trick developed through practice'. Instead of seeking 'belonging', Bauman encourages us to consider the benefits of being on the periphery, of 'continuous boundary-transgression'. Placing oneself, or being placed on the verge, gives us, as Jessica goes on to say, the opportunity to see things from different perspectives, to move in and out of what is happening, and even to move on if we need to. Perhaps this is the ethnographic researcher's inevitable position in research and even in life, and one to relish and enjoy. So, as you move forward on your voyage into ethnographic research, whether to Ithaka or elsewhere, enjoy your journey and the 'joy of harbors seen for the first time' as well as the 'Balinese cock fights' that you may encounter on the way.

References

Bauman, Z. (2004), *Community: Seeking Shelter in an Insecure World*, Cambridge: Polity.

Conteh, J. (2003), *Succeeding in Diversity: Culture, Language and Learning in Primary Classrooms*, Stoke-on-Trent: Trentham Books.

Conteh, J. and Meier, G., eds (2014), *The Multilingual Turn in Languages Education: Opportunities and Challenges*, Series: New Perspectives on Language and Education, Clevedon: Multilingual Matters.

Copland, F. and Creese, A. (2015), *Linguistic Ethnography: Collecting, Analyzing and Presenting Data*, London: Sage Publications.

Kubanyiova, M. (2008), 'Rethinking Research Ethics in Contemporary Applied Linguistics: The Tension between Macroethical and Microethical Perspectives in Situated Research', *Modern Language Journal*, 92(4): 503–518.

Lefstein, A. and Israeli, M. (2015), 'Applying Linguistic Ethnography to Educational Practice: Notes on the Interaction of Academic Research and Professional Sensibilities', in J. Snell, S. Shaw and F. Copland (eds), *Linguistic Ethnography: Interdisciplinary Explorations*, 187–206, London: Palgrave Macmillan.

Mishler, E.G. (1990), 'Validation in Inquiry-guided Research: The Role of Exemplars in Narrative Studies', *Harvard Educational Review*, 60(4): 415–442.

Rampton, B., Maybin, J. and Roberts, C. (2015), 'Theory and Method in Linguistic Ethnography', in J. Snell, S. Shaw and F. Copland (eds), *Linguistic Ethnography: Interdisciplinary Explorations*, 14–50, London: Palgrave Macmillan.

Sikes, P. (2006), 'On Dodgy Ground? Problematics and Ethics in Educational Research', *International Journal of Research and Method in Education*, 29(1): 105–117.

GLOSSARY

Advocacy Activity by an individual or group that seeks to influence decisions in political, economic and social spheres. Advocacy can include media campaigns, public speaking, letter writing, forming activist groups and so on.

Case study Analyzes of a representative or illuminative example of a phenomenon, which can include people, events, projects, institutions and so on. The case is studied holistically using one or more data collection strategies.

Communication The act of conveying intended meanings from one person or group to another through the use of mutually understood signs and semiotic rules. The notion of communication, rather than language, widens the possibilities for understanding and analyzing interactions.

Context In its earliest uses *context* meant 'the weaving together of words in language', a sense developed logically from the word's source in Latin, *contexere* 'to weave or join together'. *Context* is now most commonly used to refer to the environment or setting in which something is situated, though writers such as Michael Cole have developed a model of context that captures its original meanings.

Critical discourse analysis (CDA) An interdisciplinary approach to the study of interaction (discourse) that views language as social practice.

The focus is on investigating how societal power relations are established and reinforced through language use. CDA systematically relates specific structures of text or talk to structures in sociopolitical contexts.

Critical race theory A theoretical framework which focuses on the application of critical theory to issues of 'race' to enable an understanding of the intersections of society and culture with race, law and power.

Data collection strategies Approaches to collecting data; in qualitative research this usually involves direct interaction with individuals or groups of people and a smaller sample than in quantitative approaches. The information gathered is usually richer and affords a deeper insight into the phenomenon under study in preference to generalizability.

Discourse analysis A general term for a number of approaches to analyzing written, vocal or sign language use. Discourse analysis aims at revealing the ways people use language in sociocultural contexts, rather than simply describing text structure and language features. Discourse analysts analyze 'naturally occurring'; language use, not invented examples.

Doubleness A term connected with W.E.B. DuBois and his concept of 'double consciousness', suggesting the existence of a 'true' and genuine self which could be contrasted to a self which is 'false' and inauthentic; the two being inseparable. DuBois considered doubleness to be an inevitable aspect of Black experience in the United States.

Emic and etic perspectives Two kinds of viewpoints in social research; *emic,* from within the social group (from the perspective of the subject) and *etic,* from outside (from the perspective of the observer).

Empowerment The positive deployment of power; giving authority to others to enable them to act with authority themselves.

Epistemology The branch of philosophy concerned with the theory of knowledge; epistemology studies the nature of knowledge, justification and the rationality of belief. Much of the debate in epistemology focuses on the philosophical analysis of the nature of knowledge and how it relates to such concepts as truth, belief and justification.

Ethics The branch of philosophy that involves defending and recommending concepts of right and wrong conduct. In practice, ethics seeks to resolve questions of human morality by defining concepts such as good and evil, right and wrong, virtue and vice, justice and crime. As a branch of philosophy, ethics investigates the questions 'What is the best way for people to live?' and 'What actions are right or wrong in particular circumstances?'

Ethnographic monitoring A concept from Hymes, later developed by other researchers, which seeks to describe and analyze 'communicative conduct' in programmes to uncover emergent patterns and meanings and evaluate the programme, with the aim of countering inequity and advancing social justice.

Funds of knowledge The concept is based on the premise that people are competent and have knowledge, which their life experiences have given them. First-hand research with families allows teachers to document this competence and knowledge, and such engagement provides many possibilities for positive pedagogical action.

Grounded theory A systematic methodology in the social sciences involving the construction of theory through the analysis of data. A study using grounded theory is likely to begin with a question or problem, or the collection of some qualitative data. As researchers review the data, repeated ideas or concepts become apparent. These are tagged with *codes*, extracted from the data. As more data are collected and reviewed, codes can be grouped into concepts, and then into categories, which may become the basis for new theory.

Ideology A collection of normative beliefs held by an individual, group or society; a set of conscious and unconscious ideas which make up one's beliefs, goals, expectations and motivations; a set of ideas proposed by an elite and imposed on all members of society.

Idiographic and Nomothetic knowledge First introduced to American psychology in the 1930s, *nomothetic* is typical in the natural sciences, and describes the effort to derive laws that explain *types* or *categories* of objective phenomena in general; *idiographic* refers to the tendency to specify, and is typical in the humanities. It describes the effort to understand the meaning of contingent, unique, cultural or subjective phenomena.

Interpretivist research Interpretivist researchers assume that access to reality (given or socially constructed) can only be through social constructions such as language, consciousness, shared meanings and so on. The development of interpretivist philosophy is based on the critique of positivism in the social sciences.

Liminality The concept comes from folklore, and has broadened to describe political and cultural change, as well as rituals. During liminal periods, social hierarchies may be reversed or temporarily dissolved, continuity of tradition may become uncertain and future outcomes may be thrown into doubt. A feature of liminality is a fluid situation that enables new institutions and customs to form.

Liquidity The state of fluidity, uncertainty and change in modern, complex societies that calls for flexible research approaches. The term was introduced by Bauman, who wrote in the 1990s of the shift from 'modernity' to 'postmodernity'. Since the turn of the millennium, he has tried to avoid the confusion surrounding the term 'postmodernity' by using the metaphors of 'liquid' and 'solid' modernity.

Member checking (see also 'Respondent validation') A technique used by researchers to help improve the accuracy, credibility and transferability of a study. The data, interpretation and/or report are given to participants in order to check their authenticity. Their comments are used to develop the interpretation and analysis.

Method (see 'Data collection strategies')

Multilevel study In ethnography, a multilevel study involves understanding a social activity or event in its cultural, historical and political contexts.

Nomothetic knowledge (see 'Idiographic and Nomothetic knowledge')

Ontology The study of the nature of being or becoming. Ontology tries to answer questions that begin with 'What', and to understand questions like what is God, what is a disease, what happens after death, what is artificial intelligence etc.

Paradigm or Research paradigm A distinct set of concepts, thought patterns, theories, research methods and so on that together constitute legitimate contributions to a field.

Phenomenography A qualitative research methodology that investigates the qualitatively different ways in which people experience something or think about something; an approach to educational research that first appeared in the early 1980s, initially emerging from an empirical rather than a theoretical basis.

Positionality Since bias is a naturally occurring human characteristic, positionality is often used in the context of social inquiry as an exploration of the investigator's reflection on their own placement within the many contexts, layers, power structures, identities and subjectivities of the investigation.

Praxis A form of critical thinking that combines reflection and action; the process by which a theory, lesson or skill is enacted, embodied or realized. *Praxis* may also refer to the act of engaging with, applying or practising ideas.

Rapport A close connection marked by shared interests or similarity in nature or character.

Reflexivity Reflexivity has come to have two distinct meanings in ethnography; it refers to the researcher's awareness of an analytic focus on his or her relationship to the field of study, and also to the ways that cultural practices involve consciousness and commentary on themselves.

Respondent validation (see 'Member checking')

Strategies for data collection (see 'Data collection strategies')

Subjectivity and subjective monitoring The idea that, while it is recognized that subjectivity (acknowledging the role and influence of the self in the research context) is a vital aspect of ethnographic research, it needs to be balanced through constant checking of the perspectives of other participants in the context being researched.

Thick description A description of a human behaviour that explains not just the behaviour, but its context as well, such that the behaviour becomes meaningful to an outsider. First introduced by the philosopher Gilbert Ryle and later developed by the anthropologist Clifford Geertz in his *The Interpretation of Cultures* (1973).

Translanguaging Otheguy et al. (2015) define translanguaging as 'the deployment of a speaker's full linguistic repertoire without regard for watchful adherence to the socially and politically defined boundaries of names (and usually national and state) languages'.

Triangulation Triangulation involves using multiple data and collection strategies sources in an investigation to produce better understanding of a phenomenon.

Trustworthiness and Validation Concepts developed by Elliot Mishler to replace the positivist concepts of validity and reliability in assessing the quality of research. Essentially, Mishler's concepts argue that quality is best assessed through the research itself and the ways it is carried out by a 'community of scholars', rather than by external criteria.

INDEX

Authors are listed in the index when they appear in more than one chapter

9 781350 002630

WITHDRAWN

**Books are to be returned on or before
the last date below.**

Exhibition
Catalogue
646.407 FAS

LIBREX—